The Power of Past Life Regression

The Power of Past Life Regression

Steve Burgess

6TH
BOOKS

Winchester, UK
Washington, USA

JOHN HUNT PUBLISHING

First published by Sixth Books, 2020
Sixth Books is an imprint of John Hunt Publishing Ltd., No. 3 East St., Alresford,
Hampshire SO24 9EE, UK
office@jhpbooks.com
www.johnhuntpublishing.com
www.6th-books.com

For distributor details and how to order please visit the 'Ordering' section on our website.

ISBN: 978 1 78904 343 3
978 1 78904 344 0 (ebook)
Library of Congress Control Number: 2019933909

A CIP catalogue record for this book is available from the British Library.

Design: Stuart Davies

The author of this book does not dispense medical advice or prescribe the use of any technique as a form of treatment for physical, emotional or medical problems without the advice of a physician, either directly or indirectly. This book is not meant to be a substitute for medical or psychological help. You should always seek the help of a professional therapist or counsellor or qualified physician.

UK: Printed and bound by CPI Group (UK) Ltd, Croydon, CR0 4YY
US: Printed and bound by Thomson-Shore, 7300 West Joy Road, Dexter, MI 48130

Contents

Prologue 1

Chapter 1: How Does Past Life Regression Work? 4

Section One: Behavioural Issues 17
Chapter 2: Helen's Story 18
Chapter 3: Chris' Story 28

Section Two: Physical Issues 37
Chapter 4: Toni's Story 38
Chapter 5: Simon's Story 65
Chapter 6: Pam's Story 68
Chapter 7: Lisa's Story 77
Chapter 8: Kath's Story 83

Section Three: Panic Attacks, Anxieties, Phobias 89
Chapter 9: Amy's Story 90
Chapter 10: Rachel's Story 100
Chapter 11: Barbara's Story 103
Chapter 12: Flying Phobia: Yvonne's, Janet's and Gemma's Stories 118
Chapter 13: Jackie's Story 128
Chapter 14: Tom's Story 132
Chapter 15: Beth's Story 135

Section Four: Emotional Imbalances 141
Chapter 16: Angie's Story 142
Chapter 17: Mark's Story 157
Chapter 18: Colin's Story 161

Chapter 19: Sally's Story 171

Section Five: Unusual Cases 179
Chapter 20: Christine's Story 180
Chapter 21: Gerry's Story 185

Section Six: Depression 193
Chapter 22: Holly's Story 194
Chapter 23: John's Story 200
Chapter 24: Andrea's Story 211

Section Seven: Sexual Issues 217
Chapter 25: Lars' Story 218
Chapter 26: Mike's Story 226

Section Eight: Relationship Issues 231
Chapter 27: Benji's Story 232
Chapter 28: Jim's Story 236
Chapter 29: Mary's Story 244

Epilogue 260

Also by Steve Burgess:

Famous Past Lives
ISBN 978 1 84694 494 9

For Marianne, with all my love

Prologue

Gary burst into my consulting room like a man possessed. A bundle of anxiety and agitation, he sat opposite me and was hardly able to keep still. He exuded nervous energy, his hands were shaking and tension was etched on his frowning face. His mouth twitched and as he spoke he spat words out frenetically, his eyes moving rapidly from side to side as he poured out his unhappiness to me. Aged only 27, his lifelong anxiety state had worsened so much over the past year that he was now unable to work. He had given his job up due to constant feelings of fear and panic, and he was now barely able to leave his house. His wife was despairing and frustrated as he had become phobic about going anywhere in public. His GP had prescribed antidepressants which had not helped at all. He had tried numerous other therapies in a desperate attempt to break out of his living nightmare. As he came to the end of his story he looked me in the eyes and said, "You're my last hope; please help me out of this madness."

After a brief discussion I guided Gary into a hypnotic state, and as he lay relaxing in hypnosis I asked his subconscious to take him to the root cause of the anxieties. Suddenly he began to shake, and as he lay with his eyes closed in my reclining chair his whole body was moving and jerking. His breathing quickened, his head moved from side to side and he whispered loudly in a voice filled with fear – "They're coming, they're coming. Quickly, in here – hide, quickly, hide. Quiet – quiet – they're here – quiet – stay down, stay down – quiet." After a pause his voice began to shake as it grew louder. "No, no please – no. Don't – don't. Please don't. No – please leave us alone. Please – not the children." He began to cry and yell – "No, no please, leave them – no. Don't hurt them, don't hurt them." Tears began to flow down his cheeks, his body shook, his face contorted with rage and terror as he began yelling at the top of his voice. "NO, NO, PLEASE – NOT THAT – DON'T KILL ME – NO." His scream ended in mid-shout, as his arching body suddenly flopped back down into the chair and he lay like a limp rag doll, arms and legs splayed out, head back and mouth open. He lay perfectly still, quiet for a couple of minutes, before I asked him what was happening now. "It's over," Gary said softly, and stretched out his body in a relaxed way. "It's calm and I'm surrounded by bright light. I'm moving on now, and everything's OK." He smiled calmly and sighed. His agitation had gone and he looked serene.

I asked him what he had just experienced. "Soldiers were coming for us – with guns. I was with my wife and children. We tried to hide, me and my family, but they found us. I think they were Nazis and they took us outside and shot us all. I was terrified and unable to protect my wife and kids. Maybe that's why I've been frightened of going out of the house for so long. God, I felt it all, but what a release when I died – a wonderful feeling of calmness and peace. I've always had a terror of dying but after that I don't think I'll ever be afraid of death again."

I brought him back out of trance. Gary's anxiety state had gone as if by a miracle and it has not come back in the 22 years since our session together. Gary was able to get his life back and to function normally again in the world, something he had not been able to do for many years.

Welcome to the world of Past Life Therapy. Although not many past life regressions are as dramatic as Gary's, his experience does demonstrate just how powerful and effective this type of therapy can be. This book is all about the healing power of Past Life Therapy. From the many thousands of past life regression sessions I have completed over the years, I have selected some of the most interesting past life 'stories' that my clients have experienced in order to give a flavour of how past life therapy heals a vast range of emotional and psychological problems, and the way in which it can release deep-seated issues that hold people back from leading happy, fulfilled lives. I hope you enjoy the read.

Chapter 1

How Does Past Life Regression Work?

Before I begin to share with you the past life experiences of my clients, firstly I'd like to give you some background information so you can understand the concept of regression and why it works so efficiently. When I first began working as a Hypnotherapist in the early 1990s I had not been trained in past life regression, and Gary was my first experience of someone spontaneously regressing into another lifetime. As he began shaking, crying and screaming, I was shocked and amazed both by the strength of his reactions, and also by the incredible and rapid release that he had from his anxiety state. I realised that something extremely significant had happened and I wanted to know more. Unfortunately, as there was nowhere in the UK that specialised in past life training, I had to get some information from the United States so that I could work with people in hypnosis in previous lives. Once armed with this I was able to develop techniques that over the years have proved to be incredibly effective in terms of taking clients into traumas in former lifetimes, and releasing the problems that these traumas were causing in this present life. I have now completed over 15,000 therapy sessions, and have seen people get better from an incredible variety of problems, ranging from phobias to depressions, physical illness and anxiety states.

Hypnosis is an ideal way for people to go back into previous lives, so let me explain what hypnosis is and what it isn't, as there are so many myths and misconceptions about hypnosis, and many people have a totally skewed view of it. Firstly, hypnosis is not a sleep state. When a person is in hypnosis (or a 'trance', which is the word we give to the experience of being in hypnosis) they are fully aware of everything that is going on. Secondly, it is not a coma-type state, or an experience similar to being under anaesthetic, where someone is not aware of what's happening to them. Thirdly, the person is not powerless, at the mercy of the therapist and simply compliant to everything that is being said to them.

The truth about hypnosis is that the hypnotic state is a state of focussed awareness and is usually accompanied by a feeling of relaxation. We all enter hypnosis several times each day, either when we daydream or when we allow ourselves to relax physically and mentally. In a hypnotic (or 'trance') state we are fully aware of everything that is taking place and we can hear sounds and noises around us and respond to them if we want to. Becoming absorbed in a movie or going on automatic pilot when driving a car are good examples of everyday trance. In a therapy session we tend to become mentally more focussed on whatever is going on inside of us – feelings, thoughts, images etc., even though we are still aware of the hypnotherapist's voice and can respond to it when necessary.

So, it is not sleep or coma, just a nice feeling of relaxed inner awareness where we are still in control and not under the control of the therapist. It is in this pleasant relaxation that we can be guided back through our memory banks into previous lives.

We often use the terms 'conscious' and 'subconscious' minds without always being aware of what the two terms mean. Our conscious mind is our thinking, analytical mind. As you are reading these words you are logically making sense of them using your conscious, thinking mind. Our subconscious (or unconscious – the words are interchangeable) controls our bodily functions like walking and breathing, and it contains our emotions, our intuition, and memories of everything that has ever happened to us. If you imagine an iceberg, with its tip above the surface of the waves, that is the conscious part of our minds. Beneath the surface of the waves lies the vast bulk of the iceberg, which means that our subconscious mind is hidden beneath the thinking mind. I like to think of it as the 'engine room' of the mind. In rough percentage terms, recent research suggests that our conscious mind contains less than 1% of our mental capabilities, whilst our subconscious holds more than 99% of our mental powers. According to research quoted in *The New Unconscious* (editors: Hassin, Uleman and Bargh) whilst consciousness processes 50 bits of information per second, the rest of the mind processes 11 million bits per second!

As a hypnotherapist I use regression frequently as a means of helping my clients to heal a wide variety of their issues. Regression simply means going back in our minds to relive memories of past events. Hypnotherapists who have the ability and correct training use it regularly to guide clients back into SEEs (Significant Emotional Events) that have occurred earlier in this lifetime (usually childhood, at birth or in the womb before birth). The client usually experiences the negative emotions that have been locked into the subconscious mind from these traumatic events and releases them, often by crying, shaking or even screaming in some cases. Some clients gain a greater understanding of why they have had problems by gaining the knowledge of the causes of their problems (which can include negative patterns and behaviours), and these insights can allow deep, long-lasting healing to occur.

Some hypnotherapists also guide their clients back into past lives to clear present-life blockages, and even fewer of us work on clearing ancestral, genetically-inherited traumas to heal current life issues (these are traumas that we inherit from ancestors in our bloodline such as parents, grandparents etc.). Occasionally I have even been involved in future life progression, to look ahead into lifetimes to come. I've also used regression with people who appear to have had contact with or been abducted by extraterrestrials.

It should be said that even within the hypnotherapy profession Past Life Regression and Reincarnation Therapy is still controversial with many hypnotherapists refusing to use it as a therapeutic tool. This, I have to say, amazes me as I have seen so many incredible healings over the years and I've completed so many past life sessions that have eradicated my clients' problems that I firmly believe that Reincarnation Therapy should be regarded as a serious therapeutic discipline. The regression 'model' is that so many issues from which we suffer as human beings can stem from traumas or locked-in behaviour patterns from the past (from earlier in our present life, from previous lifetimes, from our ancestors' lives). My experience from many thousands of regression sessions supports this viewpoint.

Let me list just a few of the problems that may have their roots in former lives:

Depression
Anxieties and panic attacks
Phobias and fears
Skin problems
Physical illnesses (including migraines, asthma and cancer)
Lack of confidence and self-worth
Sexual problems
Alcohol addiction and substance abuse
Weight issues
Behavioural problems
Smoking addiction
Stress
Irritable Bowel Syndrome (IBS)

Relationship challenges
Pain

And many more too numerous to mention. The list is almost endless, but all significant 21st century ailments which inhibit us and which stop us from living our lives freely, joyfully and with a sense of inner peace could stem from events in previous lives.

Basically, many symptoms we have that usually end up with a trip to the GP have underlying emotional causes. My work as a therapist generally consists of finding and releasing the underlying emotion that has been locked in as a result of past traumas and then the issue, or symptom, can heal or be reduced. Release the emotional driver that is fuelling the problem, and then the energy goes out of it and the problem ceases to exist. It really is that simple. Reincarnation therapy is 'Cause and Effect' Therapy. This means that when we uncover the cause of an emotional problem whatever is supporting the behaviour collapses and the effect (i.e. the issue we are working on) is healed. There is a school of thought that ALL issues (yes, ALL issues) we have as human beings connect back to underlying emotional causes. Louise Hay, in her wonderful book *You Can Heal Your Life,* supports this view. When I first started working as a hypnotherapist I read *You Can Heal Your Life* and thought it a load of New Age twaddle. My dad was a scientist with a medical background and I had been brought up to show a healthy scepticism to anything outside of the Western medical model. However, as I gained more experience working with clients who came to me for help with an array of physical problems, I gradually came to the viewpoint that Louise Hay has got it absolutely right. Now I totally believe that all of our physical issues, whatever they are, have got emotional energies underpinning them.

When we are working in regression, we are working to release the five root negative emotions which have been locked in the subconscious and which are causing the client's problems. These five negative emotions are:

Anger
Sadness
Fear
Anxiety
Guilt

When a person is traumatised by a Significant Emotional Event (one that has taken place either in this life or in a previous one) the negative emotions they feel as the incident is taking place become locked in the subconscious mind and stored there. The subconscious then replays these emotions over and over throughout that person's life. Sometimes the emotions only surface when a specific event is happening (as in the case of a phobia), but often the emotions are constantly being triggered by the day-to-day stresses of life itself. In this case, the negative emotions can stop a person living their life freely and happily. However, if someone is suffering from an anxiety state they will constantly or frequently feel a sense of unease and tension that can sometimes erupt into a panic attack. If you're an anxiety sufferer reading this, you will know only too well how it feels to feel unsafe all of the time and to exist with a regular state of nervousness in the body.

During a regression session, as the client relives the events from the past that have caused their issues, they often re-experience the emotion that they felt at the time the incident first took place. As a result they may cry, shake or feel angry or guilty. It is this reliving of the locked-in feelings and the emotional catharsis that accompanies it which allows the healing of the problem to take place. The therapy is not usually fun but it is extremely effective. If it is done correctly the whole process is perfectly safe.

Having said all of that, sometimes the therapeutic process is not about releasing negative emotions from the past, but about gaining an insight into the true cause of the issue. In these cases, as a result of reliving a past life my client will get learnings, connections or understandings that they can bring from a previous life into their present incarnation. This new awareness helps to make sense of their current problem and as a result the problem is reduced or resolved.

Usually throughout a past life regression session the client is talking to me with their eyes closed, telling me what they are seeing in their mind's eye as they relive a previous life. However, some people are unable to see what is happening in the past life and they simply experience the physical feelings and emotions of the traumas. This can lead to a very powerful kinaesthetic release of the negative energies and emotions, and is often the experience of people who find it difficult to visualise.

A technique I use regularly in my regression sessions (and which I will mention frequently in the following pages) is something called an 'Ideo-Motor Response' (or IMR for short). This is a hypnotic technique which allows me to create a dialogue with my client's subconscious, without their conscious mind getting in the way. To create an Ideo-Motor Response, once my client is in a hypnotic trance I ask their subconscious mind to make one of their fingers completely light so that it floats in the air, all by itself. I watch to see one of their fingers start to rise up gently, as if it were a helium-filled balloon. As this takes place many of my clients are amazed, as they are just lying in a comfortable chair with their eyes closed thinking that nothing unusual is happening until one of their fingers starts to move of its own volition. I then ask their subconscious to remain in control of the finger throughout the session, using the finger to signal the word 'yes' to me by floating the finger up in the air whenever I ask a question that requires a 'yes' response. If the finger remains stationary whenever I ask a question that would be the subconscious' way of answering 'no'. I can then ask the client's subconscious questions about the client and their issues and receive 'yes' or 'no' answers which are not influenced by the conscious mind.

I mentioned earlier that the subconscious is the engine room of the mind. However, having worked for over 26 years as a hypnotherapist my experience is that the subconscious is even greater than that. It seems that it has an innate wisdom and knowledge, and that it knows everything there is to know about the client. My model of the subconscious is that it is not simply an automaton which blindly does what it is told to do, without thinking or reasoning. I believe that the subconscious mind has an innate intelligence and it is desperate for us to be physically and mentally well. It is just waiting for us to connect with it so we can achieve physical and mental freedom. Some people believe that we all have a 'Higher Self', an awesomely wise and knowledgeable part of us that operates at a much higher spiritual level than our mundane conscious minds. I feel that if this is the case, then our subconscious either IS our Higher Self or is intimately attached to it. I believe that the subconscious has an all-knowing intelligence which we can tap into simply by accessing trance.

Using the Ideo-Motor Response I can ask the client's subconscious about the causes of the issue we are working on. For example, have there been any Significant Emotional Events in their present life which are connected to causing the issue? Are there any past life traumas causing it? If so, how many past lives? Quite often there are frequently several past lives that contain SEEs that are causing the issue. Once I have diagnosed the causes of the problem, we can then work directly on those causes rather than using guesswork (which is what many therapists do, I'm sorry to say).

Where there are multiple past lives that need to be worked on and 'cleared' (i.e. cleared of their negative emotions), sometimes clients will begin by exploring the most traumatic one first, whereas others will go into the least traumatic ones firstly, and then as we do more sessions they go into the really unpleasant ones. I explain this by saying that sometimes the subconscious saves the best till last! However, the process is led by the client's subconscious which knows the best healing process for the client. This means that if I, as the therapist, allow it to do the work, it usually does so in the most effective manner. In therapy terms we call that a 'client-led process'. When I first see a client for a consultation, although I may suspect that there could be past lifetimes causing their issues, I do not mention this as I do not want to lead or influence the client in any way. Also I could be wrong in suspecting that past lives need to be worked on, so I simply have the attitude that I do not know where the issues are coming from but their subconscious does know. I then get myself out of the way and let the client's all-wise subconscious take us wherever we need to go.

Although many therapy sessions with my clients over the years have become past life sessions, very few people come to me with either knowledge of, or a belief in, the subject of reincarnation. Still fewer feel that the cause of their issue is something that happened in a lifetime before this one. However, once they access trance in many, many cases their subconscious mind (the deep, inner mind in which all distant memories are stored) has guided them back to the source of their problems which is usually some trauma or series of traumas in previous lives. Often this is a death in a past life that has been so traumatic that its energy has been locked into the client's subconscious and carried with them into this present lifetime. The energy of that trauma then bubbles up under the surface of the conscious mind causing the issues which are blighting or limiting their lives. By re-experiencing the death or trauma in the past life (which can sometimes be quite dramatic but perfectly safe to go through provided the therapist is properly trained) the problem is healed.

There are those who mock or question the reality of the process but usually from a position of fear, ignorance or prejudice. Sceptics will say that the past life is simply a metaphor of the client's problem, and their mind has created the metaphor in the form of a past life so that they can get better. Others would say that it is simply someone's imagination or they are recalling something they once read in a book or saw on a TV programme (this is called cryptomnesia). I admit that this can happen, but it does not explain those cases where people in past life regressions come up with historically true facts which they could not have known and which are verified after the regression sessions. You may like to read my book *Famous Past Lives* for a whole host of such examples. Neither is anything implanted by me into my clients' minds during the sessions. I do not suggest anything which could lay me open to the accusation of leading them. I use what in therapy terms is called 'clean language' so that all of the information they come up with during the regression comes through quite spontaneously from the client. Personally, I feel that if this was not a real phenomenon it would surely not be happening so often and with such breathtaking results. People just keep getting better, often from issues or illnesses they had suffered from all their lives, regardless of whether they believe in the concept of past lives or not. I must say that most people who come to me for therapy do not believe in (or have any real knowledge of) reincarnation, but they still get better once they've relived their previous lives. The reality is that past lives cannot be just explained away simply as imaginary fantasies by those who experience them. This makes what follows all the more intriguing.

One of my aims in writing this book is that when people read about the benefits of past life therapy they may be less sceptical about the process and more open to the possibility that previous lives are a real and not an imaginary phenomenon.

My view is that past life therapy should be accepted as a credible hypnotherapeutic discipline, which deserves serious consideration within the world of psychotherapy.

Even though I have completed many thousands of past life regression sessions and many hundreds of my clients have experienced substantial or total relief from their issues, I have chosen just a few of them to include in this book. The reason is that a large number of those sessions do not have enough detail in them to describe in a way which would be useful to the general reader. This is particularly the case where my clients have been unable to visualise the events in the past life when they are experiencing them. In these cases clients experience the feelings and emotions of the traumatic incidents which they have regressed into, but they cannot see any pictures that provide a narrative about those incidents. When in trance they may cry, scream or shake as, for example, they relive the death in the former life, and this release of emotions or physical feelings (I call this 'Kinaesthetic Releasing') is enough to get them better and heal the issues they came to me with in the first place. However, for me to include them in this book would not be of any interest as I would simply be describing them rolling around and crying whilst they were being regressed. I have, therefore, chosen client cases in which they were able to visualise their past life during their regression sessions and to describe to me the pictures that they were seeing in their mind's eye.

I have grouped the cases into several categories – e.g. physical issues, phobias etc. – in order to give a balanced overview of the range of issues that can be alleviated by using past life regression to get to the source of the problem.

As you read through my clients' stories, you will notice a wide variety of experiences, some of them more dramatic than others. However, dramatic or not, I feel that they are all fascinating in their own ways, particularly as in all cases they brought about real improvements in the issues that had been troubling my clients. For some of these people their lives had been severely restricted, sometimes even damaged, by the problems that we worked on. Opening up the real emotional root causes of these problems, the traumas from previous lifetimes, had a life-changing effect for them. The life of a therapist is not an easy one, and to bring about major changes in the lives of our clients is what drives us on. I feel proud to have helped so many of them to get their lives back, and to help them to live their lives freely and joyfully. So, without further ado, let me introduce you now to the first of my clients' past life experiences. Please note that all clients' names have been changed to preserve anonymity.

Section One

Behavioural Issues

Chapter 2

Helen's Story

Helen came to me as a long-term alcoholic. For over 20 years she had been classed as a functioning alcoholic, which means that she was able to hold down a full-time job whilst at the same time, every evening after work, she would consume at least half a bottle of Scotch. As she explained to me during our first meeting, "every night over the past 20 years I've got home at 6pm, started drinking and been pissed by 9 o'clock." She was living alone, very overweight, suffered from poor sleep and had chronic asthma. She was unhappy and she knew that she was not living a satisfying life.

Helen had tried many of the standard routes to help her with her drinking, including counselling and the usual agencies, but nothing had worked. She was extremely sceptical about anybody or anything being able to help, and she was VERY sceptical that regression therapy might help. She was almost aggressive when I mentioned that the roots of the problem lay in the past. I explained to her that the reason she was drinking so heavily was that the alcohol was simply a means of anaesthetising her inner emotional pain, but she couldn't understand this as she felt she didn't really have any inner pain. Her life had had no real traumas and she had enjoyed a good childhood (the cause of so many issues in later life for most people). However, I stuck to my guns and we agreed to do some hypnosis to check out the emotional causes.

Once I'd taken her into a hypnotic trance, I asked Helen's subconscious to take us back to the roots of her inner anxieties, anxieties which were being masked by her drinking. She lay with her eyes closed, her body relaxed, and after a few seconds I saw a quizzical look appear on her face. She was obviously seeing something in her mind's eye, and I asked her to describe what she was experiencing. Haltingly, and with an air of surprise, she spoke softly:

"I'm outside, with a lot of other people. I'm a girl, wearing a long dress but with no shoes. It feels itchy on my skin."

SB: "How old do you feel?"

"I think I'm around 20–25 years of age. I feel as if I'm waiting for somebody, in a marketplace. Soldiers are arriving, and a girl is with them. She gets off her horse and starts talking to the people, laughing with them. I'm too far away to hear her. The men are stood behind her, as if they're joining her. She comes over and looks straight at me and tells me to join them. She puts her hand on my shoulder and says that it'll be alright."

At this point Helen, who so far had remained a little detached from the experience, became quite emotional. The feelings of the past life began to come through, all by themselves. However sceptical she had been initially about the concept of previous lives, she now was being carried along by the strength of the feelings. As she continued it became obvious that she was reliving a past life in which she had met Joan of Arc. (I should emphasise that it is highly unusual for anyone in a past life session to relive a previous lifetime in which they were around a famous person. In the vast majority of the past life sessions I have completed over the years my clients have been totally ordinary people in ordinary situations. Having said that, in my book, *Famous Past Lives*, I write about some of my clients who appear to have been very famous in their former lives.) Through her tears Helen carried on speaking:

"I'm crying and she gives me a hug. She's wearing armour and it's cold. I put my basket down and follow her. She's talking about a fight, but she doesn't mean a battle or a war. I don't understand. Everyone's listening intently and nodding, she's talking about beliefs and rights and freedom. She gets on her horse and before she goes with the soldiers she tells everyone she'll come back. She looks me straight in the eyes

and says, 'It's alright, you will understand.' Everyone's going home happy. I don't understand."

Helen paused in her narrative at this point, as if the scene she had just witnessed had finished. I asked her subconscious to take her to the next significant part of the experience. After a few moments of silence, her face changed as she began to see another scene. She spoke quietly:

"I'm in somebody's house now and people are talking about her. Her name's Joan. They keep talking about a fight but I don't understand. All I know is that we have to follow her but I don't know why. They believe in what she's saying. I say that I'll come, even though my father says I shouldn't as I might get hurt. We're walking through fields now, a long way. There's a cart with food on it. I don't know where we're going, but I know we're going to see Joan.

We've arrived now; she's standing on some rocks. There's a big light around her. Everyone's very quiet. She's talking about religion and God, saying that many people will die. I don't know who she's going to fight, but she says it'll be alright and eventually she'll have eternal life. She tells us that she has dreams, visions that God talks to her. God told her it'll be a hard fight and she knows that she's going to die, but she's not scared. Everyone's very quiet. She keeps saying it'll be alright, to have faith and courage. I believe her. I don't want to die but I believe her. She says that we all have to go home and wait, when the time is right she'll let us know. We don't want to go but we know that she'll tell us when she's ready. We go back home and sit in an inn talking about what she'd said. Apart from one other lady and myself they're all men."

Helen sighed and was quiet for a few seconds, and then she moved on to another scene:

"I'm in the marketplace with my basket. She's come back with her soldiers. She wants me to go with her – I can't, I'm too scared. She keeps saying it's alright and it's meant to be. She puts her arm around my shoulder and we walk out of the village. Everyone's cheering, but I don't want to go."

SB: "How do you feel?"

"I feel really scared. I don't know where we're going but I know everyone's going to die." Helen became agitated, her breathing quickening and her body began to tremble slightly. *"Whatever she says it's not worth it. I'm not that brave. Everyone else doesn't seem to mind. She's knelt down with her sword pointing into the ground, praying. They're all going to fight. Everyone's praying and asking for victory. They're all following her. I'm begging them not to go but they're just laughing."*

She was quiet for some time, not speaking but breathing quickly with her body tense as she lay in the chair. Her eyes screwed as her face became more and more tense, her hands wringing together as she experienced something too traumatic to recount to me. After a while I asked her to tell me what was happening. Hesitantly, she continued, her voice stern and quivering:

"There's been a lot of fighting. People are dead. Hundreds of people. There are bodies everywhere, as far as the eye can see. I'm hidden in some trees next to a big field where the battle is. I tried to tell them. There's a smell of death and blood everywhere. Some people are hiding with me, saying that Joan's been captured. I can just smell blood and death everywhere."

Again Helen paused for a while, relaxing at the same time. I asked her to move to the next significant part of the past life. After a few seconds, she began to cry, and her words came between her sobs:

"No, they can't. They can't. It's not fair. They say she's a witch and they're going to burn her. A man's reading a piece of paper; he says she's a heretic. People are crying. I'm in a market square with stone buildings around and there's a large crowd. I can't watch as they set fire to her." Helen became very emotional, spitting out her words as she sobbed: *"I can't watch. What a waste. Everybody's crying. It's so sad. She doesn't look scared though. Such a waste. Those of us who saw it say that it should never happen again."* Helen simply cried for

a while, saying nothing. I allowed her to vent her sadness, and eventually she stopped crying and gave a huge sigh. She spoke again, softly: *"We're all going home. I'm not well, I've been caught in the rain. They take me to see an herbalist in a small village. He gives me something to take. Ugh, it tastes awful.* (She was grimacing at this point.) *It's foul. He says that I've got to drink it. I'm ill for a long time. He keeps bringing me the stuff, drinking it is worse than being ill. Eventually I get better and I marry the herbalist. He makes me feel safe. He works very hard, a lot of people come to him."*

It was obvious that Helen had worked through the most important parts of the past life. As a matter of completeness, I asked her to go to the end of the life and experience her death. She whispered softly to me:

"We're both old. I'm sick. I feel tired. I'm dying. My husband's crying. I can't touch him. I'm sad to be going, but I'm happy leaving. I can see people who died in the battle, they've come for me. I leave him crying and go with them."

Helen took a deep breath and relaxed fully, her body lying calmly in my reclining chair. I brought her back out of trance to full consciousness. She expressed amazement at what she'd experienced but she felt remarkably calm, much more at ease than she had felt for some time. We discussed the session for a few minutes and then she left with an air of confusion about her, but still feeling very peaceful inside herself. She'd agreed to come back the following week to explore more past lives.

Just as a reminder, I should emphasise that at no time did I lead Helen or implant into her subconscious anything to do with Joan of Arc. Everything came through to her totally spontaneously, and she insisted that she'd never read anything about Joan of Arc and knew nothing about her. She was, however, overwhelmed at the strength of the emotions she had felt. Had she really been in a past life with Joan of Arc? I can't give a definitive answer to that, but if not, why did she create such a fantasy in order to help her drink problems? To have done so makes no sense at all, particularly as at the start of the session Helen was quite aggressive in her disbelief in the possibility of previous lives.

Helen arrived a week later for our second session together in a state of confusion. She could not understand why, but she had not had a drink of alcohol all week, and what's more at no time did she feel that she wanted one! She couldn't understand why this had happened after just one session of regression, but she was obviously very happy that for the first time in two decades she had not had any alcohol for several days. As well as this she was feeling healthier and she had lost half a stone in weight. The scepticism which she had exhibited at our first meeting was fading fast!

However, all was not sweetness and light as she told me that a couple of times during the week she had felt angry for no reason, so this showed me that her therapy was not yet complete as there was obviously still some negative emotion in her subconscious which had not been released in our previous session. Helen agreed to go into trance again to see if we could work on the roots of the anger, and she relaxed back into my reclining chair and closed her eyes as I guided her into a pleasant hypnotic state.

I asked her subconscious to take control of a finger by making it very light and free (the Ideo-Motor Response) and then checked with her subconscious if there was anything else that needed working on in the Joan of Arc past life. It signalled, "No." I then asked her subconscious to take us into another life that contained significant emotional events that were causing the emotions that were 'driving' her drink problem. After a pause, Helen sighed loudly and began speaking softly:

"I'm a soldier in the trenches. It's World War I. We're all sat in a trench smoking. It's cold and it's muddy. We're going to go forward." Helen became tense, her face and jaw tightened. *"We've all put our cigarettes out. There are bangs and flashes, I can see barbed wire."* Her body stiffened and her breathing quickened, her words staccato and loud: *"It's madness – we're running towards the enemy. I'm all*

by myself in the middle of nowhere; I don't know where anyone else is."

Suddenly, she softened and was quiet for a few seconds before she began to weep. I allowed her to cry for a time before I asked her to continue:

"I don't know why but I'm laid in the mud. I know I'm dying. I'm drifting off, there's no sound, I can't hear any guns anymore. I can just see a clear light and I feel warm and safe."

Her crying had stopped and she breathed deeply and calmly. I asked her how she was feeling and she told me that she felt peaceful. She had obviously left the body and moved into spirit. I allowed her to relax for a few minutes before I asked her subconscious if there were any other lives we needed to go to. Her Ideo-Motor Response finger indicated, "Yes," so I moved her into another lifetime. Immediately she began speaking:

"I'm outdoors, looking at vast American plains. I'm in a village of tepees, a Native American village and I'm a girl. I feel as if I'm around 20 years of age. I feel happy, this is where I live. There's an animal skin on the floor and I'm scraping the underside of it with a knife. There are a lot of people coming and going and dogs wandering around. I have a small child with me. Some men are coming back to the village, laughing. One of them is my husband. He gets off his horse, they've been hunting. I love him very much. I run to meet him and the child follows me. He lifts the child on to the horse and we go back to our tepee."

Throughout all of this Helen had a big smile on her face as she was feeling the happiness from the past life that she was reliving. I asked her to move to the next significant time in that lifetime. The smile vanished from her lips and her body stiffened. Her breathing quickened. Her voice whispered before becoming a shout:

"We're eating. There's shouting. I'm scared. There are blue-coated soldiers firing at us. People are being killed. My husband's grabbed his rifle and run towards the fighting. I'm left with the child, she's crying." Suddenly she became emotional. *"He's been shot. He's dead."* She

began to sob uncontrollably. *"I loved him so much. They've shot all the men in the village. I've escaped with my child, but inside me I feel completely empty. I've lost my husband."*

I allowed Helen to release all of her sadness and after a few minutes she began to calm down, so I asked her to move to the next significant time in that life. She moved on to her husband's funeral.

"We're outside the village and the medicine man is offering my husband's spirit to the Great Spirit. I don't want to leave him up there in the trees. I feel sad that he's died but I'm happy that he's with the Great Spirit."

Helen was fully composed again, relaxed and at ease. There was nothing else for us to work through in that past lifetime so I asked her subconscious to move on. Once more, after a pause, she became tense and her hands began to grip the arms of the chair. I asked her to tell me what she was experiencing. After a few seconds she took a deep breath and began speaking quietly, her brow furrowed:

"I'm outdoors and it's daytime. I'm in a Roman amphitheatre, in the crowd with a lot of other people. I'm a woman, maybe 28–30 years old. I don't want to be there. It's horrible. There are lions fighting people. They're Christians and they won't fight, they're just standing there being killed. Everybody's cheering and shouting for more. I ask some important official to stop it but he just laughs at me." After a pause she continued: *"They believe in a new god, but they won't fight. One after another, women, children, old people, they all die. Every time one dies everyone cheers. I keep pleading with him to stop but he just laughs. It goes on all day, I want to leave but he won't let me. I'm his wife. He won't let me leave. Afterwards there's a party at our house, they're all eating and drinking and laughing but I just feel sick. They're all so superior, they've got no heart. I feel so ashamed. I go out into the garden and sit by myself. I don't understand why they didn't fight. They must have been so scared but they didn't look it. A servant comes out with a glass of wine. He says that they knew they'd*

be alright as they were going to a better place. How can they believe in one god? We've got dozens of them." Again Helen was quiet for a while as she moved through the life.

Eventually she spoke again. *"I'm in a cell now, a prisoner with the servant and some others. It's because I'm a Christian. The servant told me about his god and I just felt it was right. I go with him to meetings in a house. They explained it all and we prayed. I'd been going for a while when soldiers came and took us all away. They knew who I was but it didn't make any difference. My husband's washed his hands of me."*

SB: "How do you feel?"

"I don't feel scared, because I believe in their God. We're going out now, the crowd's shouting. We stand there holding each other. I can see my husband in the crowd. A lion's walking around us and a man with a sword is in the arena too. He's going to kill us. He stabs me and the servant. I'm on the floor but it doesn't hurt. It's alright." Helen became a bit emotional as she whispered: *"I know we're both dying. It doesn't hurt. I'm going on a journey, I feel happy, not scared. I'm in sunshine now, and peaceful."*

Helen breathed a big sigh of relief and was quiet and calm. It was obvious that she had died in the past life. Her death experience was similar to many others that I have witnessed as a Past Life Therapist. Features such as a bright light and feelings of complete calmness are reported by many people once they leave the body. I allowed Helen to relax as she left that lifetime and then I slowly brought her back to full awareness.

Once she had come out of trance, Helen sat for a while as she came to terms with her experiences in those past lives. She found it hard to understand where the memories had come from, but she felt very free and light inside herself, both physically and emotionally. We talked for a while and then Helen left, feeling calmer than she'd felt for years.

These sessions with Helen took place in 1999, and she has never touched a drop of alcohol since. More than that, she has never even wanted to drink alcohol. She has moved on massively in her life since then, with a new-found sense of confidence that has seen her lose lots of weight, exercise regularly and take on some very demanding roles at work. She is also in a long-term relationship. Although she still doesn't know whether or not she fully believes in the concept of reincarnation she doesn't care because, as she herself says, "I have got my life back."

Chapter 3

Chris' Story

Chris' case has always stood out for me because of the nature of the reaction he had when he tried to stop smoking. I had treated his wife successfully for an anxiety problem and she had recommended him to see me to help him become a non-smoker. This is usually a simple issue that is treated very successfully using one session of standard hypnosis (in which the therapist feeds post-hypnotic suggestions into the subconscious mind whilst the client is in trance. This reprogrammes the inner mind to create the required changes in behaviour). The aim is to use the power of the mind in hypnosis to help a smoker to let go of their smoking habit quite easily, without suffering from the side effects (e.g. cravings, irritability, the need to eat more) that often bedevil a smoker if they try to give up by going 'cold turkey' and only using willpower. My understanding is that hypnotherapy has a higher success rate than any other method in terms of helping someone to give up smoking. I have helped many hundreds of people to become smoke-free over the years, and many of them have been amazed at how the hypnotherapy has made it so much easier than they would ever have imagined. So, when Chris' wife told me that he wanted to stop smoking and she booked him in to come and see me, I envisaged a fairly standard, routine process that would help him to become a non-smoker quite effortlessly. What transpired was quite the opposite.

Chris was an ex-professional rugby league player who at the age of 40 was still powerfully built but who was now working in a manual job. He told me that since retiring from rugby he had started smoking and was now smoking 20–30 cigarettes a day, and he was starting to suffer from chest problems. His breathing was becoming more laboured (especially when he did anything physical), he had a wheeze sometimes, he had to clear his throat regularly and he could feel his old levels of fitness fading away rapidly. In short, his smoking habit was having a significantly negative effect on his health (and sooner or later it would probably cause some form of smoking-related illness). I explained to him the hypnotherapy smoking cessation process, and when he was ready I then began to take him into hypnosis.

Chris went beautifully into trance and I proceeded to go through my standard smoking cessation routine with him, feeding his subconscious mind with very powerful suggestions about being a non-smoker. We finished the session, he professed himself to be a non-smoker and he left my office happily smoke-free. Another job well done, I thought to myself.

Imagine my surprise when, about three weeks later, his wife rang me. "Steve," she said, her voice sounding fraught on the phone, "since Chris left you three weeks ago he hasn't had a cigarette. He hasn't even wanted one. However, he's been like a bear with a sore head, firstly just being grumpy all of the time, and then as the days have passed becoming more and more irritable. He's always had a bit of a temper, but last night, he just went berserk. We were sitting in the kitchen at the dinner table with the children and I made a remark about something, nothing at all really, and he just flipped. He started shouting at me, screaming and yelling like a madman. I shouted back for him to calm down and he went crazy. He swept the crockery off the table and started smashing cups and plates on the floor, screaming and shouting as he did so. He then ripped doors off the kitchen cupboards, and then got a hammer and started smashing the new floor tiles. Our new kitchen which we only had installed a few weeks ago is completely wrecked. The children were terrified, screaming and crying, and I was petrified that he was so out of control he was going to hurt us too. I grabbed the children, pushed them into the car, locked the doors and drove off with Chris chasing us down the drive yelling and waving the hammer above his head like a maniac. We've spent the night at my parents' house and I haven't slept a wink, the children are still crying and I don't know what to do. Steve, does this normally happen when someone comes to stop smoking with you?"

I reassured her that it wasn't! I had never heard of anyone having such an extreme reaction, but it was obvious that there was some connection with Chris stopping smoking and the irrational rage that had been building up inside him since he came to see me. She told me that she had spoken to him on the phone that morning, and that he was distraught over what had happened and utterly ashamed of himself. I told her that he must come back to see me as quickly as possible so that we could work on this and lay it to rest. She booked him in a couple of days later, and when Chris arrived for the session he was embarrassed and contrite about his actions. In tears he explained how terrible he felt about his flare-up. I explained to him what I thought had happened.

You will sometimes hear people say that when they stopped smoking they became more irritable and angry than usual. What this means is that without realising they have been using their smoking habit as a means of anaesthetising their inner emotional pain. Basically, there are three aspects to anyone's smoking habit: firstly, it's a habit, and most smokers build up a range of habit patterns around their cigarettes (always have a cup of tea with a cigarette; always have a cigarette after they've eaten; always have a cigarette after sex; etc., etc.). Secondly, smoking is an addictive habit. Nicotine is one of the most addictive substances known to man and most smokers become addicted. However, the third aspect of smoking, the emotional aspect, is hardly ever discussed and not many people know about it. Having treated many hundreds of smokers over the years, my estimation is that around one in ten of all smokers do not merely experience the first two aspects (the habits and the addiction), but they primarily are what I call 'psychological smokers'. This means that their main reason for smoking is to use the cigarettes as a way to subconsciously anaesthetise their inner negative emotions (anger, sadness, fear, anxiety or guilt). The EFT (Emotional Freedom Technique) and TFT (Thought Field Therapy) 'take' on addictions is that ALL addictive substances are a means of anaesthetising anxieties and inner emotional pain (EFT and TFT are two very powerful and effective therapies that involve tapping on selected acupuncture points on the body whilst tuning into the problem). My thoughts about Chris were that he was probably a psychological smoker and that once we took his cigarettes away we had taken away the lid from his 'emotional pressure cooker' containing his anger and emotional hurts, and they had bubbled up to the surface causing his horrendous outburst. I explained that the way forward was to work on releasing the causes of the anger by emptying his 'emotional pressure cooker' in a safe way. Then, he would be able to stop smoking without any further problems. Chris understood my reasoning and I took some details about his personal history. I was looking for any emotional traumas that could be causing his anger issues, but to my surprise I found none. He had had a happy childhood, and the only significant emotional event in his life had been the death of his father a few years previously. However, he was already smoking prior to his father's passing and he had always had a short temper. It was obvious that there was something else under the surface that needed investigating, and once I had taken him into hypnosis and elicited an Ideo-Motor Response (the IMR technique I explained in Chapter 1) his subconscious used a finger to signal that there were four past lives that were causing the anger problem. Very quickly Chris moved into the first of them. He started to shift around in the chair, and a worried frown came over his face. I asked him where he was and what he was experiencing. His voice took on a degree of harshness as he spoke:

"I'm outdoors and it's dark. I'm a soldier, about 25 years old and I'm lost and alone. I've lost my comrades, and I'm looking for other helmets like mine. I don't know which way to go, but I know I'll have to make a decision in a minute; I can't just stay here. I feel indecisive. I'm used to being told what to do. Something tells me to go forward. I've got to find somebody, I can't stay here. I feel tired and dazed. I'm a long way from home. I start walking through the night. It's warm and I'm hungry. The sun's coming up and it's a beautiful morning but there's no one to share it with." I asked Chris to tell me what had happened to bring him to this situation and he started to cry. As he explained he became more and more emotional and animated. *"Losing your mates – there's no point to it all. You get sent to do something and you lose all your fucking mates. Take the bridge they said, but after we took it I lost all my fucking mates. One fucking shell. All good men and now it's just a pile of fucking bricks. It's not right. I just walked away. It's not right."*

Chris lay sobbing quietly for some time before eventually the emotions subsided and he was calm. There was nothing else to experience in that particular life so I brought him back out of trance. He was solemn as we debriefed the experience, but he felt much calmer than he had felt for days. Surprised by what had happened, and certainly not a believer in the concept of reincarnation or past lives, he expressed scepticism that past life therapy would help with his problem. He agreed to trust me though, as the work I had done with his wife had made a big difference to her, and he had seen such positive changes in her as a result of the therapy.

In Chris' next session he went into the second of the past lives, and he saw himself as a woman in her thirties on board a sailing ship. She was emigrating with her young son after the death of her husband. She was obviously very poor since she spent the entire voyage on the deck of the ship as she couldn't afford a cabin below decks. Fairly soon, however, he began to feel anxious as a storm started to develop:

"It's night-time and there are waves breaking over the decks. I feel really worried, it's a bad storm. I'm trying to protect my little boy. We're above decks getting knocked about. It's cold. The boat's rocking left and right, there's lots of noise and the wind is screaming. I'm trying to hang on with my right hand and hold my son with my left hand, but my hands are tiring and I don't think I can hold him much longer." Chris started to blow out through his lips and his body started to twist as he felt the tension and the physical effort of his situation. *"All our clothes are wet and my son's frightened and screaming – 'Mum.' The deck's full of water and there are barrels and ropes and wood floating on the deck. I don't want to let go of him but I can't hold on any longer. I let go and we slide down the side of the deck into the water. We're swilling around as the boat tosses up and down. I can't do anything for him, it's too cold. He's been hit on the head by something, he's not moving. I can't help him, I can't help myself. I'm cold, weak and numb; I feel I'm blacking out. I know he's not going to make it, and I know I've lost him. I keep drifting in and out of consciousness. I can't even hear the noise now. I'm trying to hold on, but I'm really cold. The stupid clothes that women wear. I'm blacking out now."* Chris relaxed and his body lay still for a couple of minutes. He continued his narrative in a softer voice: *"It's morning, the sea's calm and the storm's gone. I'm cold. I'm asking people where my son is. What a mess there is on the deck. The bodies of some people are lying, covered up, at the front. I go and have look. One of them's my son. I have no feelings; I'm numb with the cold. There are three men lying there and my boy. I've never been so cold in my life. I go below decks to a warm stove and put some dry clothes on. I know my boy's dead but I just can't feel for him as I'm so tired and cold. I lay down to sleep."* After a short pause he continued: *"It's later that day and whoever's in charge wants to bury him at sea. I want to take him to our destination and bury him so I'll be able to visit his grave. We have a discussion and I feel a lot of soul-searching but we decide it's the best thing to do. They've put the three men's bodies*

over the side. My son's wrapped in a black blanket and pushed over the side. He's gone now. I can't feel anything, just cold and empty. I've no husband and no lad now. I'm tired. We eventually dock and it's a warm place. There are horses and wagons and a church. It's a fairly new town. I've got nothing, but everyone's helpful. Later on I meet a man and get married."

Chris sighed deeply but the trauma was over, and he came out of trance feeling quite subdued, albeit with a sense of lightness inside. A feeling of calmness stayed with him until our next session, in which we worked through the remaining past lives. The first of them was very kinaesthetic, with Chris feeling lots of sensations in his body, and as he regressed into it he began to groan loudly and squirm in the chair. I asked him what was happening. He spoke in a broad, Northern accent:

"I'm underground. I'm a miner, a man around 30 years old. I'm alone at the moment, although there were others here. My right arm and leg are trapped. The roof's collapsed. I feel pressure on my right side. I'm frightened." His breathing came faster and shallower and he continued to moan: *"There were five or six of us, on our way back to the surface and I was at the rear of the group. I can hear them trying to come back for me. I feel a lot of pressure and pain in my right side. You always know that it's likely to happen someday. I'm worried about being able to work again. I'm starting to feel cold, even though it's warm down here. I can see me mate's lights coming towards me. They give me some water to drink. It's not been a bad fall and I don't think I'm too badly hurt. They're moving the big timber off me."* Chris jerked and began to writhe, speaking through gritted teeth: *"I can't feel my right hand. They're putting me on a stretcher. It's hurting more now as they're walking. I'm in the basket now, there's only room for two of them and the stretcher. I can't wait to see the light again. I'm at the top – daylight. I go in an ambulance to hospital. It's not as bad as it might have been, I've broken my ankle and fingers and some bones in my hand. My wife and sons come to visit me. I know I wasn't trapped too badly so I wasn't too scared, but I don't want to go*

back down again. I tell my wife and later on we move and I get a better job. That feels much better. I've forgotten about the accident now."

Chris was calm again by this stage, so I asked him to move on to the final life which we needed to explore. After a few moments he sighed and he looked serious and upset by something:

"I'm outside in the countryside and it's a beautiful day. I'm a man in his late 50s, standing on a fell-side looking after a flock of sheep. I'm contemplating my life and feeling sad. I never got married and I feel lonely. I've no relatives left alive. Winter's on its way and I know I'm going to struggle. I won't see anyone for weeks. The cold and harshness is getting too much for me. The thought of another winter..." His voice trailed off for a minute or so, before he started to shiver. His voice shook as he continued: *"There's loads of snow. I'm sitting in front of a fire but my fingers, knees and ankles are stiff. Nothing in my body wants to work. The sheep are in trouble but I haven't got the strength to see to them. I think that's my lot. I'm sitting in my chair looking at the fire. I know what's coming. I feel sad that I'm on my own but I'm tired and I close my eyes. I can't be bothered to bank the fire up. I feel sorry for my sheep but I feel a quiet contentment. I just drift up and away. I feel calm now, lighter."*

Chris let out a big sigh and we moved away from that life into this present one. As he continued to relax in trance I gave him some suggestions about letting go of all the negative effects that the past lives had had upon him, and I fed his subconscious new instructions about being a non-smoker. We finished the session and Chris came out of trance ready to stop smoking. We had cleared all of the subconscious emotional drivers that had been pushing him into smoking. As a result he was able to become a non-smoker without any problems, and the last time I spoke to him several months later he was not only a non-smoker but he also felt a lot calmer.

Section Two

Physical Issues

Chapter 4

Toni's Story

Toni came to me with a combination of issues, each of which fed into the other. An intelligent 42 year old, she felt depressed, was overweight and had a severe back problem that caused her constant pain. As a result of the pain Toni was unable to go to the gym, she was depressed because of the constant pain, and she was overeating because of the feelings of depression. As she ate more, she put on more weight which made her more depressed, and her low mood made it harder to put up with the back pain; a cycle of unhappiness that Toni was finding it hard to cope with. She had had surgery for the back problem but the surgeons could not find anything wrong, and had merely discharged her and told her to live with the pain. She had undergone many physiotherapy sessions and the frustration of sundry appointments with her doctors but nothing had helped, and she felt forlorn and hopeless about her future.

I usually find that if there is a mystery illness in the body it comes from past lifetimes, and although I didn't tell her this (she was certainly not a believer in past lives) this turned out to be the case.

I took her into hypnosis and once Toni was in trance, I asked her subconscious mind to take her back to the emotional root source of the back problem, and via an IMR it indicated that this was in a previous life. I guided her back through time, and after a few minutes I watched her eyelids start to flicker. I asked her to talk to me with her eyes closed and describe the images that had begun to appear in her mind's eye. She began to talk to me in a hushed voice with a sense of bewilderment in her tone. At this stage she could not believe that what she was seeing was not just in her imagination, but that is often the case when people first go into a previous life when in trance. I asked her not to analyse whatever she was experiencing but to simply go with whatever came to her.

SB: "Tell me what you are seeing, Toni. Are you inside or outside? Is it day or night?"

Toni: *"I'm outside. I can see a big lake with mountains in the distance. It's daytime, and there's a haze over the lake."*

SB: "Are you a girl, boy, man, woman, or something else?"

T: *"I'm a teenage boy, with my family."*

SB: "How do you feel?"

T: *"I feel good; I'm throwing stones into the lake."*

SB: "What happens?"

T: *"My father comes to me and puts his arm around me, he wants to speak to me. 'Well young man, what are we going to do with you?' I feel that we are only physically close, but not emotionally close. He tells me that I should become more involved, I'm too quiet and isolated. What am I going to do with my life? I tell him I want to study art but he is scornful. He has been a soldier, now he's in local government, and he thinks I should join the army. There's nothing I would hate more, but he insists I really should be in the Hitlerjugend. He says I must join all teenagers, 'it's for your Fatherland. You must feel this sense of community; we will become a strong nation'."*

Toni sighed deeply, her face as she lay in my reclining chair showing the tension and conflict that she was feeling as the young man in the past life. Slowly she was beginning to go deeper into the life and let go of her conscious scepticism. This enabled her to start to feel the emotions of the character whose life she was reliving.

"It's difficult to tell anybody that I don't believe in this, it's stifling; stamping out the individual. But Father's delighted with it."

SB: "Do you get a sense of the year, or perhaps your name in that lifetime?" Toni paused for a few moments and replied:

T: *"I think it's 1936 and my name is Manfred Zeller. I'm somewhere in Bavaria. I'm still at high school. There are many arguments with*

Father because when I graduate I want to study art but this is not what he wants me to do, he wants me to have a good career in the army. He is some kind of local hero; he fought in the first war for a united Germany. He is proud of that – 'We showed all those Prussians, they think they are the only fighters,' he says.

I am due to leave school but things are looking bad. Europe is restless and there is a very strong Nationalist political feeling, they're trying to build a strong country and rebuild the economy. The Chancellor says we Germans must build a proud, secure, healthy, strong race."

SB: "How do you feel about this?"

T: *"I understand, because the country was bowed and humbled. We need to reshape our identity. This man thinks there is no end to the things we can achieve, but things are becoming more regulated to create a strong structure in the country."* Toni paused for a few seconds, before she continued in a melancholy tone: *"I agree to my father's wishes and I will join the army for four years to please him, then after that I intend to go to art school."*

SB: "Move to the next significant part of the life."

T: *"I'm a little older now, around 18. I'm just outside Berlin at a training school. It's a very beautiful place with a lake and there's a group of us training together. It's just like school – theory, maps, firearms, physical exercise, calibration, firing distances. We wear uniforms with high collars that feel very hairy. There's a sense of comradeship, and we eat and drink well. The others tease me for being the quiet one. I draw cartoons of my comrades."*

Throughout this description of her military training school, Toni had a slightly amused look on her face. Then her bearing changed and she frowned as she continued:

"There's been a sudden change. Everyone's stopped laughing. We're listening to the radio. We are at war. This is serious now. I feel scared and apprehensive. This wasn't what I had in mind when I joined up. I can see myself over the next little while in lots of places, in a car, in the Rhineland, back home, in Berlin. I'm always in a state of panic, trying to keep my head above water, but I think my senior officers

know I'm never going to be really successful. The war's started and I've been sent into Holland. I haven't been sent to the front-line. My job is in supplies, but I've been given a new brief, for the protection of art. Everywhere I go in Holland I have to visit local galleries and art collections and assess whether it needs protecting from a potential Allied invasion. I must not reveal any of this though because it must not be known that there is a question of an Allied invasion. I'm staying in a Dutch town; we've taken over the best accommodation and it's very comfortable. I feel so alone and unwelcome. The locals have to talk to us but the resentment and disgust they feel is almost palpable. Some of my fellow officers relish this feeling of superiority and power, getting what you want when you want it. I think it's a high price to pay."

SB: "Move to the next significant part of that life."

T: *"I can smell dampness. I'm sitting in a car, part of a convoy travelling east. It's summer and it's wet. I think it's 1941 and there's a big movement of troops. I'm in Group Central. There are massive troop movements all over Europe and a lot of troops moving east. Our instructions are to take Moscow. So far it's been easy. I've seen spasmodic fighting but I've avoided hand-to-hand combat."* Toni was quiet for a while as she moved on in time, then she resumed: *"I'm sitting at a big dining table in a country house. It's the Officers' Mess. The Schnapps is flowing and the older officer on my left is telling me that the plans are to clear the lands, move out the Slavs and the Jews and send them back to support the war machine at home, and to bring in Germans from the Fatherland to settle here. He says that there are rumours that some senior officers are unhappy with this treatment of the Slavs and the Jews so some of them don't want to be here. There may be requests for transfers."* Again she paused for a while and was silent. Then she became tense, her body stiffening and her face serious. She shivered and continued:

"We're stuck. It's October and we should have been in Moscow by now but the weather's closed in. We've been caught out as we need winter supplies. It's snowing and the weather's bad. We're not

properly equipped for this, no one expected it to close in so quickly. I'm permanently cold. We have to sequester supplies locally, which means the locals will have to go without. They don't like this. They think we're soft as we're not used to these conditions. There's been fierce fighting. I'm dressed in my long grey coat with two brass buttons, a belt, thick leather gloves and a peaked hat. There's a vehicle waiting for me. We're leaving, part of a troop movement."

Toni's voice became a whisper as she continued to shiver, her hands knotted together. The tension that she felt was visible to me as I watched her. Her jaw was set, her brow furrowed:

"Everybody's edgy. Vehicles are getting separated because of the weather, trucks are getting stuck. It's all very messy and progress is slow. We've had warnings that Russian troops have been seen. We're a long way behind. We're coming through what seems to be a deserted village. Not a good place to get stuck. I've been put in charge of a group of men. We're being fired on from a four-storey building that's been bombed. I order everyone out of the vehicle, keeping down low. This is what we'll do. The driver will move the vehicle forward, we'll move with it. Get as close to the buildings as possible. I'm the most senior so I have to go with them."

Toni's speech had become more rapid, as she experienced the terror of the situation. I asked her how she felt. She almost spat out the words in a hushed, breathless tone:

"My stomach's in knots, I'm so scared. We go inside the building. My clothes are big and bulky so it's difficult to move quietly and quickly. We go up to the first floor. There's paper, desks, rubble. I hear something higher up. I take four men. Quietly. Amazingly, the stairs are intact. We're out on the top floor." Toni flinched and jerked. Loudly and rapidly she went on: *"Suddenly, things are happening all around. There are people all over. Somebody comes for me. I have to shoot. There's fighting going on all around me, I've just shot someone. It's the first time I've ever shot anyone so close. He's only a boy. I didn't want to but I had to. I have to make sure he's dead so I push him with my foot. He's thin and pale with dark hair. I feel terrible. In my*

mind I'm thinking this is wrong; wasteful, pointless. What does this violence achieve? Two of my men are hurt. There are six Russians, five of them dead. One of them's groaning but the Sergeant's shot him again to finish him off."

Toni relaxed and her body softened in the chair. Her speech was less panicky, but she spoke with sadness in her voice:

"Our job's done. We have to keep moving or we'll get further behind. We just leave the bodies there. The boy that I killed was somebody's son or brother. We continue moving east, but I just feel quiet and down. These people fight with such determination – they'll show us no mercy. After the Netherlands and Poland, which was so easy, this has been a terrible awakening. I've seen mankind stripped of all humanity. Is this what we're really like? I hate the violence and the ugliness. I don't belong here."

She was silent again for a while, as she moved on to the next important scenes in the life. Unwittingly, she began to move to the most significant part of the past life, the event that had caused the back problem in this lifetime.

She continued to look anxious, every now and again shivering with the cold of the Russian winter that she was reliving. Sometimes her hands knotted together; sometimes they rubbed up and down the arms of the chair in an agitated manner. What happened next was not anticipated by either of us. She spoke again, quietly:

"We've taken over an old schoolhouse and there's a boiler there. It's so cold but we're frustratingly close to Moscow. I think we're near a town called Smolensk, maybe 40 miles from Moscow. The spring will soon be starting and we've had orders to go on the offensive as soon as the weather turns. I've heard about a painting in a church nearby, a triptych. I decide to take a motorbike and take a look at it. The village which it's in is north-west from here. I've found the village and I go to the church. I'm desperate to look at the pictures. I'm walking around the church. I can't get in. I walk back towards the road. I'm furious – where's the motorbike? OW!"

At this point Toni screamed and her whole body jumped about two feet in the air. I was so shocked I too jumped up about three feet! She lay in the chair at an awkward angle and began to moan and gasp:

"Something's hit me. I've been shot. In the right side, my back. I can't see where it came from. There's no one around and my back's gone. I should have brought someone with me. I can't get up out of the snow. Maybe my coat's stopped it doing too much damage. Who am I fooling?" Throughout all this Toni was coughing and moaning, as if coughing up blood. *"I don't even get to see the pictures in the church. I'm lying there for some time. It's getting dark now. Surely they'll send somebody."* She began to squirm in the chair, all the time coughing and panting as her life ebbed away. She whispered: *"I feel really cold. I can see one red flower."* Gradually her movements and breathing slowed down. After a long pause, she simply said, *"I'm looking down on myself. I feel peaceful, still and light. I'm leaving, into warmth and light. I'm glad to leave the panic and the cold."*

The life was over, and the young man who had never wanted to be a soldier but an artist was dead. After the session, once Toni had come back out of hypnosis she said that she felt very aware that as he was dying he realised he had made a big mistake in going to the village without an armed escort. She realised that there was now an energy moving around in her back and she said that the point of impact of the bullet was exactly where she had felt considerable pain for many years. She also insisted that she knew nothing about the Nazis' campaign in Russia in the Second World War, and she was shocked and surprised at what she'd experienced in the session.

From that day onwards her back began to improve and within a few weeks was completely healed as if the pain had never existed in the first place (and remember she had even had surgery which had not found anything wrong). Her consultant at hospital discharged her and she was now able to make inroads into losing weight.

Of course, just eliminating the back pain made a big difference to Toni, because the pain had stopped her from doing any exercise which meant she could not go to the gym to help with her weight problem. Once her back pain was no longer there she was able to start exercising again. However, her depression meant that she kept overeating to anaesthetise her unhappy feelings (also known as 'comfort eating'), so it was obvious that to help Toni with this cycle of problems we had to work on the emotional root causes of the depression and the need to overeat (she was snacking a lot and eating large portions of food at mealtimes).

Although in our next session Toni spoke to me in a matter-of-fact way about her problems, the tone of her voice and her body language gave away the sadness she was feeling about herself. It was as if she was trying to remain distant from the emotions that were buried inside her. She was an attractive, highly intelligent woman whose life was being spoilt by her negative mindset and her unhappiness about her weight. Despite being sceptical about the concept of previous lives (she was a left-brainer working in the legal profession), she accepted the need to look for the reasons behind her issues and she was happy to be hypnotised in order to do so. Once again I guided her into trance, and her subconscious mind indicated that there were several past lives which contained significant emotional events that were causing the problems. As she drifted deeper into relaxation her closed eyelids began to gently flutter, a sign that she was seeing images on her mental picture screen. I asked her to describe what she was experiencing.

After a few seconds, she breathed deeply and softly replied:

"I'm standing in a cornfield in strong sunshine, with a small boy by my side. I'm a young woman, about 20 years old. The wind's blowing and it's a beautiful scene. There are mountains in the background and I'm wearing a white bonnet, a long dress and a white apron. I can feel the apron crackling in the wind. I have long hair which is escaping

from underneath my bonnet."

SB: "How do you feel?"

"I'm happy to be here, I feel joyful. I'm smiling and holding the child's hand. I can see a man in a black hat and coat on a grey horse. We go inside our house, a small wooden house with a rail outside for the horse. My house is special; it's got an indoor water pump." She was quiet for a few moments, before she continued: *"I'm serving food at a table. We say grace, there's the man and the boy and another man sitting. I feel content; it's good food – biscuits, gravy, home-made bread, stew. There's coffee – ouch! It's hot coffee."* Toni jumped a little as she felt the burn and her hand jumped in the air. *"I need a cloth to pick it up."* She appeared to be living a past life in America, in the Old West. She didn't speak for a couple of minutes, as if enjoying the feelings of domestic bliss, so I asked her to move on to the next significant time of that life. Initially, she spoke lightly with a half-smile on her lips, but after a few seconds her face became serious:

"I'm in my room at the back of the house and the boy's bouncing on the bed. I can see him now in the bed wearing a white nightshirt. I think his ears hurt. He has a fever, he's sweating. I feel scared." Toni began to breathe heavily and she started to cry. *"There's snow on the house, melting. The boy's gone. I wish I was dead too."* After a while, she stopped crying and sighed. There was a tremor in her voice as she continued: *"Spring comes. I feel lonely. I can see a buckboard outside, all loaded up. I'm going away."*

Again, she was silent for a while so I asked her to move to a later time in that life. After a minute or so, during which she was moving through the life, she spoke:

"I'm sitting on a garden bench, outside a town house. I'm wearing a brown dress with flowers on. I'm alone and it's years later. I'm middle-aged now, feeling calm. I live here with another woman, younger than me, wearing a straw boater and a long skirt with a tiny waist. She's carrying books; I think she's a schoolteacher. We're friends, I'm her housekeeper, I think I look after her. There's a grandfather clock on the

stairs and it's a modern house in a row of others, with a small backyard and a street out front. People know me here, but I wish I was back in the country. I know I can't be but that's where I lost my boy and that's the reason why I left. I haven't moved on though, there's still a big hole inside me." Once more she sighed deeply and was quiet for a time, and when she continued it was obvious that she had again moved on in time:

"I'm in the general store and there are big barrels in front of the counter. There's a man behind the counter wearing a white apron. He's bald with glasses and a moustache. He's called Seth and he's jolly and helpful. I'm buying flour and raisins. I think he likes me. He calls me Maisie and he jokes with me. I've moved on now and I'm in a long nightgown in a bedroom. I've let my long grey hair down and I'm brushing it. I'm around 50 or 60 years old now and I'm in a different house. I sit in another room on one side of a fire with Seth. He's reading a paper. I feel content and happy with him; we're two old people together. He lights his pipe and I'm scolding him for the smell, but he doesn't mind."

Toni had a gentle smile on her face, but after a few seconds she began to cry softly. *"It's near the end now. I'm in bed with a blanket round my shoulders. Seth's sitting next to me on the bed. I don't feel well, tired. I'm saying I'm sorry but I'm so tired I want to go. I don't want to leave him but I have to go. I'm peaceful as I pass away. It's like a big stone's being lifted off my chest. I'm sad to leave but I know I'll see my boy."* Smiling, she started to cry tears of joy. *"He's there, he's just the same. I feel pure joy, and light."*

The life was over, and the troubles from that lifetime that had so worn down Maisie as a result of losing her son were over. She was reunited with him in Spirit, and Toni felt as if a great weight had been lifted from her. She surfaced from trance and told me that she felt lightness inside, a sure sign that the negative effects that that past life had had upon her in this present lifetime were dissolved away.

As you can see, when I'm working in therapy I don't usually go looking for particular details (names, places, dates etc.) from the past life as those are just distractions from the main aim of the process. I'm aiming to let my client relive the negative emotions from that lifetime so the emotions can be released and the client is able to feel free of the problem they have caused in this life. Although the past life appeared to have been in America in the 1800s, we didn't need to find out any specific information about it, we simply had to let Toni re-experience the locked-in feelings. Neither do we have to analyse the connections between the past life experiences and the problems in this life. It is simply enough to release the emotions, and the problems fade away. Toni had been overeating as a means of anaesthetising the emotional pain from that life.

At the start of our next therapy session Toni said that she'd noticed a big improvement in her eating habits as a result of our past life session, and she felt the need to snack had considerably reduced. She also felt stronger in herself, and one or two issues in her home life that would usually have bothered her hadn't troubled her. She was a bit less sceptical about past life therapy now, and she was ready to go into trance to explore the next life that was causing her eating problems. She lay back in my reclining chair and closed her eyes as I talked to her gently and induced a pleasant hypnotic trance. Her subconscious took her back through time into another lifetime, and soon she began to tell me what she was seeing:

"I'm outside and it's daytime. There are people with horses. I'm a young woman, around 20 years old. I have a bird – a falcon on my hand with a hood on its head. I'm standing near a horse. There are lots of woods and fields. I'm hunting with the bird. Other people are attending me. I feel happy. I'm the daughter of somebody important. These people are here to serve me. A man next to me is wearing lots of leather and the horse has a strange headdress. I have long dark plaits. My shoes and the hem of my gown and my long green cloak are wet

and muddy. I'm sending the bird to fly – it's a merlin. I wear a very heavy cross with rubies on it. Oh, but I walk badly; I don't know why. They call me, 'Lady', and help me to get on my horse. I'm going home. I ride through the trees across a small bridge over water with swans swimming in it. There's a long stone wall and a wooden top and I go through some gates into a big courtyard with straw on the ground. Men come to hold the horses. We've had a good day's hunting. There's a dead boar. Father has not been with us today, he's had to talk to someone. He wants to talk to me now. 'Child.' Ah, when he calls me 'child' I know he wants to talk seriously. Like the time my mother died. He says that it's good news as a suitor has been found for me. I was promised to William when I was 14 but he died and Father feared no one else would have me because I'm not sound of limb. But a widower is looking for a new bride and would consider me because of Father's land. I don't like this as he lives three days away. I am unhappy but Father says I must obey him and I can take things with me – my chest, my prix dieux, Oswald and Matilda and two of my birds. I'm crying and Matilda is comforting me. Half of me is excited and half is scared. When he comes he will bring his own priest but Father says we will use our own priest for the marriage. He gives me a gift of a heavy gold chain for a marriage token."

So, the stage is set for an unhappy scenario, the negative feelings of which Toni will have brought from that past lifetime into this present life. From her description of things I guessed that she was living a life in medieval times in England, the daughter of a wealthy landowner either living in a castle or a large stately home. She paused for a time, during which she moved on in the lifetime to another day, possibly just a few days later:

"I'm at home next to a big fire, arguing with my father because I want to be by myself. I'm annoyed that I'm expected to be kind and polite to the people all the time. There are people around all the time and I want to be by myself. I have to learn languages, music, poetry, and there are people in waiting all the time." Toni looked irritated as she lay in the chair, her brow furrowed and she spoke through

gritted teeth, sounding like a petulant teenager. *"We're expecting visitors. I usually like visitors but not now. I have to go and check the wine and the beer. There are many people in the kitchen and dogs and straw on the floor. There are people outside washing, they smell. My father has said that we are privileged to have such a visitor, and that the union will be good for both houses. I am to be introduced to a prospective suitor."*

The last words were spat out with a harshness that showed she wasn't too keen on the possibility of marriage. I asked her how she felt about this. She almost growled at me:

"Disgusted; I have heard that he is old and ugly. I have to get ready.

My maid is fussing with my headdress. I'm shivering, partly as I'm nervous and also because my room has no glass in the window. My gown comes in pieces, a top and a skirt over it, pulled tight. I'm cross with her so I slap her. She's so pleased with my shoes; they're so delicate and mustn't be worn outside. I can hear a party coming – horses and dogs. There are 20–30 people and banners – it's quite ostentatious. Everybody has to be accommodated. My father's fussing and he sends his steward to show them in. He says I must look more modest. I try because I want to please him. I feel so anxious." Toni *was breathing quickly, her hands fidgeting nervously. "He comes in. His cloak is strange, made of ermine and he's wearing long boots. He doesn't look as bad as I expected, but he is grey. He looks as old as my father with his grey beard. I curtsy and he takes my hand. He's wearing gloves with rings on the outside. He calls me, 'My Lady Bertha.' His name's Edwin. The two men are talking. What do I do now? Have I passed the test? It seems it's important that I make good beer and wine – is that all? This is a good business arrangement; I am to marry this man. He looks acceptable but as long as he's not cruel. He has a lot of followers who are very noisy and rude. They all want feeding. His steward is kind and gentle and thoughtful." She continued to look anxious, and then her face saddened. "I sit down to dine and suddenly I think I have to leave this place and my father. I have no mother. I'll leave all by myself with this strange man. I hadn't thought of that. I suppose it happens to all who are like me. I can take my maid and one or two other servants but I will know no one there. Is he going to be good to me? I don't want to leave my home. Hmmm; my wine must be good as everyone's had plenty and there are a lot of red faces. There's a lot of noise and clamour, with people shouting but I just want to go to bed. Why do men always shout at one another? Now they're starting to make jokes at my expense, even my father's doing it. It's like being a horse or a cow."* She breathed a big sigh of relief. *"Finally my father takes my hand and says I may be excused and that I've done well. I take a torch and go up to bed. Tomorrow I leave. I'm sad to be going, leaving my home and going into the unknown.*

I'm worried what things will be like. I'm taking my birds and my maid. Oswald will care for my birds, I know he understands." Suddenly, she began to shake and her breathing came quickly. *"Now it's the day. I'm so scared I'm shaking. There are rows of porters outside. Matilda's closing the chest and everything's taken downstairs. I go to the chapel and Father Richard is there. I'm shaking so much. Why? The man doesn't have a bad reputation. He smiles kindly enough at me but he's still an older man. When we played as children the girls always said never marry an older man."* After a long pause, during which she was obviously reliving the marriage service, she sighed and her shaking subsided. *"It is done. I feel sorry to leave all that is familiar. Edwin has said he'll take care of me but that's only words. I'm leaving now. Father embraces me, but he doesn't seem so sad. I travel in the wagon and it's very uncomfortable. I ask if I can ride but they say not now as it's not safe. Matilda laughs. Edwin is 53 and he has three children already but he may not want to have anymore. We're stopping under a wooden canopy. We're staying here tonight."* Toni began to breathe nervously again, her hands shaking slightly. Her body was stiff and tense. *"Matilda is saying, 'Go on, child.' The only person I've ever shared my bed with is her. My hand is in his nightshirt. There are grey hairs on his chest. I'm so nervous. He takes my hands and we say our prayers. He takes me into bed. He tries to make me laugh. He says that he calls me his leaf because I shake so much."* Toni was silent for a few moments and then she went on:

"His home is very grand. He has two sons and a small daughter who expects me to be a mother to her but I know nothing about children. She's ten now but she's had no mother since she was seven. She likes me. How can I do this? His sons are older than me." Toni was quiet again for a while, and her body relaxed as she moved on in time. *"I've moved on now and it's maybe a year later. I'm seated at my window talking to Matilda. I have prayed but it's like living in a wilderness and there's no joy here. Nobody's cruel or unkind but I don't know how I can live here and I don't like the priest."* She began to shiver. *"It's dusk now and I'm walking outside on a hillside. I just feel I have to be away. 'Mistress' – Oswald's calling me, he's carrying a cloak. 'You shouldn't be here on your own.' He puts the cloak around my shoulders. He's so gentle. 'You must come in.' He takes me by the hand and draws me in. It's the first kind, thoughtful action from anyone for weeks. I realise that I care more for Oswald than I do for my husband. Matilda sees me and is shocked – 'Rather one of his sons than his servant,' she says."* Toni sighed again, deeply, and began to wring her hands. *"What am I going to do? I have to go to confession. It's coming up to Lent and I have to be shriven. I cannot say this to that priest, but I have to make my peace with God. I go to the priest but I cannot tell him, he makes me uneasy. I'm sure if I tell him something dreadful may happen – I may lose Oswald. I don't tell him, just make up all the sins. My penance is fasting from dawn to dusk every day throughout Lent and prayers at dawn and night. I still mistrust the priest. He makes me shiver."*

Our time was up for this session so I brought Toni out of trance. She was thoughtful and sat for a few moments without saying anything. Although she was back in the present and the door to the past life she had been experiencing was closed until our next appointment, she knew that there was still more to come in that lifetime. With a shrug of her shoulders she agreed to see me again a few days later.

I too knew that the past life held more traumas that were affecting her in this life causing her to overeat. I also suspected that it had something to do with her depression, which had affected her for some years. I knew that we were doing good work and making excellent progress towards her goals of taking control of her eating habits and overcoming the darkness of the depression. It was just a matter of time, and a few more therapy sessions, before we would help her to get her life back on track and she would be able to live freely and in a more balanced way.

When Toni came for the next session, she told me that although the past life had not been on her mind much, she had realised that in her present life there was not much fun. Her husband's business was the all-consuming focus of his life and she felt that she was playing second fiddle to his work. A part of her yearned for other things, other places and a different way of life, just as she had in the past lifetime. This is a common feature of past life therapy as I often find that my clients are running patterns in their present life that mirror the events or feelings from their previous ones. Sometimes having this awareness is enough to create 'shifts' inside them that begin to make changes in their present life. Other times we still have to work to release the negative emotions that are driving their negative behaviours.

Once she had shared her realisations with me she made ready to experience hypnosis and lay back and closed her eyes. Within a short time she was back again in that same past life, coming up to the most important events that were causing the problems in her present life.

"I'm still young and I'm sitting at the table with my lord. I have a sore tooth. He tells me he's leaving in the morning with a party of men but he's leaving some of the household to defend us. I'm in my chamber now and Matilda's bringing me wine and willow bark for my tooth. It's like a tea. Ugh!" Her face grimaced and she stuck her tongue out as if trying to get rid of the taste. *"She says it will feel better.*

I don't know why but she's cross with me and she's been like this for days. I sometimes tell her it's because she's a dried-up old hag! My lord comes to me this night and leaves early in the morning. It's a shame the priest stays behind. I get dressed in my chamber and I can feel the year is turning as it becomes colder. Oswald comes and tells me that one of the birds is sick so I go down to the barns with him. One of the birds is sat looking ill. It has dull eyes. He's not sure why it's ill, but he thinks we should take them out later. I'm standing with a bird on my wrist. Oh! I felt something touch the side of my neck." She wriggled a little and her voice was gentle yet excited. *"Oswald has kissed the side of my neck. He apologises. I put the bird down carefully and turn to him. 'Do that again.' So he does. I've never felt anything like that. He smells of the outside, of fresh air and earth. We're holding one another and he keeps apologising. We draw apart as we realise how difficult this could be. But then we can't let it go. This is like nothing before. I have to go now but I want him so badly."* Toni's breathing quickened and she began to blush slightly. *"He's coming to me in my room. 'Lady, are you sure?' He says that I'm taking a terrible risk but I don't care. The leather he's wearing is warm and moulded to him and he has a scar. It happened to him when he was a soldier before he came to my father's."* She smiled. *"I can't believe this, but this is what it's meant to be like. Oh, I want to shout and laugh and cry. I feel so light and I want to stay like this forever. He says, 'Lady, believe me I am honest and true and I will do anything for you.' We are lovers – real lovers. This is the happiest time of my life. He's a true man, strong, kind and gentle, and he makes me feel like the most important person in the world. We are together a lot. The bird dies. My lord will want to know why when he comes back. He is like water or wine to me. I couldn't live without it.*

My maid Matilda knows what's happening. She is still cross with me but she can see how happy I am. The priest comes to tell me that he's been summoned by his bishop and must leave. Thank God! He says, 'Madam, you are not as pious as you would have us think.' Does he know? He says he will be speaking to Lord Edwin when he comes back. Is that a threat? 'Unless I look with favour upon him.' He's gone. He wears rings on every finger. I tell Oswald what he's said and he says that we must be careful now."

Toni was quiet for a couple of minutes as she moved on in time. When she resumed her narrative her voice was softer and her tone flatter. Her body shook slightly as she lay in the chair and her face had lost the happy smile she had worn when she was reliving the joy of her feelings for Oswald. Occasionally she coughed as she talked.

"Now it is colder and darker. The house is full of people. My lord is home and I am not well. I'm constantly cold. Chances to be with Oswald are fewer. We have to decide what to do. Matilda says that I am looking pale and thin. I am, but I don't know why. I feel unwell but there's no fever. We go through Christmas. I can't walk anymore and I have to be carried to my chamber. My lord keeps saying that I must eat. Matilda tempts me with broth and I eat some of it. I don't think I'm meant to get better. I should tell my lord about Oswald but how can I? I could not dishonour him. All my life I've lived for the purposes of others. I don't want to go yet. I've so much to give. My lord is sitting by my bedside but I truly want Oswald here." Her voice was just a whisper now, and her breathing was very slow. After a long pause she heaved a sigh and began to cry: *"That's it. I've just got a gentle feeling of floating. I feel happy and regretful at the same time. I know I will always be with Oswald."*

Her crying stopped and she shifted slightly in the chair. The life was complete and so I brought her out of trance. She looked lighter than she had at the start of the session, as if something had been lifted from her. We talked about her experience for a few minutes. As usual she expressed amazement at what she had seen and felt, describing the awful despair as the reality of the loveless marriage with Edwin closed in upon her. The young woman who she was in that life had felt helpless and desperate, and only the passionate love affair with Oswald had brought any joy into the situation. However, as a Christian woman she had experienced a massive amount of guilt, and it seemed that the conflicting emotions inside her had combined to weaken her physical strength, bringing about her early death. She did feel relieved that it was over and she knew that already she felt different inside. I looked forward to seeing her the following week as I knew that by 'clearing' that past life she would feel improvements in her present life.

Toni bounded into my office a week or so later and she proudly told me that her problems with food had simply not been an issue. She had not snacked once or felt the need to snack, something which she had been unable to do for years. She felt healthier and lighter, and she knew that now she could begin to lose weight. The only cloud on her horizon was her marriage, which she felt was dull and her relationship with her husband was not as loving as it should be. She realised that it mirrored the state of her marriage in her previous life. I did wonder if we should explore in trance whether Edwin in the past life was her present husband (in other words whether the soul who was Edwin had reincarnated with her in this lifetime to become her husband), something which I often do if my client is working on a difficult relationship with a partner. However, once in trance her subconscious took her into a new past life, which was contributing to causing her depression. As usual her eyelids began to flutter as she started to see the past life, and she began to talk quickly with a slight cockney accent and a clipped tone:

"I'm indoors. There are high walls and small windows. I'm alone. I'm a young boy, about nine or ten years old. I'm sitting on a sack."

SB: "How do you feel?"

"I'm tired, cold and hungry. I'm being punished by a large, fat woman. She's the matron. I've not worked hard enough. I live here in the workhouse sorting fabrics or sacks. I hate it. We get up early; cold water wash; say prayers; say we're thankful for charity; porridge breakfast; work till your fingers bleed; 15 minutes for lunch; sometimes cheese and water; supper – sometimes porridge, sometimes stew; sleep. I'm tired all the time. Men wearing chains on their coats come and

watch us. We must be polite and grateful to them. I've got no boots, but I don't go out much. We try to play sometimes but we get beaten if we're too noisy. I have no family and no way of getting out."

SB: "Have you been here for long?"

"Yes. I'm on my own. My mother left me here when I was a baby. I wish I knew her. She could take me away."

SB: "What's your name?"

"Jacob. They give us Bible names here. I feel helpless. If God is good then why am I in here? We're always supposed to be thankful, but for what? I'm frightened all the time. People sometimes come and buy the boys. I'm in trouble again for being sullen and cheeky. She's hitting me on my head. I curl up in a corner so the stick doesn't hurt so much. The men in chains are nicer than her, at least they smile. One of the boys is going off to be a butcher's boy – we won't see him again."

As she lay in the chair Toni was curled up into the foetal position, her face a picture of woe. She coughed occasionally as she spoke and her voice sounded childlike.

"I'm trying to get to sleep. When we're 12 we'll move on. She wants to get rid of as many as possible before they're 12 then they won't be a burden to the church. People keep coming to look at us but they say I'm too small. I'm no good and I've got a cough as well. They pinch my arms saying I'm puny. I've always been a weakling. She says she doesn't know how I've lasted so long. She's getting cross with me now 'cos my coughing keeps everyone awake. She gives me some hot, strong drink. It makes me feel fuzzy and I stop coughing. 'And don't you get blood on them rags.' I'm coughing so much now that my chest hurts and I feel tired. The other boys say, 'Shaddup.'" As if to emphasise this, Toni began to cough more regularly and held her hand to her chest. *"I've been taken away from the other boys. When I cough I get to spit into a bowl. I'm frightened as it's blood. The vicar comes and he's being nice to me. He doesn't say I have to be grateful."* After a few minutes her coughing subsided and she lay quietly in the chair, her breathing heavy and laboured. Finally she whispered: *"At least I'm going to be getting out of here. I turn my face to the light*

and I hear somebody calling me. I'll just go." She breathed a big sigh of relief as she straightened herself out in the chair. The life was over. *"I feel warmth and light and content."*

With a smile on her face she came out of hypnosis and stretched contentedly. The tensions of that life had dissolved away and she felt clean and relaxed inside herself. We spent a few minutes chatting about her experience as a boy in a Victorian workhouse before she left my room with a spring in her step. I knew that that past life was now cleared and the negative effects it had caused her would be no more. I looked forward to our next session as her subconscious indicated that we still had one more past life to explore. This next one proved to be the most traumatic so far.

Toni came for her next hypnotherapy session in a mixed frame of mind. On the one hand she was greatly improved as a result of the therapy she had experienced, but on the other she knew that she was not fully 'free'. She was probably 70% better, but she knew that there was still room for improvement. She was happy to go into hypnosis again, so after a short chat I laid her back in my reclining chair, and she closed her eyes and I guided her into trance. I asked her subconscious to take her back through time, as though there was no such thing as time, back to the past life which we needed to explore. Little did I know then that this past life was going to be a very significant one for Toni, with a lot of negative emotional events of a deeply unpleasant nature.

I knew that Toni had begun to access the past life because her body stiffened in the chair and after a few moments she began to breathe heavily. Although she didn't cry, her face was very sad and she looked as if at any moment she would break into tears. I asked her where she was and what she was seeing. Softly, and with a tremor in her voice, she spoke:

"I'm outside in a churchyard and I'm a young girl, maybe 12–13 years of age. I feel a terrible sadness as I stand by a graveside with my mother and a priest. It's my father's funeral. Mother's so sad. I'm

more sad for her than I am for me." She paused for a few moments, as if receiving more information about the life, before she went on: *"Father was a minister too. He was kind but distant. He died from a seizure. I'm not crying but I feel like I have a stone in my chest. I keep swallowing but it won't go away. Mother holds me on one side with my brother Daniel on the other. She calls me Eliza. We live here in the village but we are not to stay here. We go home and there are people who have come here after the funeral. Mother's talking near the window to a man; he's my father's brother-in-law, Edward. She calls him brother. He is a publican and he is to take us in and look after us. The money that my father left is to go to him to look after us, but I cannot see my mother in such a place."*

Toni paused for a while, experiencing the passing of time before she continued:

"We're standing outside the inn; it's a white building with black around the windows. It's called The Three Tuns. I'm excited as we go inside. There are wooden floors, long wooden tables, and benches and side booths around the walls and a big fireplace. Edward and his wife greet us and apologise that there's not a lot of room. There'll be one room for mother and Danny and one small room up the stairs in the eaves for me. It's rather cold though and I can tell that Edward's wife doesn't want us here. I'm listening outside the door to her complaining about us, but he says, 'Hush, it will work to our advantage.'" Again Toni was quiet for a few seconds, before she went on excitedly: *"I'm downstairs in the kitchen now and Uncle's explaining that my aunt's not well and I have to help out. He says that they've taken us in and they will take care of us but I must help. He gives me an apron and I can serve the food, and if I do that well I can serve the ale. He's laughing, saying that I'm wise for my age. Aunt gives me a cap to wear. He puts it on me and tucks my hair out of the way – it's nice to have people who care about you. I can hear noise now and voices outside as the place is filling up. Uncle takes me out of the kitchen and a red-faced man says, 'Who is she?' I take food out to them. People are talking loudly and the fire's burning, everyone's happy. Uncle seems*

pleased with me. He's always patting me and giving me a hug and lots of praise. He's so unlike my own father. This goes on for some time, and soon I know how to serve the drinks. Uncle Edward says, 'Go on, have a taste.' I don't like the taste of the ale or the porter, but I like the wine. He says I'm good at keeping the customers happy. I'm taking trays of ale and porter and the place is stuffy and smoky and too hot; there are red, sweaty faces and the laughter gets harsh." Toni jumped suddenly and caught her breath: *"One man grabs me by the waist and tries to make me sit on his knee. I rush into the kitchen but Uncle just laughs. Mother has a huge argument with him but he says that they are keeping us and I should do my bit to help and that includes keeping the customers happy. Sometimes there are other women there. They wear gaudy clothes and tall wigs and very low-cut gowns, and they laugh a lot. I feel detached from this. One day he says I'll be good enough to work in the kitchen and Aunt can take it easy as she's not well. It's hard work, tiring."* Again, she jumped a little and held her hand in the air. *"Ouch, I've burnt my fingers making hot soup. Uncle puts my hand in water and holds it there; then he kisses it better like Mother does."*

So far, all of this had been spoken in either a matter-of-fact way by Toni or with a degree of excitement in her voice. Although her father had died and she was forced to work in her uncle's public house, nothing had occurred that could be viewed as traumatic or particularly unpleasant. However, I suspected that sooner or later we would begin to move to the grist of the past life, and sure enough after a brief period of silence Toni looked sad and uncomfortable as she lay in the chair. A few tears fell softly from her closed eyes. It was obvious that something was happening that was troubling young Eliza.

SB: "What's happening now?"

"Uncle Edward has bought me a new dress. It's green and I thought it was because he cared for me, but I've put it on and I think it's much too old for me. It's just like the dresses those other women wear. He insists that I wear it when I'm working. He says that if I don't it will

be the end of our free accommodation and we'll be put out on the street. What choice do I have? I'll have to split myself in two – the outside me that does the work and the inside me that no one can get near. He says that it's most becoming and we drink a small toast – it's hot and strong. It's later now and they've all gone and I'm bolting the door. He says get yourself off to bed and I give him a kiss."

Again, another pause as time passed, but before she continued Toni began to cry and she started to wring her hands. Her whole body was tense and she spoke in a whisper:

"I go to bed but the door's opening. He comes in and closes the door carefully. 'Now this is between you and me. No need to tell anyone about our arrangement. You want to continue living here, don't you? Then you have to be good to me.' He's unlacing the back of my dress. I feel scared."

Toni began moaning and her body was twisting in the chair, as if trying to get away from her assailant. Her hands were pushing outwards, trying to fend him off. Her breathing quickened and her words were spoken rapidly. *"He's got his hand on my mouth. What's he doing to me?"* She continued to writhe and whimper, saying nothing as she relived the horror of the attack. I allowed her to experience the trauma, telling her gently all the time that it was OK to do so and that she was safe to do so. I realise that that must seem a horrible thing to do but in regression therapy we have to work through and release all of the physical and emotional pain in order to let go of the impact that it's had upon us in this present lifetime. After a time Toni went on:

"He says that next time it won't hurt so much. 'Next time you'll begin to enjoy it.' He's doing his buttons up and he leaves me. I curl up into a ball. I feel sore and my shift has got blood on it. I don't know what to do with it; I'll either hide it or burn it. I don't want to wake up again. No wonder his wife doesn't want us here."

She was quiet for a time and after a while she began to relax again. It was obvious that time was passing again. When she spoke, it was in a flatter, more serious tone, as if the life she was now living was heavy and hard:

"I'm going upstairs with a glass of brandy for my aunt as she's ill. Then I go into my room and my uncle comes in. I'm trying to talk to him but as I call him 'Uncle Edward' he pushes me against the wall and pins me against it. He puts his hand over my mouth – 'Don't call me uncle – just call me Edward.'" Toni nodded her head, as if nodding in compliance to him. *"I'm asking him about my aunt. 'She is your wife, it is wrong to come to me.' He just says that she can't be a wife to him. I'm so worried that in the eyes of God and the church this is wrong and I will be damned. It's later now and she's died. Things have changed. He used to just come to my room and take me and then leave. Now he stays all night and he's not so rough. He says that he's going to call me Rose because I'm like a rosebud turning into a rose. I don't feel as frightened now. This is just part of my life. If my aunt's not there anymore is it such a bad sin? Will I go to hell? I feel guilty because sometimes what he does makes me feel good."* Once more, Toni paused in her narrative before going on: *"I'm older now. All these years and I thought nothing would happen. Now it has. I'm with child. Oh no, it's not right. Everyone will know, all of the village. It couldn't be anyone else's. I feel like I've got a big stone inside of me. I lie awake for days. I can't see any way out. No one else knows. I try to talk to him. He says that he'll fix it for me to go away and have the child and then come back without it. If I bring a child back here or have the child here, I'm branded and so is the child. He leaves but I know there's only one clear answer. There's only one thing that will give me peace. I've got to protect my family."* She started to cry. *"I'm damned anyway. I can't see a way out. I'm sorry. I feel dead inside anyway. He's taken everything I ever had – the family money; then he pretends he'll look after us and he takes my innocence. I can't tell anyone as Mother's health is frail but I suspect that she knows anyway. I can't think straight. What will happen to Mother and Daniel afterwards? I can't protect them. I can't fall any lower. How could my father have been so naïve?"*

Toni's crying turned into anguished sobbing as she moved

with a sense of inevitability to the ending of the life. Her head moved from side to side as she relived the young girl's agony and helplessness. Through the sobs she continued:

"I've taken a bottle and drunk a lot from it. I'm walking through the fields to the side of the river. I'm by the mill and I'm walking along the bank looking for the best place. I'm unsteady. I've found a place where the bank's been washed away. My cloak is heavy. I just do it. I'm in the water. My clothes are filling up with air so I push down and lie back and let go. I'm so sorry. It feels like there's a stone inside me weighing me down. I have a sleepy feeling and I can see lots of bubbles and my hair and the weeds." She stopped crying and her body began to relax again, letting go of the tension she had displayed as she was approaching her final moments. She sighed deeply and spoke peacefully: *"There's a light, pulling me up through the water. I feel warm and clean and dry, as if I'm wrapped in something soft. I can hear a voice saying, 'It's alright, you're safe now.' It's my father. He says, 'I'm sorry, my child.' At last there's someone to take care of me. I feel peaceful now."*

Poor Eliza was free at last of the horrors of that lifetime, and Toni lay in my chair with a deep sense of calmness and ease. She had worked through the significant emotional events in that life and she had released the emotional pain that had been inside her all of her present lifetime. I asked her if she could get a sense of the year in which she died and she told me that she thought it was 1763, and that she had lived and died somewhere in the UK in the West Country, perhaps in a village that sounded like Dulverton or Yelverton. I brought her out of trance and she looked radiant, as if a great weight had been lifted off her shoulders. She felt free and light inside, and she said that she understood now why she had felt so depressed throughout her life. The feeling of hopelessness that Eliza had felt was exactly the same feeling of depression she had felt so many times before. Now, though, the feeling was completely gone and she felt safe and at ease.

I'm pleased to report that as a result of our regression therapy sessions Toni's life was radically changed. Her back problem was cured, she was able to lose weight (three stones in total!) by eating sensibly and her lifelong depression was healed. She was more confident and positive in her approach to life, so much so that she separated from her husband as she realised her marriage was no longer fulfilling her. I often find that when one door closes another one opens, and indeed this was the case here. Just after the separation she happened to bump into an 'old flame', a man whom she hadn't seen for years. He was her first love when she was in her late teens and he too had just recently divorced. They began a deep and happy relationship which continues to this day. Past life therapy had totally transformed her life!

Chapter 5

Simon's Story

Over the years I have often used regression to help migraine sufferers to either significantly reduce or completely eliminate their migraines. As with any physical problem, there are always underlying emotional causes to migraines, and I usually find that they have been caused by deaths in previous lives, where there have been blows to the head. It appears that the person brings into this life the energy of those deaths which is stored in some way in their head, and the pain and trauma of the deaths is constantly being replayed in the subconscious, leading to the pain of the migraine. The same is often the case for people suffering from regular headaches.

Simon was a 13-year-old schoolboy who had been getting debilitating migraines from the age of two. They were occurring frequently, sometimes as often as every few weeks, and as a result he was missing a lot of school as the migraines were so severe that he was unable to get out of bed for several days at a time. As he was still a minor his mum insisted on sitting in on the sessions, and what she observed took her breath away!

Once Simon was in trance his subconscious indicated that there were nine past lives causing the migraines, and Simon went straight into each one, one after another. It was as if his subconscious was taking the opportunity to clear out the negative memories stored within it. Simon was what I call a 'quick worker', in that when he was in hypnosis he moved rapidly through each past life, experiencing the traumatic events before speedily moving on to the next lifetime.

In the first life he described being a man whose grandfather had just died, and he felt a lot of sadness at this loss. He became a bit emotional for a time and then relaxed, before moving straight into the next of the eight remaining lives:

"My daughter's just been born. I'm a man, aged around 30, and I'm holding her and smiling. Oh, it's a later time and I'm in my garden watering plants and my wife's come up behind me and hit me on the head with a spade. I fall over. We've had an argument because she was seeing someone else. I just lie there and I don't wake up. Everything's white and peaceful. From above I can see her being arrested and people taking my body away. I feel calm now." Simon paused for a few seconds before he continued: *"I'm a woman with my head on a guillotine. I feel really scared and there's a crowd cheering. I feel angry too as they said I'd killed someone but I didn't do it. My head's been chopped off. I'm calm again now. I've moved on again, I'm outdoors, running. I feel scared because I'm being chased. I'm a boy, around ten years old and I stood up to a boy who was bullying me. I tripped him up and ran away. I'm running home but he catches me and pushes my head into the wall of a house. He's banging my head against the wall. I fall over and start crying and then I run home. My mum comes to see if I'm OK but my head hurts and I fall over. I'm in the car now on the way to hospital and I feel really tired. I can't keep my eyes open. Mum's crying and hugging me but my head falls limp. I can't feel anything now, it's all calm."*

Throughout this he had been crying softly, but then Simon sighed deeply and was quiet for a minute or so, before he moved into another life. In this one he experienced dying of old age with his family crying around his bedside. There was no sense of trauma in this, just relief at the end of a long life. Soon he moved into the next life, which did carry a lot of negativity in it:

"I'm a man in a bar having a drink. Someone insults me and I feel angry so I punch him. He punches me and we start fighting, then two of his friends join in and they knock me to the floor and start kicking me in the head. No one helps me and I can't get up. I feel frustrated and then I feel myself floating up out of my body. It's all white and I'm at peace again. Now I've moved into another life. I'm shouting at someone in a weird language. 'How dare you, how could you do this to

me? I thought we were friends.' I feel really angry and I hit him and there's blood on his face. He gets up and starts bashing my head. I fall down. Everything's peaceful now." Once more Simon was quiet for a couple of minutes, before he moved into the final two lives, both of which continued the theme of deaths from head injuries:

"I'm driving a car and a lorry runs through a red light and crashes into the side of my car. I'm banged about by the impact and I hit my head on the steering wheel. I feel angry with the other driver. I'm too weak to get out of the car. People run over and open the door and I just fall out. I'm dead. Now I've moved into another life. I'm seeing a big old clock, slowly ticking. I'm outside the old clock house and I'm walking up wooden stairs towards it. One of the stairs breaks and I fall and land on my head. For a moment I feel angry because I'd told someone to fix the step but they haven't done it. Then it's all gone and I just feel peaceful."

Simon breathed deeply and relaxed, feeling a sense of ease and lightness in his head. There were no other past lives to work through and so he came out of trance. Simon's mum sat with her mouth wide open, amazed at what she had witnessed. Neither she nor her son had any belief in the concept of past lives and they were both shocked at what he'd relived in the session. Remember, this was all without any leading or prompting from me. His subconscious had simply taken him from one life into another.

He came back to see me after six weeks to tell me that for the first time ever he'd been free of migraine attacks for over a month. He'd then experienced a bit of a headache so he felt that there might still be more to do. We spent the session exploring some minor events from this lifetime and releasing a small amount of emotion from an ancestor's life which he'd inherited, but there was very little to work on as the bulk of the trauma causing the head pain was from the past lives which we had cleared. We finished the session and he left my office completely free from migraines.

Chapter 6

Pam's Story

Pam came to me with severe psoriasis on her arms, legs and body. This skin problem is both unpleasant to live with and unsightly, and Pam had tried various types of medication, none of which had helped. A former senior executive of a major national company, she told me that she had experienced a lot of stress in her business and personal life. She had been "stabbed in the back" (her words) by a few people several times, and the psoriasis had started just two weeks after her father's death 12 years earlier. A dynamic, voluble 52 year old, Pam also felt 'blocked' in her life, unable to move forward in ways that would lead her to feel that she was achieving something with her life.

As I mentioned at the start of this book, my world as a regression therapist is based on the idea (which for me is a fact) that all physical problems are caused by emotional causes. When we hold locked-in emotions inside us from previous traumas, then these emotions have to come out in some way. For many people they come out in the body in the form of some kind of illness. I have worked with skin problems often over the years and have usually found that they are caused by locked-in anger. The anger cannot come out in any other way, so it comes out through the skin. Pam herself was angry at the way she had been treated by others in her life, but being a kind-hearted, spiritual soul she had never wanted to retaliate at the people who had hurt her.

Although Pam had given me a sizeable clue as to one of the main causes of the psoriasis (her father's death had triggered it), I wondered if there was more to it than meets the eye. Once she was in hypnosis, I asked her subconscious to use one of her fingers to signal to my questions. As well as emotional causes in this present lifetime, the IMR also indicated that there were past life causes. We began the process of regressing back into the past lives, of which there were several.

As Pam lay in trance in my reclining chair, initially she was calm and very relaxed, and her breathing was slow and deep. Suddenly, however, she began to shake and her whole body stiffened, her hands clenched into fists and she began to breathe quickly through gritted teeth. I asked her to tell me what she was experiencing. She replied tersely:

"I'm being held and I can't move. I'm manacled. Being tortured. I think I'm in a dungeon. I can't see; there's something over my head. I'm a woman."

SB: "How do you feel?"

"I feel sadness and grief. Loss. A child's been lost to me, maybe it's been killed. I'm being persecuted for being a witch. I'm not though, I'm just an herbalist. A man's doing it and he takes pleasure out of taking me away and torturing me. He's taken the child and he's trying to make me say things. I can't sacrifice my belief in what is good." Pam began to cry as her body writhed in the chair as it remembered the physical assaults from the past life. *"I feel this connects to a pattern in my current life. Because I'm good at what I do people have been jealous and I've been knocked back by them. Also I haven't had children because they can be used as a weapon against me."* Pam moaned loudly as if in agony. *"He's taking pleasure in doing this. Part of him wanted me, part of him wanted to destroy me. I think he's some sort of Puritan."*

Pam continued to move in the chair before she started to relax. She spoke quietly:

"I've moved to a later time. I survived but I live a long time alone in a cottage. I have to live with the weight of whether I'd done the right thing because I lost my child. I carried on helping people but I lost my heart." Suddenly she began to sob and she writhed in the chair with her hands covering her face. She was feeling all the anguish

of that life, all of the unfairness of what had happened to her at the hands of her torturer, of the death of her child as a result of refusing to accede to his requests. *"I have to keep it all in – I can't tell anyone."*

Pam continued to cry for some time, before she finally began to soften and relax. After a period of silence, she spoke again: *"I've moved on now, to another life. I'm a man in my late 30s and I'm standing on a heath. I'm apart from the others. I'm on guard, wearing a Cavalier-type hat with feathers in it. I'm in charge of a group of men."* She became tense and her body started to jerk. *"I can't work out if we're hunting or being hunted. Perhaps both. There's a lot of fear. We have to go down into a town but I don't know if we'll make it. I'm apart, trying to think of the best thing to do. I decide we should make a move. We're not full military. We're landowners with their men. A battle's being fought all around, Roundheads and Cavaliers. We're going down into the town. I know it's a huge risk."*

Pam paused for a few seconds, and then she flinched and she spoke quickly, the sound of panic in her voice: *"We're under attack. We're fighting. There are too many of them. We're being killed. I feel all the responsibility of this. I feel guilty because they trusted me and now they're being killed. I cared about them; they were my family and friends. My name is Jones, I think Cavendish Jones or Jones Cavendish."* Suddenly she jerked and lay still. *"I've died. I'm aware of feeling guilty as I pass over."* Pam relaxed again and was quiet for a minute or two before she told me that she had entered another life:

"It's daytime and I'm outside standing gazing at a river. I'm an Egyptian woman, about 28 years old, with servants around me. I feel powerful, but I'm thinking things through. My life is under threat. There's a lot of hatred at the court. Part of my family is jealous of me. I can't relax as I have to be on my guard all the time. I have to watch and observe everything because things can change at any moment. I even have to watch my food and drink. Finding people to trust is difficult."

Throughout all of this her body was jerking with anxiety. Her breathing quickened. *"I feel that I'm always under attack from spells and magic, incantations that affect the generations. I have a son but he's taken away from me. I have too much time to think and so I'm fearful all the time. It's almost like being a prisoner. I've got everything I need but it's a silken prison. I think we've lost the game, we're not going to survive."* Suddenly Pam's body contorted and she began to choke. *"I've been poisoned. They took my son; there was nothing I could do."* She continued to cough. *"I was a widow. I had to manage on my own and try to protect my son. I feel helpless and angry."* These last words were almost spat out as she writhed in the chair, her body obviously feeling the effects of the poison. Suddenly she lay still and sighed. *"I've died. I can see that I was diminished gradually. My power and authority was slowly taken away; all because another woman was jealous of me. Poison is a woman's weapon. I was a junior priestess or princess and my whole life was one of duty, loneliness, responsibility. I also had spiritual abilities, of which others were jealous. I can see a lot of parallels with this present life."*

Pam was silent again, her body relaxed as she moved into another lifetime. Once more she began to jerk and her face became tense. I asked her where she was and what she was experiencing. She spoke quickly:

"I'm outside, in a concentration camp. It's Poland and I'm a woman in my early 30s with long dark hair. This is the life before this present incarnation. I'm Viennese. I'm being taken away to be killed. I have a daughter aged about two or three and I had to service the German officers to keep her alive. They promised but I've betrayed them to the prisoners. There was an uprising because of the hunger. One of the officers cared about me. I'm Jewish, petite and educated in music. This is such a waste. I gave information to the prisoners about shift changes and where the officers and troops were so they could attack the weak spot. It happened when the commandant was away with some senior officers. I feel defiance and anger and triumph because I managed to betray them, but also anger and impotence because I can't do anything.

I was betrayed to the commandant. I know my betrayer is in this present life – she's my ex-business co-director. She's betrayed me in this lifetime too, again." Pam began to writhe as her body jerked as she became more agitated. *"There's a sense of the awfulness of the place. I think it's Treblinka. One of the officers is very brutal."* She began to breathe heavily and quickly, and then she started to cough. Her words came quickly and she started to cry. *"I feel total grief that I'll never see my daughter again. I'm with a group and we're being sardined in, some being thrown in and pushed on top of others. The doors are shut and we're being gassed. We fall into a pile. I'm dying."*

Pam continued to cough for a short time before she lay quietly again and she let out a large sigh. I brought her out of trance back to full awareness. She quickly became composed, and although she'd been through the rigours of some horrible past life experiences she was very relaxed. She told me that she felt as if she'd let go of a lot of heaviness, and she felt a real sense of relief. I asked her to be gentle with herself for a few days as she processed the session and the events she had relived, and she agreed to return for another session.

Pam arrived for our next session a few weeks later with a big smile on her face. She told me that the psoriasis had begun to improve and had started to clear up quite dramatically. It had virtually gone from her arms and her upper body, and now it only remained on her legs. As you can imagine, she was overjoyed that the treatment was working so well and she was looking forward to working through the other previous lives. As you will see, we spent the session working in several past lives, all of which had one common theme – namely, anger.

I guided her into hypnosis and once she was in a pleasant, relaxed trance I asked her subconscious mind to take her into another past lifetime that contained events that were causing the skin problem. After a few moments of relaxing, her body began to jerk violently and her breathing came quickly. I asked her to tell me where she was and what she was experiencing. She spoke hoarsely and with a voice full of tension:

"I'm at sea, on board a ship. I'm in the hold."

SB: "How do you feel?"

"I feel ill, very bad. I think it's cholera. I'm scared. All the people here are ill. I'm scared, my children are here somewhere. I'm a woman. We're going to America and we've got to stay in the hold. They won't let us up on deck. I'm angry – they won't let us near any air. We've got no chance to make it and we've given everything to do this. It was going to be a new life, but we're going to die. I'm furious – we've paid them and they treat us like this. We try to get out but they beat us back. I can't see my children."

Pam had been shaking throughout all of this, but finally with those last words she sighed and her body relaxed again. It was obvious that she had died in that lifetime. I allowed her to rest for a few moments before I asked her to move on to something else. She then began to move in the chair, draw her shoulders back, and she pushed her chest out. She looked stern and her body looked strong. I asked her to tell me what she was experiencing. She spoke slowly and determinedly:

"I'm in Egypt; at Karnak. I'm a man, a priest, aged about 44. I'm in a procession, going inside. It's a ceremony to Osiris, an important festival. I feel very powerful, as if I rule Karnak. I am close to having absolute power. Nothing will get in my way. There are probably around 100 people here, high priests and temple guards, and this procession is a symbol of how important Karnak is and how powerful I am. It is my responsibility to make sure everything is correct."

As she spoke, Pam's body looked more and more powerful and her jaw was set. She began to assume the energy and physicality of her past life character. She held up a hand as if to signal for people to stop. A look of disdain was on her face. I asked her to tell me what was happening. Again, with a masculine-sounding voice she spoke:

"We're inside the temple and we're moving towards the inner

quarters. There's been a death, a pharaoh has died. We have people to send with him. His handmaidens and servants are being brought. It's an honour but they make such a noise. They are to be sent with the pharaoh. We must do it in order that it is done correctly. Why do I have to explain? Someone has to be strong enough to do it. It is a responsibility I have – the ultimate responsibility and power is not pleasant."

Suddenly she jerked and her arms flicked up into the air. *"There is unrest. The temple is being attacked. Agh!"* Her body jumped and she began to moan. Through clenched teeth she groaned: *"I've been stabbed in the back, three times. I'm dying."*

I asked her to tell me what she was thinking as she died. *"I feel angry, as if I've been thwarted. It mirrors things that happened in my current life, in which an unexpected attack stopped me from getting to the top of my profession."*

She relaxed but after a few seconds she began talking again, this time about another past life that she had spontaneously entered:

"I'm outside, in a forest. I'm a man, wearing a jerkin, hat, boots and tight trousers with a belt. There's a bag on the ground and I'm standing, listening. I'm hiding, avoiding a group of the Sherriff's men as they travel through the forest. I've stolen something. They wear black and leather. Everyone flees to the forest if they fall foul of the Sherriff of Nottingham's men. There are around 16 of them and they see this as a sport. I stole food for my family – a hare. I'm out of work and I'm hungry. I can hear them." She began to jerk and breathe heavily, her face full of anxiety. A few moments later and she started to cry. *"They've found me. They sword-whip me, play with me before they stab me in the stomach. They enjoy it. I'm helpless. It's so unfair, the cruelty of it. I'm living in poverty, a young man with three children. I was a joiner but the carpenter I worked for was a bully. He bullied another apprentice and I stood up to him. I lost my job and he put the word around to others so I can't find work. I feel so angry at the unfairness of it all."*

Pam had been sobbing as she said all of this, but finally she fell silent and breathed a sigh of relief. Once more she had passed into spirit and was leaving that life and its rigours behind. After a short time she had a sense of a past life as a Cossack, killing relentlessly in an orgy of bloodlust before dying in a fire (she had torched a village as she helped massacre its inhabitants but was caught in a burning building). However, she felt no deep emotions other than relief when that life was over, and within a couple of minutes she began to settle into the final past life of our journey. Initially she was quite calm as she recounted to me what was happening:

"I'm wearing sandals and a long dress like a toga. I'm a woman, about 42 years of age and I'm outside. It's daytime and I can see olive trees. I feel cross, irritated. I can sense a lot of responsibilities and a large family. I'm trying to sort out a difficult situation. My husband is a senator, close to Caesar Augustus. I'm on our estate outside Rome. We have three sons and two daughters. I think he's making a big mistake getting so close to Caesar but he's stubborn and won't listen. I feel powerless. I have to keep all of the estate running but there's a lot of unrest. I must go to the temple. Oh no." Pam began to shake her head, and then she put her hands up to her head and began to cry. *"My husband's been arrested and charged. I knew this would happen. Everything we've built up."* She held her hands over her face, as if experiencing the shock and horror of the situation. *"We've been disgraced. We'll lose everything. After all our work."* She sobbed bitterly. *"I've no alternative, I must die with him. I had so much to live for, but the children – I must free them of this shame."* She started to gasp and writhe as she lay in the chair. *"I drink poison. He was tortured and put to death as a traitor. Everything he had was confiscated, and I chose to die as a matter of honour. This would leave the family free of shame."*

Pam began to relax again, and I asked her to tell me what she was aware of as she was dying. After a short pause she spoke quietly: *"I'm so sad and angry that he didn't listen to me. I could see it all. On the one hand I had the responsibility of running everything, the estate, the crops, wine etc. Yet on the other hand I was totally impotent as I was considered unworthy and he thought he was too important to listen to me."*

With these sad words Pam was silent and our session was over. I brought her gently back to full awareness and she spent a few moments in silence, considering everything she had experienced. So much of it made sense to her as she had felt so many of the same emotions in this present lifetime. Some of the events in the past lives felt like they had parallels in this life too. She felt sadder and wiser at the same time.

I didn't see Pam again for any more regression sessions but later she reported back to me that she had seen a great improvement in the skin problems and that she was happy to leave things as they were at that time. I feel that with more work releasing the emotional causes of the psoriasis we could have achieved a total cessation of it, but I have to respect her decision, and although I still view her as 'unfinished business' I am pleased with what we achieved as it was another positive result for past life regression.

Chapter 7

Lisa's Story

Lisa was a 20-year-old hotel receptionist who was suffering from panic attacks and irritable bowel syndrome (IBS). She had been experiencing the panic attacks for a couple of years but there appeared to be no reason for these to be happening as she had not experienced any traumas in her life in the two or three years before they began. They would happen several times a week and sometimes when she was feeling the anxiety at its most severe (as well as the usual symptoms of shaking, breathlessness etc.) she would feel sick and her throat would feel as if it was closing.

IBS is an awful illness. When a person has it at its most serious level it can totally dominate that person's life to such an extent that they will not want to leave their house in case they have an episode when they are away from home. Typically, irritable bowel syndrome causes stomach pains together with either diarrhoea or constipation, or alternating diarrhoea and constipation. Throughout her life, since childhood, Lisa would regularly have very bad stomach pains and constipation, and as a result was constantly too ill to go to work. She also had a phobia of being sick (emetophobia) and was frightened of dying. Her anxiety state, although separate to the IBS, was undoubtedly making her stomach problems worse. One of the first questions I ask any client once they have shared their issues with me is if they have experienced any major traumas in their life, particularly in childhood. Sometimes these experiences are the events that we have to work on in therapy to clear or to neutralise their problems. In Lisa's case, though, she had had a fairly unremarkable life with no significant emotional experiences that she could remember. In regression terms this either meant that there were some unremembered incidents in this lifetime causing the problems, or some past lives (or ancestral trauma) at the heart of the matter. Usually, if a person has a substantial fear of dying (as Lisa had), I suspect that there are some traumatic incidents in previous lives that are lurking around in the mind. However, as I said at the start of this book, my standpoint is that I do not know where a client's issues are coming from so I let their subconscious tell me. In Lisa's case, once she had slipped into hypnosis, her Ideo-Motor Response finger indicated that there were four past lives that needed working on.

She regressed back into the first of them, and soon she started to shiver. She pulled her arms in tightly as if trying to ward off the cold. She told me that she was a little girl, maybe seven or eight years old, and that she was sitting alone at a deserted railway station. Her voice took on a child's tone as she spoke through chattering teeth:

"I'm shivering as I'm waiting. I'm wearing a long white dress with short sleeves and sandals on my feet. I'm so cold. I'm waiting for my dad. I can't wait to see him but I'm scared in case he doesn't come." I asked her whereabouts in her body she felt the scared feelings and she said it was in her stomach. *"I keep waiting. A steam train goes past but it doesn't stop. I wait for the next train. I'm scared that I won't see my father again. He should be on his way home from work and I've come to meet him. Some people come on to the platform. That means a train should be coming. Even though other people are there I feel so alone. I'm so scared he won't be coming. What would I do if he doesn't come? I hear the train coming in and people are gathering in front of me. The train stops but I can't see him."* She started to cry and her voice was frantic: *"Where's my dad? Where is he? I can't see my dad; he's not there. What shall I do? People are leaving and I'm all on my own again. The train's going out."* Lisa started to shake and she was wringing her hands, her breathing coming quickly as she relived the child's panic. *"I'm cold and alone and scared. I*

sit in a corner gripping my legs to my chest. My hands feel numb. I'm holding them tighter and tighter and my hands are tingling. I'm tired and sleepy. I drift off and feel calm, as if everything's going to be alright."

Lisa relaxed in the chair and breathed softly again as her hands slipped gently by her side. I checked with her subconscious via the IMR signal if there was anything else to do in that past life and it responded with a 'no', so I asked her to move into the next life that needed exploring. Soon her eyelids started to flicker as images came on to her mental picture screen. Her body went rigid and I could see that she was tensing her stomach muscles. With a tone of desperation she blurted out:

"I can't feel my arms. My legs are numb. I feel frightened because I'm unable to move. I'm a woman, maybe around 24 years of age and I'm in a hospital bed. I think that part of my right leg is missing from the knee down. My arms won't move; I can't feel them at all. I don't know why I'm here or where I am." Lisa was quiet for a few moments so I asked her to become aware of what had happened to bring her to this place. She started to shake and she spoke haltingly: *"I'm in a car; a passenger sitting in the back seat. I can feel butterflies in my tummy. We're going down a long, narrow road and it's raining so I can't see very well. I'm scared. Slow down! We're going too fast and the rain's pouring down. I don't know who's driving. Where are they taking me? Ouch!"* Suddenly she jumped and held her head. She started to rub her forehead with her hand. *"I've got a terrible pain in my head. It's been hit in some way. Then I'm concussed and I wake up here in the bed. My stomach feels very tense. I know that there's nothing they can do for me. I'm starting to feel warm and calm; I'm passing away. I feel at ease – heaven's a nice place."* With those words Lisa relaxed and was quiet. I asked her to come out of trance, and like most of my clients she expressed amazement at what she'd experienced. She left my office with a smile on her

face, telling me that she felt calmer than she'd felt for a long time and the stomach pains that she was feeling at the start of the session had vanished. This could, of course, simply have been down to the fact that she had enjoyed the relaxing elements of hypnosis, but I believe it was because her body had released a lot of locked-in fear and tension from the past lives.

When Lisa arrived for her next session a couple of weeks later, she told me that although she was not 100% better she had certainly seen considerable improvements in her IBS, and her anxiety state had reduced immensely. She had been able to go out much more often than usual without any tension, and she had coped much better with the stressors in her life. However, one extra benefit was that as a result of feeling a lot less stressed she had spent time calmly thinking about her life, and she had come to the conclusion that she did not enjoy her work and so she had started looking for another job. She had even had an interview for a new job and she was pleasantly surprised at just how calm she'd been throughout what had been a very long and intensive interview. I reassured her that as long as we cleared the remaining two past lives that we had to work on she would almost certainly get to the 100% improvement she was hoping for.

She went into trance and we began to explore the third of the four past lives. I can't write about this in detail as Lisa experienced it kinaesthetically, with very few images in her mind about what was happening, but lots of feelings. As in our first session, there was a great deal of tightness in her stomach, although her whole body felt the tension too. She cried and shook, her breathing was panicky and at times she writhed as she relived the horrible past life events. Eventually this all dissipated, and she moved into the final past life. Once more her voice took on a childlike inflection, and she told me that she was a seven-year-old boy who was just starting his first day at a big, new school. Her hands held on to her stomach as she told me how scared she was:

"I've got pains in my stomach because I'm so scared. I've started halfway through term so I don't know my way around. I'm in a long corridor looking for my classroom. The lesson has started but I'm scared to go in in case they laugh at me. The teacher shouts at me for being late so I run out and hide under a bush at the edge of the playground. My stomach hurts. At playtime the other children come out and I crawl out and walk over to them. They just stare at me and then ignore me as they play. We then have to get in lines to go back into school but I get pushed to the back of the line. The boy in front of me has stolen my spectacles and in the classroom they're passing them around and trying them on. I get them back but they're all dirty so I can't see clearly. I don't like those boys but they're sitting right behind me calling me names and flicking things at me. I feel upset and scared. When the class is finished it's time to go home but I wait until everyone has gone and the teacher asks me how I'm getting on. I tell her what's happened, and she says that she'll move me to a different table away from them and she'll speak to them. I don't want her to because it might make it worse. I'm worried that they'll wonder why I've moved tables."

Throughout all of this Lisa was shifting around in the chair, clasping and unclasping her hands and looking very troubled, a deep frown on her forehead. After a short pause she continued:

"I go outside and my mum's here to pick me up. I run to her and feel safe. I tell her that they've been picking on me and I don't want to go back there. She says that I have to ignore them and it'll be OK. The next day I go back and my tummy's really sore. I'm at a new table but in PE I can't get changed because I haven't got the same shorts as the others and I think they'll laugh at me. I tell the teacher I'm not feeling well so he says I can watch. The children are staring at me as they play ball. One of them throws the ball at me and it hits me in the tummy. They're

laughing at me and pulling faces at me. At home time I tell Mummy about it but she says it was an accident. She doesn't understand."

She was quiet for a while as she moved to another time in that life and she went on:

"I'm in my last year of primary school now. Nothing improved; I was bullied all the way through it. I do well in my exams though and they're jealous. They punch me in my tummy. There are four of them and they won't stop. I tell the dinner lady but she can't do anything. She takes me to the Headmaster and I tell him. He says that I've done very well in my exams and I should take a week off school while he sorts it out. It's not fair; it feels like I'm being punished. He lets me go home early and the pain in my stomach's easing as I don't have to go back for a week. When I go back it's all been sorted out. The other boys don't even look at me. I sit in the class and they don't bother me. My stomach hurt at first but I feel relieved now and I know it will start getting better."

Lisa breathed a big sigh of relief and told me that her stomach was feeling completely calm and the past life images had vanished. This was a sign that the session was over and so she surfaced from trance with a big smile on her face. Although none of the lives had been very dramatic, they still contained a good deal of tension, and by going into trance and reliving the emotions from the past she had released them, particularly from her stomach which was the place in her body where she had stored them in this life. I knew that her 'presenting problems' were cleared, but it was nice to receive confirmation of this when her mum phoned me a few weeks later to tell me that Lisa was completely well, and that since our session she had not experienced any stomach pains or a single panic attack. Job done!

Chapter 8

Kath's Story

This may come as a surprise as we are so used to being fed the medical model that physical problems have to be treated by the use of chemicals, but I have regularly found that the true cause of infertility is unresolved negative emotions from the past. As a result, I have had a substantial number of women who were unable to get pregnant actually become pregnant once they had cleared the underlying emotional causes that were blocking them. Standard Western medicine ignores the power of the mind by believing that everything needs to be fixed with chemicals, which nowadays more and more people are waking up to is just a means of making massive financial profits for pharmaceutical companies. Many of us involved with psychotherapy know, however, that the mind is one of the most powerful forces on the earth and when it's used correctly can effect far greater changes than your average doctor is trained (or brainwashed) to believe.

In terms of past lives, some of the ladies I have helped to get pregnant have found that they have died in childbirth in former lifetimes. This means that the energy of death by childbirth is brought into this present lifetime in the subconscious mind, which blocks the woman from either conceiving in the first place or from successfully giving birth in this life. The subconscious, although it has a great wisdom, is also very literal and once something is in the subconscious it keeps replaying the same pattern over and over. Death by childbirth in a past life means that the subconscious equates childbirth and death together, and all the time in this present life it will be saying to itself, "If we get pregnant and give birth we will die, if we give birth we will die." As the subconscious has a desperate need for us to survive and to be healthy and well, it can therefore stop a woman from getting pregnant or carrying to full term, as it believes that by doing so it is helping the woman to stay alive.

Having said all that, my next client whose case I'm sharing with you didn't have any death-by-childbirth past lives preventing her from becoming a mother. She did, however, have some past lives that contained trauma which was blocking her in this life. Kath had been unable to get pregnant despite wanting desperately to start a family. In her early 40s she was physically well and working as a hypnotherapist so she understood the concept of regression as a healing tool. However, before this as she had been unable to conceive she had gone down the route of spending her and her husband's life savings on IVF. Consequently she became pregnant, but during the pregnancy she felt constantly tired and became progressively ill. She put this down to the high level of medication she was taking which was causing severe nausea. She spent most of her time resting but after seven weeks she had a scan which showed that there was no foetal heartbeat. She had to undergo a medically managed miscarriage which was very unpleasant, and she told me that her body felt wrecked. As well as this she said that she felt emotionally very raw and traumatised by the whole experience. I assured her that if we used her mind it was still possible to become pregnant, especially if there were any blocks in the subconscious that needed to be removed. Of course, initially I couldn't tell if this was definitely the case, but once Kath was in trance and her IMR indicated that there were some past lives causing the difficulties I knew that we had a good chance of being successful.

I gently regressed her back into the first of them and in a quiet voice she told me what she was experiencing:

"I'm inside, in a big, old-fashioned kitchen. There's a stone floor and a big, open fireplace. I'm a little girl, around three years old, sitting on the floor near to a wooden table. I'm wearing a bonnet and a shabby, dull-coloured dress and I'm watching a plump lady sitting at the table darning clothes."

I asked Kath to move to the next significant experience and after a few seconds of silence her face, which had so far shown only signs of relaxation, became serious. Her frown was accompanied by a tremor in her voice.

"I've grown up now; maybe I'm about 13 years of age, and I have long black hair. I'm a servant in a big house. I walk in on something that I shouldn't have seen. My mistress is in her room, in bed with a man. She's very angry. I'm shocked. I run out of the room and she shouts at me that I have to leave and never come back. She throws me out of the house with only the clothes that I'm wearing. I have nowhere to go, it's dark and I'm all alone. I feel devastated, cold and frightened. I have no one to turn to. I just start to walk." Softly, Kath began to weep. *"I've been living rough for a long time now, and my body is emaciated. My long hair has been cut short and my eyes are sunken. I'm sitting on some cold, stone steps, begging. I'm lucky if I get anything to eat, just scraps sometimes. Some people spit on me as they go past. I feel really sad. I'm starving to death. No one helps me. I can see red crosses painted on doors; I think it's the plague. I die, and I can see my body being dumped on a cart with the bodies of other people who are just as unimportant as me. I just don't count. I can see a big bonfire and a man with a cross. They burn our bodies because we were diseased."*

Kath sighed heavily and was quiet for a while as she moved into another lifetime. This proved to be just as traumatic as the first one:

"I'm lying on my back looking up at the sky. It's daytime and I'm surrounded by tall trees. The sky is a beautiful blue. I'm a girl, wearing a dress and I have bare feet. I'm around six years old, and I feel carefree and happy. I feel loved by my family. I have a little brother and loving parents, we live in a house in the woods and we grow our own vegetables. Something happens to spoil it though." Kath's face darkened and she began to cry and shake. Her voice came in between anxious gasps: *"I lose my family. It feels as if my whole world is spinning. I run back to the house and find that whilst I wasn't*

there they've been murdered. The house has been ransacked. I feel as if my whole world has been ended. My mother's head has been cut off. I see my little brother – he's so tiny and he's dead. He was only three. My parents' bodies are outside the house. My little brother must have come out to see what the commotion was about and been killed. I have no one to turn to. I want to bury them but I'm too small, so I just cover them with branches and sticks. I have to leave and I just start walking. It gets cold and dark. I don't know the way out of the woods; I just get lost and go round in circles. I choose to die as I know I have no hope." She started to sob and moan. *"I'm starving. There's nothing left. I've no strength or energy. It's such a shame. After a while I die, and I'm reunited with my family in spirit."*

Kath continued to weep for a few minutes without saying any more, before the tears ceased and she sighed deeply and relaxed. She came out of trance and expressed both surprise and a huge feeling of relief.

Our last session took place a few weeks later, and Kath told me that since the regressions she had felt quite different in herself. She felt as if a huge weight had been lifted off her, and the sadness which she had always felt each day throughout her life had gone. As with many people who undergo regression therapy, she felt lighter inside.

Once in trance she moved into the final past life that needed to be released. As she began to access it, her breathing quickened and her body stiffened. Her voice sounded gruff as she choked the words out:

"I can see the plank of a boat from underneath, it's the bottom of a hull travelling through water. There's lots of spray. I'm in the water, helpless, looking up at the ship. I'm a man, weighed down with something and a rope attached to me. I'm desperately trying to reach the boat but my legs are weighted down. I can feel myself drowning and my body's becoming limp." Kath was twisting around in the chair,

as if trying to get out of the water. Suddenly, she flopped down and lay motionless, before she sighed and continued quietly: *"I can remember what happened. I'm a crew member on the ship and it's a rough journey. We've got goods stored in the bottom of the hull, but there's a problem. There are some holes in the bottom of the boat. I was sent down on a rope to look at what's happened. We've hit something which has caused the damage. I got trapped and couldn't get back up. No one's trying to pull me up – where are they? They're drunk. They don't care about me. They didn't care about the water coming in and that we were slowly sinking. I was the only one who did anything about it. Nobody helps me, it's like they've forgotten I've gone down. How could they do that? I can't believe it. I was the only one who cared."* The amazement and anger in her voice was plain to hear. She paused for a while, as if she was processing the shock of the realisation, before continuing:

"I feel that they do get me back to the surface and they lay me on deck. I'm not quite dead and I come back to life. They're laughing, they think it's funny that they left me and I almost died. I thought I had died. It's not a joke. We're still sinking, and if we don't do something we're all going to die. We're in the middle of the ocean and as the ship goes down we all jump into the sea. Fortunately it's calm, although the rest of them are so drunk that they sink and drown. I'm the only one left alive, holding on to something, bobbing up and down in the water. I feel helpless, and I'm losing my strength. Eventually I get washed ashore and I fall unconscious. I wake up with my head in the sand. I'm on a tropical island and some natives find me and look after me. I feel relieved. A brown-skinned, tanned native woman with long hair is caring for me, feeding me. They help me to get well again and I wait for a passing boat. After a time they take me out in one of their boats with oars to a ship and I say goodbye to them. The ship's going home. Although I'm safe I look back to when I was abandoned by my shipmates and I feel really angry. Not caring about me and almost drowning was unforgivable."

Kath sighed and told me that the images in her mind's eye

were dissolving away, a sign that the past life experience was finished. We did a little bit of work to release the residual feelings of anger that she felt and then she came out of trance. Although Kath's past lives had not contained any traumas relating directly to childbirth, for some reason her subconscious had held on to the negative emotions in these three lives and it had prevented her from becoming pregnant. I do not bother to analyse the connections between the past life traumas and the problem in this life, as sometimes it is impossible to see any connection. I just know from experience that releasing the emotions and energies from the past is enough to allow healing to take place. Sure enough, this is exactly what happened. Less than one year later Kath phoned me to tell me that soon after our sessions she had conceived naturally and she was now the proud mother of a bouncing baby boy.

Section Three

Panic Attacks, Anxieties, Phobias

Chapter 9

Amy's Story

Most hypnotherapists find themselves regularly treating clients suffering from anxiety states, and as with any issues that we see in the consulting room there are degrees of severity of the symptoms. Some people experience just a light state of anxiety, which means that they go through each day feeling mild symptoms, but others suffer severe anxiety which not only can stop them from living a normal life but also lead to panic attacks. The high number of people I have treated over the years with anxieties makes me think that there's an epidemic of anxiety in the Western world.

Although some anxieties are caused by physical issues (e.g. hormone imbalances, thyroid problems) most are caused by negative feelings from the past churning around all day in the subconscious.

Amy had been suffering from panic attacks, on and off, for a number of years. Now 25 years old and working as a hairdresser, the panics had first started when she was 15 and taking her mock GCSE exams. The pressure she felt as a result of the exams caused her to feel sick every day (she even had to undergo an endoscopy to ensure that nothing physical was causing the sickness) and after her genius doctor put on her antidepressants (when are these people going to realise that this is not the answer?) she spiralled deeper down into anxieties and depression (not many people know this but Prozac, for example, can lead to an increased risk of suicide). Eventually she even tried to take her own life by taking an overdose of the tablets. A course of counselling, combined with coming off the medication, helped her to get back to some sense of normality. However, the anxieties had never really gone away, and for ten years she had experienced panic attacks regularly. As a result she felt that she had lost a lot of confidence, and in recent weeks the panics and feeling of sickness were present most of the time. She was struggling to hide her feelings at work and was generally unhappy with her life.

She eased her way into trance and her subconscious indicated that there were four past lives causing the anxieties, but as well as these it also indicated that Amy was carrying two spirit attachments with her. Now, I realise that this may sound weird (and even more controversial than past life therapy), but I have found over the years that some of my clients have spirits attached to them which can cause all sorts of problems. I'll just digress a little in order to explain this in more depth.

It appears that when some people die, instead of leaving this earth plane and moving in their light body into the spirit world (for more info on what happens in between lives read Michael Newton's book *Journey of Souls*) they remain stuck and stay trapped on the earth plane. This can happen for several reasons: if they die suddenly and the shock of dying stops them from passing over; if they are frightened of being judged in the spirit world for negative actions they have committed whilst alive; if they are frightened of going to hell (which I don't believe exists, by the way, as I have never, in all of the thousands of regressions that I've facilitated, had a client report such a place when they were in the Spirit after death); if they have a strong desire to stay around loved ones who are still alive. Sometimes they are just baffled at not having a physical body anymore and don't know what to do or where to go. Occasionally these spirits, because of their confusion and fear, connect to living people. These people may or may not be known to them, as often they attach themselves to people whose energies are low. It seems that if we are feeling down or depressed our energies are attractive to them, and they become stuck to us, often in our aura but sometimes they can get stuck in our bodies too. We then become affected by their negative energies and the subsequent lowering of our energies affects us both emotionally and physically.

I first became aware of the concept of spirit attachments when I read Dr Edith Fiore's book *The Unquiet Dead*. An American psychologist, Dr Fiore found that many of her patients had attachments, and she was able to move the spirits on and help her patients to get better.

I have to say that, and I know this may sound bonkers to you, I feel many people with emotional or psychological issues have spirits attached to them, contributing to causing them to feel 'wobbly' in so many ways. Certainly, for me over the past few years I am doing more and more spirit release work than I have ever done before (and bear in mind that I do not lead my client by suggesting that they might have attachments, I simply ask their subconscious the question and if it raises the finger and makes a 'yes' signal then we work with them). Sometimes, having done this the improvements in my clients' issues have been amazing.

Once Amy's IMR had signalled that she had spirit attachments, I went through a process of releasing the spirits from her and sending them 'home', sending them fully into spirit to where they should have gone when they died. This was duly done and I asked Amy to imagine herself protected by a cloak of healing light energy which surrounded her aura and which would help stop her being vulnerable to any more spirit incursions. Amy felt an immediate release of anxiety, as if she'd let go of something which had been troubling her for a long time. We were now able to begin work on the previous lives that were also contributing to causing the panic attacks. She regressed nicely back through time into the past, and began explaining to me what she was experiencing:

"I'm a woman, around 30 years old, and I'm in a market, shopping. I'm thinking about buying myself a new wig, a big, white, curly one. I'm not well-off but I'm not poor. It's busy and noisy, and from houses

around the market square people are throwing rubbish out of the upstairs windows, including buckets of excrement. I feel lonely, but I'm also looking after a young girl wearing a bonnet. She's dancing around a big concrete stand, like a bandstand, on the other side of the marketplace. I feel happy when I look at her. She's fallen and cut her knee, so I comfort her. She's my niece, and now her mum has come for her and takes her home. I'm left alone. I've got nobody in my life." Amy started to cry and then she became anxious. *"I'm remembering the day I gave birth. I'm in bed and a lady's there with me. I feel empty as my husband's left me. This is my first child and I have a baby boy. He's crying really loudly and I can't make him stop. I don't think I'm going to be a good mother, but the lady shows me what to do. She's a nursemaid. A doctor comes to check on me but the baby's not well, he's got something wrong with his chest."* She began to sob, her words jerked out through gritted teeth. *"He's not breathing, he's dead. They put him in a small brown box. I can't see him. I've got nobody. I go to the cemetery for his funeral. It's a sunny, autumnal day with leaves on the ground. He was called Matthew, and I'm saying goodbye to him."* For a while Amy continued crying, holding in her arms an imaginary infant and every now and again making a shushing sound as if she was trying to soothe her dying baby. Eventually she became calm again. For a time she was silent, before she began to tell me about another past life, this time much more recent than the first.

"I'm in a university and it's my first day at college. It's 1975. I'm a girl and I feel excited. I'm with some friends, sitting on the grass outside an old building with a bell tower at the top. There's a boy with us called Freddy who's really good looking and I sit next to him in the first class. It's a science class and we have a female teacher. Some boys at the back are messing around, being noisy. Freddy's being kind to me, helping me with an experiment. The other boys are being disruptive and throwing things around so Freddy tells them to be quiet, but they start picking on him. I'm worried in case they hurt him. That night I go for a drink with everybody. I'm staying in halls of residence and

there's a bar downstairs. Freddy's with me and my friend Natalie. The gang of boys from the science lecture are there, all drunk and causing trouble. They keep coming over and one of them's not nice, he's very angry. I don't like him so I tell him to get lost. Freddy's sticking up for me. The boy's touching my face, he's creepy. Just leave me alone. He says that he'll see me later and they leave. I don't think so. We have more drinks and I'm a bit drunk." She laughed and as she spoke she was slurring her words. *"Freddy says he likes it when I laugh. He kisses me. He's taking me home but I can't walk straight. I'm giggly when I'm drunk. It's cold outside and he gives me his coat. He's so nice. Those boys are coming up the road towards us. They're pushing Freddy around and the angry lad's touching my face. Leave me alone! They're holding Freddy, and he's grabbed my wrist and pulls me into him. He's kissing me. I feel scared as there's no one else around."* Throughout this Amy had been becoming more and more tense, and then she started to cry and wring her hands. *"Freddy can't get free and the boy's dragging me down an alleyway. He's pulling his trousers down but I can't get free and I don't want him to. The others are just watching, holding Freddy down. He's raping me. Freddy's crying and shouting. When he's finished he pulls his trousers up and they all just go. Freddy comes and cuddles me, saying that he's so sorry. He's comforting me and we're both sitting on the ground crying."* By this stage her whole body was shaking and she was gasping and shivering. *"He takes me home and we call the police. I just can't talk, I'm in shock. Freddy can't look at me as he feels responsible. I'm sat on my bed now, curled up in a ball and a policewoman's there but I just can't talk. Freddy tells them what happened and they take me to hospital to be examined and then the police go out looking for the gang of boys. I don't want to be examined but the policewoman keeps telling me I'm safe now. It hurts when they take samples from me. A stupid man, a counsellor, comes but I don't want to talk to him. I just want to get back home to my mum. There are bruises on my arms and face. The policewoman comes back and tells me that they've caught him."* Suddenly she became angry and she shouted out: *"I hate him for what he's done to me. I want to kill him."* She paused and spoke quietly again: *"They take me back home to my mum. Freddy can't look at me. I just feel dirty."*

She continued shaking for a while as her body released the trauma of that dreadful night. After a time she was calmer, and she had moved on in time. Her voice, though, was flat and devoid of emotion, as if the impact of being raped remained with her in that life for a long time.

"I don't want to go out anymore and I don't go back to college. I'm sad because I'll miss my friends. I don't want to talk about it, and it never gets mentioned again. He gets jailed. I don't see my friends again, I just get a job but I don't go out much. I'm not happy; it feels like my whole life has been spoilt."

Amy was silent and began to relax again. I brought her out of trance and we spent a little time debriefing, in order to make sure that she had let go of the trauma of both lives. She was shocked but she felt a great deal calmer than she had for some time.

When Amy returned a week later, she told me that she had made great progress since our last session. She had not only felt much lighter in herself, but a lot more confident too. So much so, that she had given her job up at the hairdresser's (she had never liked the boss there but had been too timid to do anything about it) and had had an interview for a job at another salon. She was delighted that they had offered her a place there and she was looking forward to starting work in a few weeks' time. Although in a morning she still felt some anxiety in her stomach, it was vastly reduced from how it had been before our first session. I knew that we were going to get a really good 'result' for Amy; it was now just a matter of working through and neutralising the other two past lives in order to achieve this.

Once she was in trance again, she relaxed deeply and she was soon in another lifetime:

"I'm outdoors and it's daytime. I'm in a field and I can see tepees.

I'm a boy, around 15 years old. I've been away for the day, hunting with my dad. He's a Native American too. We've killed a deer and brought it back to camp. There are lots of children running around, including my younger sister who's playing with friends. She's about six years old. My mum's just come out of a tepee. There are lots of tepees, it's like a community. Dad's big and stocky, and I think he's a chief. We're a happy family. Mum starts cutting up the deer to make a stew. I'm comparing hunting stories with my friends. I've got a female friend. I like her; she's got a feather in her long, dark hair and she's shy." She suddenly looked serious and her body gave an involuntary jerk. *"There's another boy who likes her. I don't like him as he's arrogant as he thinks he's better than me. I'm the chief's son so I get to pick who I want. We have a fight and I punch him in the face. We're scrapping on the floor but we get pulled apart. We have to fight properly, in a ring made by stones on the ground. We have to fight for her. It's a fight to the death; whoever wins will be the one who marries her. The whole village comes to watch, standing around the ring. I can hear drumming and chanting. I don't feel scared as this is part of our culture. I want to do this to please my father. We've both got daggers but first we have to fight with fists. He's around four years older than me and he's taller, but because I'm smaller I've got good movement and I can duck and move around."* Once more, Amy's body started to jerk uncontrollably, a sign that her body was feeling and releasing tension.

"Everyone's cheering; we're fighting and wrestling on the ground. The chief decides who wins the fist fight but he has to be fair. He has to be honourable so he won't just choose me because I'm his son. He decides I've won the fist fight but I don't have much experience with a dagger. Everyone's gone quiet and I feel nervous. This is the first time I've fought with knives. They're all staring at me. I can see my sister watching anxiously. She's scared she'll lose her brother." Suddenly Amy jumped and she started to breath heavily. *"He's stabbed me in the stomach. I can't breathe."* She jerked violently, and she began to gasp and whimper. She coughed and wheezed, as if

coughing up blood. Her body was twisting around in the chair as she held her stomach. The coughing and spasms continued for a minute or so until she began to relax and her breathing came back to normal. When she sighed I asked her what she was experiencing. *"I'm calm now. I've died, and I can see my mother kneeling by me, stroking my face. It's over."*

Quite often, the death in the past life is all that we have to relive in order to release the trauma that the client is carrying, but I usually check with the client's subconscious to see if there are any other significant incidents in that past life that have also been traumatic. When I did this with Amy, her subconscious signalled that there was something else that we had to experience. She regressed into an earlier time in that life and relived a horrific event:

"I'm around four years of age and I'm crouched in the corner of the tepee with my knees tucked up to my chest. I feel really frightened. My older sister who's about 15 years old is being pulled outside by some men. We're being attacked and I feel so scared. I don't want them to take her away. Mum's tied up. I don't know where my father is. They're strapping my sister to a horse to take her away. I run out of the tepee shouting at them to leave her alone. The man grabs me and picks me up from behind. He stares at my sister and then they take her off the horse. She's so scared. I'm crying. I can't do anything. The man takes me back into the tepee whilst the other men bring my sister." Amy became emotional and very tense, and her body started shaking as she cried out: *"He's – I can't watch – he's holding my face – she's screaming. He's making me watch. My mother's crying. I can't do anything. He's making me watch."* Amy was sobbing by this stage, her fists pressing down into the arms of the chair, her body stiff with terror. *"She's just laid there while they do it. She's numb. Where's my father? There's no one to help. When they've finished the man slits her wrists and then stabs her with a knife. He looks at me and says, 'Nobody gets away with what your father did to me.' She's dead, just laid there. He throws me towards my mother and ties me up*

to her. They leave and set fire to the tepee. It's night-time. We have to wait for someone to come. My sister's body is just laid there, dead. My mother's cold, not moving, just staring. Eventually, two men and my father come and they take her body away and bury her. My father says that we'll never speak of it again. I can see my mother's eyes and they look empty. She's so sad. But I'm a good boy and I don't speak of it again. There was nothing I could do." Slowly she started to relax. *"We just carry on living our lives and we slowly forget what happened. After a while I get a new baby sister and my mother's happy again."*

By this stage Amy was no longer tense and she lay calmly in the chair. I asked her how she felt and she said that she was relieved. I brought her out of trance and took a while debriefing her in order to make sure that she had let go of the negative emotions after the horror of what she had remembered, but she was at peace and feeling very much at ease. Even though she had had a harrowing experience, the entire trauma of it had been neutralised and she was ready to move on with her life.

Amy's final past life session came a week or so later, and she told me at the start of the session that she was feeling so different in herself to how she had been before we began working through the past lives. She felt much more assertive and the anxieties were virtually non-existent. Only occasionally had she felt a tiny feeling of anxiety but it merely lasted a few seconds before it disappeared. She was looking forward to working on the last of the four past lives, and once she had settled into hypnosis she was soon reliving it. I asked her what she was experiencing:

"It's night-time and I'm standing at the front of a church. I'm the minister and I can see other people praying. There's a choir and quite a few people in the congregation. They're poor people, not well-to-do. It's a big, cold church and they look to me for guidance. They listen to me and respect me. There are lots of lighted candles and it's Harvest Festival; everyone's brought food. My wife's there, she's quiet and kindly. After everyone has left we're tidying up. Some men come into the church, they don't look very nice and I feel scared. I ask if I can

help them but they want money and I don't have any. One of them pushes my wife out of the way and then they tie us up and disappear into the back of the church. I can hear banging and they come out with gold plates and goblets. They knock a candle over when they leave and start a fire." Amy started to jerk and breathe anxiously. She was shaking and coughing, wheezing as if gasping for breath and crying. *"We need to get out. My wife's screaming and screaming. There's nothing I can do. The flames are getting bigger. I'm trying to get free, it's so hot. I hope God hears us but I don't think he will. It's so hot and things start to fall from the ceiling. I'm coughing but my wife's not breathing."*

She spoke no more but continued struggling as she lay in the chair, until after a time her shaking subsided and finally her breathing was relaxed. I asked her what was happening and she told me that she had died and she felt calm. I finished the session by giving her some positive post-hypnotic suggestions and then brought her out of trance. The therapy was complete and she told me that she felt totally at ease and there was not a trace of anxiety left in her body. She said that she was looking forward to her future life free from anxiety. I have no doubt that this has been her experience ever since our sessions took place.

Chapter 10

Rachel's Story

Rachel was a 42-year-old hairdresser, a competent businesswoman running her own hairdressing salon. However, for a number of years she had been suffering from an anxiety state which was making her life very difficult, particularly when she was at work. She was finding that in her salon she felt stressed a lot of the time, and she had started to feel that she couldn't talk to her clients as she felt uptight and embarrassed. She would sometimes get panic attacks and a nervous skin rash would appear on her chest and throat. As a result of all of this happening, she was constantly 'on edge' and she felt less confidence in herself. Feelings of anxiety wouldn't go away, and she was getting to the stage where she was dreading going to work in a morning. The struggle to keep things together at work all day whilst trying to hide a constant feeling of dread and anxiety was exhausting her, and she felt drained a lot of the time.

Our first session consisted of talking about these issues and her feelings, and then we did some hypnosis to check out where the anxieties were coming through from. Her subconscious indicated that there was a past life at the source of the problem and, although we didn't open up the past life in the first session as we didn't have enough time, Rachel felt a great deal calmer at the end of the session having enjoyed the benefits of the relaxing elements of hypnosis.

When she returned for her next session, Rachel told me that she had felt a lot calmer for a few days after the first session before the usual anxieties had started to come back again. She was intrigued to know more about the past life that was causing her anxieties. She told me that she didn't understand the concept of previous lives; in fact she was quite sceptical, but that she was willing to give it a try. She settled back into my reclining chair and soon was relaxing deeply, and I began to guide her back through time, deeper into her subconscious mind, and after a few minutes she was sharing with me the visions she was seeing in her mind's eye:

"I'm a little girl, only about five or six years old. I'm playing outside, near to a wagon. It's a bit like a smallholding, and my dad's there tying hay on to the wagon. I feel happy. Dad gives me an apple and then says, 'Come on, poppet.' He lifts me on to the wagon and we move off, singing, 'Hey ho the rushes oh.' We're going home. When we get there, he lifts me off the wagon, throws me in the air, catches and kisses me. We go into the cottage and he puts his arms around Mum from behind. There's a table in the middle of the kitchen and Mother's cooking. She calls me Millie. I pick up a doll and go out into the yard and chase some chickens. I'm skipping and humming the same tune. I feel really happy."

Rachel had recounted all of this calmly, in a slightly childlike voice, with a gentle smile on her face. From experience, I know that quite often when a client firstly moves into a past life, they begin to relive parts of it which are neutral or pleasant memories. However, this is usually just a preamble before the most significant part of the life comes through. After a few moments' pause, Rachel's body began to stiffen and her breathing rapid. Her words became snatched between gasps for breath. She started to cry as she went on:

"I can hear the sounds of horses' hooves, and some men with guns appear. I'm frightened so I run into the barn and hide. I see my father come out of the cottage and they shoot him in the head. They pull my mother out of the house and they're hitting her. One of them's trying to

kiss her. He's hit her in the face with the end of a long gun and knocks her out. They tie her up against a tree. One of them has gone into the house; another's coming round the back of the barn. I'm hiding and watching. I feel terrified. He bangs on the wooden wall with the gun and I jump. I'm trying not to breathe in case he hears me. I feel like I'm going to faint. The door opens and I hear footsteps. He's got me by my hair and he drags me outside. I'm struggling and he kicks me on to my dad's body. I see blood trickling down his face. I'm laid on my father; I can feel his hairy chest and his chin." Suddenly Rachel jumped. *"They've shot me in the back, my body's exploded. I've died now. I feel calm."*

Rachel breathed a big sigh of relief and the tautness in her body softened as she began to relax. The terrifying ordeal was over, and so I took her back through it a few more times to completely release all of the fear she had brought through from that past life into her present life. The last time she relived it there was no emotional charge, and she recounted it to me quite calmly. She came out of trance and expressed amazement at what she had seen and felt, but also surprise that she now felt so calm inside. This calmness continued to stay with her. In fact, I met her again six years after our regression session and she told me that it had completely got rid of all of her anxieties and panics, and that she had been able to work stress-free since then.

Chapter 11

Barbara's Story

Barbara was a quietly-spoken 40 year old who was suffering from a severe anxiety state coupled with claustrophobia. A learning provider who tutored adults, she was hampered in her work by the anxiety feelings which she said were always there with her. She constantly had to yawn as she felt that she couldn't get her breath, and she had a history of panic attacks throughout her life. She had been a nervous child and her claustrophobia now meant that she was unable to get in elevators and other confined spaces. At times she felt that she was being smothered, her chest would feel tight and her breathing would feel constricted. The anxiety feelings had been getting worse over the previous few years. She had tried CBT (Cognitive Behavioural Therapy) which had reduced the anxieties for a while but they had since come back with a vengeance. Her doctor (as usual in these cases) had put her on medication, in her case Prozac, which was definitely not working (and was possibly making things worse). Fortunately, as she progressed through our sessions she was able to reduce and then come off the medication completely as it was no longer necessary.

Barbara was brilliant in hypnosis, having a natural ability to go in to trance (as do approximately 25–30% of people), and once we had elicited her IMR her subconscious indicated that there were seven past lives causing the anxieties and claustrophobia. This is quite a high number of past lives (the average number of past lives causing issues is three) and on the basis of 'the bigger the problem the bigger the cause' it meant that Barbara's phobia and anxiety state were going to be more severe than usual. As well as this, she told me that she had had a terrible early life, with a hideous mother who had bullied her mercilessly throughout her childhood, and as you would expect during our therapy sessions we did work on healing her childhood wounds and helping her Inner Child to feel calmer, safe and valued. However, it was the past lives which contained a substantial energy of trauma and which really were at the heart of the problem.

Barbara began by regressing into a childhood memory from this life in which she was trapped under a bed and unable to get out, and then suddenly she was in the first of the past lives, as a young eight-year-old girl in medieval England:

"I'm outside in the countryside and it's a warm summer's day. I'm with my family and I'm skipping. We go to our village and there are lots of animals around. The house has a straw thatch and there's a fire burning outside. At first I'm feeling happy, then suddenly I hear horses thundering towards us and I feel terrified as I see soldiers setting fire to things. People are screaming and shouting. I run into the woods to hide with my mother. Eventually we creep back when it's over. They've killed my father and brother. Then the soldiers come back and round up all the people who are left alive. They put us in a wooden carriage and take us into a castle. It's dark and cold. We have to work as servants in the kitchens and the cook is a bully and is really cruel to us. My hands are red from scrubbing. One day I do something wrong and they're screaming at me and they throw me into a dark cellar for a long time. It's pitch black and the floors are wet and there are rats. I just want to get out, I'm screaming." By this stage Barbara had become very tense, her breathing in gasps and her body shaking in the chair. *"There are no windows and no air in here. I keep shouting but they ignore me until the morning when they let me out. I feel cold and traumatised."*

She continued shaking for some time, before she started to calm down. I asked her to move to the next significant event in that life:

"I'm a few years older but still in the castle. Something bad's happening in the courtyard. Soldiers are putting black hoods over the

heads of some prisoners and hanging them. I don't know what they've done wrong, but I'm frightened it could happen to us. I feel very scared." After a short pause she moved on: *"A few years later I get married and live in a cottage near the castle. I have a baby, although we're very poor."* Suddenly, she started to jerk as she became agitated. For the rest of the session she continued jerking and shaking, her hands clasping and unclasping and her breathing coming in short, rapid bursts. She was twisting around and squirming as she moaned and whimpered: *"My husband has gone away to fight. He's gone overseas and I don't hear anything for a long time. I'm distressed in case anything happens to him and frightened because I'm on my own. He doesn't come back. I feel vulnerable so I take my daughter to the castle for my mother to look after. I stay in the cottage, but soldiers come and burn it down. It's terrifying. I run but they knock me over, and they're kicking me and laughing. I'm screaming – I know they'll kill me. They're going to bury me alive. I'm kicking and screaming as they throw me in a hole in the ground and throw mud on me. I try to get out but I can't. There's mud on my face and in my eyes and nose. I can't breathe. I can't breathe and I can't move my body. I'm lying face up and the jeering and shouting is getting fainter. There's so much earth on me. I can't move or breathe."*

Eventually Barbara was still and her distress and agitation eased right down. She began to breathe slowly again, and I allowed her to regain her composure for a few minutes before I asked her subconscious to move her on to another of the seven lives. Very soon she was there:

"I'm outside in a marketplace. I'm a young woman in my early 20s, doing some shopping. It's very busy with lots of noise and the unpleasant smells of livestock and there are horses and carts. It's cold and icy and my hands are cold, and I'm shivering because my clothes are threadbare and ragged. I buy some fish. People are jostling me and the stallholders are shouting. It's too crowded; I just want to get out. Beggars are grabbing at my skirt. The noise frightens me. I'm panicking and I can't breathe properly. I walk quickly down some alleyways to

get home and there are beggars and pickpockets about. I feel vulnerable and feel relieved when I get to my mother's house to pick up my little girl. I've been working as a maid and she's been looking after her. It's winter and it's getting dark so I wrap her up in a coat and a hat, and leave for home. She falls over in the snow and she's screaming. There's blood on the floor so I wrap the wound up quickly. When we get home I make a fire and boil some water for the fish. It's a small, dark house with small windows. My hands are shaking with the cold. My daughter plays with a doll by the fire and after we've eaten I put her to bed. I sit by the fire, sewing, feeling anxious. My husband's late and I don't know where he is. After a while there's some loud banging at the door and it shocks me. He's angry because I locked him out. He's been drinking and he starts shouting. I try to placate him with his food but it's dried up so he shouts at me and throws it on the floor. He's pushing me around and shouting. I feel really tense and scared. He bangs my head against the wall and then he gets his coat and slams out of the house. I feel relieved once he's gone. This is a regular thing and he's a brute all of the time. My little girl's been frightened by the noise and she's crying. I usually try to keep quiet whilst he's around. I clean up the mess and go to bed." Barbara became calm again and was silent for a couple of minutes. Then she went on:

"It's a few weeks later and my little girl's poorly. She's in bed with a fever. My husband's not understanding. The doctor comes and says that she's seriously ill with her lungs. I sit in candlelight mopping her brow but she dies and we put her in a little wooden coffin. There's thick snow in the churchyard and I'm crying. Even my husband's upset. Back home I feel sad all the time as the house feels empty without her. Everything I see reminds me of her. But we're poor so I have to go back to work. My husband was nice to me for a while after her death but now he's slipped back into his old ways and he's drinking more again. There are lots of arguments and he hits me. I feel depressed and hopeless so some of my friends take me out for the night. I've made a pretty dress and I come home late. There's a big row as he's very jealous and he doesn't want me to look nice. He starts pushing me and pulling my hair

and I'm trying to get away. I'm screaming and I kick him really hard and run upstairs to the bedroom but he chases me there, screaming at me. I try to get out but he punches me in the head and throws me on to the bed. He's trying to smother me with a pillow and I can't breathe." Once more as she was experiencing this Barbara was squirming, crying and gasping for breath. She put her hands up to her face as if to ward off the blows and was trying to pull off the pillow that was smothering her. *"He won't get off me, I can't breathe. He's pressing down on my face with the pillow. I manage to push him off but he kicks me to the floor. I get up and run to the door but he grabs me and he's screaming in my face. His hands are round my neck and he keeps pressing. I can't get away. I can't swallow. I try to kick him but I've no strength left. Everything's going black. He's strangling me and I feel suffocated. I can hear him shouting and then it's over and I'm outside my body watching him push me down on the bed. I don't feel anything now, only calmness. I'm going to join my little girl. It's all peaceful now."*

The life was over and Barbara relaxed again, this time very deeply as a result of letting go of so much trauma. I brought her out of trance and she sat calmly for some time, shocked at her experiences. She didn't believe in past lives and so she was surprised that not only had she been in two of them, but also that they had been so powerful and vivid. I reassured her that she would get better as a result of the work we were doing, and that she only had to continue working through the remaining past lives and her anxieties would be a thing of the past. As you can see, the traits of her anxiety states (claustrophobia and a need to take panic breaths) were mirrored in the two past lives that we explored. In the first she was buried alive and felt trapped and couldn't breathe, and in the second life she was strangled and unable to get away at the same time as not being able to breathe. As I mentioned earlier, this does not always happen in therapy, where we can be left scratching our heads and wondering what the connection is between the past life trauma and the client's issues, but here with Barbara there is a clear link.

She returned a few weeks later and she was pleased with her progress after the last session. She had felt more assertive at work, and more confident and energetic generally. However, when work became more stressful than usual she felt a little anxious, and the need to take deep breaths came back. I told her that I wouldn't expect her to be completely better just after one session because we obviously had a lot more to do, but I was pleased that she'd experienced some improvement in her confidence levels. Something was obviously working!

Once she was relaxing in hypnosis again she began to regress into another life, this time in WWII. A frown came over her face as she spoke:

"It's night-time and I'm in the kitchen of my house. I'm a woman in my 30s and I'm alone, reading some Christmas cards and a letter from my husband. The windows are blacked out as it's wartime. It's late at night and I'm sitting drinking a cup of tea. It's a few weeks before Christmas and I feel scared and lonely, worrying about my husband and my son. My husband can't come home on leave from the Navy at Christmas and my 10-year-old son is an evacuee in Cornwall. I have a letter from my son and he's drawn a picture for me. I'm worried about air raids, and then I hear an air raid siren and I start to panic. I put my coat on, get my gas mask and torch and a blanket, and run outside to the shelter. It's pitch black outside so I'm stumbling around. I feel very vulnerable in the shelter and it's cold, damp and dark. I put a blanket around me but I can't get warm. There's a lot of noise outside, of aeroplanes and bombs whistling and dropping. It's terrifying, I can feel my heart racing." Barbara now was breathing heavily, her body rigid with fear. Her hands kept jumping up and down, as if she was reliving the impact of bombs falling close by. *"It all sounds quite near and I can hear people screaming and sirens and fire engines. I'm frightened they'll hit the shelter."* She paused for a while and began to relax again. *"It's gone quiet and I can hear the all-clear. It's getting light when I come out of the shelter and I see two*

houses down our street are on fire. People are crying and screaming. It's depressing and I feel on edge all of the time." Again she was quiet for a short time, and then she continued:

"It's the next day and I'm working in London in an underground factory packing munitions. It's very noisy and dark with hundreds of people, many of them women, and lots of metal everywhere. I don't enjoy it as it's monotonous with long hours but I'm trying to help out. On the way home afterwards I go for a Christmas drink with some of the women. The pub's crammed with people jostling around and I feel uncomfortable. I just want to go home. When we come out people are trying to rush for the bus but there's another siren so we run for the shelter. It's down in an underground station, and it's really crowded with people and smelly. Everyone's packed in and I feel claustrophobic. I'm frightened we might get trapped down there." Once more she had started shaking and panic breathing. *"There's so much noise, babies screaming and people crying. I don't like it here and I want to get out and I can feel myself starting to panic. More and more people are coming on to the platform and I'm trying to get out but I can't get past them. I'm squashed against a wall. Eventually the crowd starts to disperse and the danger's over. I'm so relieved when we get outside and I can breathe again. Big buildings are on fire and there are ambulances around. It's really sad as lots of people have been killed. I walk home past lots of bombed buildings."*

She sighed deeply and paused again as time passed in the life:

"It's after Christmas and I'm packing my suitcase as I'm going to visit my son. I really miss him. I don't feel well; I'm feverish so I go to bed. There's another air raid siren but I don't feel well enough to move. I'm fed up of it all. I'm really unwell but also panicky so I put my dressing gown on and go downstairs and sit in the cupboard under the stairs. I can hear bombs dropping and the house is shaking. I don't think I've made the right decision. I should have gone outside to the shelter. The noise is deafening – planes, bombs and the house is shaking. I cover my ears with my hands." Suddenly she jumped

and she screamed loudly: *"There's an almighty loud crash – the house has been hit. I try to open the door but I can't – it's blocked. I can't get out and I'm panicking. There's brick dust everywhere and I can smell burning. I push against the door but I'm trapped. I need help."* Her voice was agitated and she breathed in short bursts. She was twisting around in the chair and she began to cough. *"There's a fire and smoke everywhere. I'm being smothered and I can't get any air. There's a really strong smell of burning and flames licking at the door. I'm suffocating, choking. I can't breathe."* She continued to writhe and cough for a minute or so, until finally she eased down into the chair and she lay quite still. *"I'm looking down on my body and I feel sad. It's finished."*

Once more I asked Barbara to relax and let the rigours of the past life dissolve away from her body. She drifted deeper into trance, and as she did so I moved her into another life. She spoke softly:

"It's daytime and I'm alone in a forest. I'm a young girl, around eight years old and I'm wearing a rough, hessian dress. I'm collecting berries and bits of wood into a basket but I think I'm lost as the woodland is very dense. It's starting to get dark and I can't find a path back to my village. I'm panicking so I start to run but I trip over a log and fall and hurt myself. I don't know what to do so I sit down behind a tree, shivering. It's cold and dark and I'm frightened of ghosts and things. There are things rustling in the trees and I've torn my dress and lost my basket. I'm really scared and I'm there all night. The next morning I find my way back to the village, where my parents are really upset. It's a Celtic-type village and I sit by the fire to get warm. I feel safe now." After a short pause she continued: *"It's two years later and my father and brother and the other men are getting ready to battle with another tribe. Everyone's frightened. They daub themselves with paint. I don't want them to go and Mother's crying. When they leave I'm just really worried that they might not come back. We're all alone in a bleak village. They're gone for a long time and they come back bloodied and injured. I feel agitated because the fighting doesn't seem*

to stop as they're always fighting. I wish we could go somewhere safer. One woman has lost her husband and she's crying, whilst another's son hasn't come back. I just feel fear all of the time." Barbara had been tense throughout all of this, but then she started to tremble and cry. *"It's night-time and I can hear horses' hooves and people yelling. Soldiers are attacking us in the middle of the night. The men rush out to fight and the women huddle the children into the houses. We've been caught off guard. I'm terrified, listening to the noise and the screaming. We're forced out and there's blood everywhere. Most of the men have been killed and my father's dead. Everyone's crying, the women are wailing and the children are screaming. They tie our hands and make us walk. I don't know where they're taking us but we walk a long way. They're really rough men, jeering at us and I'm really frightened. They take us to a village and lock us in a building. It's dark and I don't know what's going to happen. They keep us there for a few days. One night they come and take some of the young women and the girls. It's winter, it's cold and they're pushing us around. They push us towards a hill where there's some kind of ritual or ceremony going on. I can see a full moon. There are lots of people and some Druid-type people there. I think they're going to sacrifice us. We can't escape. They're all chanting as they push us towards a stone altar. They put a hood on my head so I can't see and someone lifts me up on to the altar. The stone's really cold on my back."* Her hands were out in front of her, her arms rigid as if she was trying to stop something happening. Her breathing came quickly and she started to moan and sob. *"I'm screaming. I think they're going to kill me. I'm terrified. I'm lying face upwards and they stab me in the heart. I die quickly."* She slumped down and her body softened as her breathing slowed down. *"I'm at peace now."*

I allowed Barbara to let go of all the tension she had been feeling throughout the horrors of that life and gently brought her back to full awareness. She was relieved that it was over but she felt very calm inside, as if something had shifted inside her. The smile on her face was warm and serene as she left my office.

When she arrived for our next session Barbara looked radiant, with a quiet sense of composure that I hadn't seen before. She was happy to report that she felt a lot better in herself, nowhere near as anxious as she used to feel, and her breathing problem (the need to yawn and take big breaths) had hardly happened at all, despite a stressful Ofsted inspection at work. Although she had initially expressed doubt about the concept of past life therapy, now she was beginning to realise the importance of it since she had improved so much as a result of our therapy sessions and she was far less hesitant about going into trance to relive her former lives.

Once more she settled into a pleasant hypnotic state and I guided her back into the past. This time we moved into a more modern past life:

"I'm a young trainee nurse in a hospital. It's an Edwardian period of time. I'm making beds, wearing a uniform and a white apron and black shoes. There's a strong smell of disinfectant. I'm on a women's ward and I feel nervous. The matron's unkind, it's hard work and the hours are long. She shouts at me when I do things wrong, but I'm not sure if I like the work or if I'm cut out for it as I don't like to see people suffering. I feel homesick and lonely, living in nurses' digs in an old, gloomy Victorian house. I don't want to go back to work and when I'm there I feel anxious. One day I'm ushered in to help a woman who's having a baby and she's screaming in agony. I've not seen anyone in labour before and it's all going wrong, I feel frightened and I don't want to be there. There are horrible instruments and I just want to get out." By now she was wringing her hands and breathing anxiously. *"I feel helpless as I can't do anything so I try to mop her brow. I feel trapped and the doctor's not been kind to her – he shouts at me to get more towels. There's blood everywhere. The baby's born dead. They try to revive it but they can't. The woman's crying and her husband comes in to comfort her. I feel distraught and traumatised by it all and I just want to get out. The experience is so unpleasant and it makes me ill so I go home early. I feel trapped as well because I can't*

leave the job. I stick it out for a short time but one day I've had enough and I have a row with the matron so I hand my notice in. I spill some drinks so she's screaming at me but I throw the mop down and start shouting back at her. I get the train home but when I get there my dad shouts at me for wasting my life, he's angry and wants me to go back but he doesn't understand. We have a screaming row, I'm crying and he says that I'm a disgrace and he hits me across the head. I run out of the house and run to my grandma's house."

After a while Barbara began to calm down and her silence indicated that she had moved on in the life, and she saw herself in the future much happier, married and working in a haberdashery shop. Although the past life had been less dramatic than the previous ones she had relived, there was still a lot of fear and trapped-ness in it which meant that it had a depth of trauma contributing to her issues. As usual I waited for her to regain some composure before we moved into another life, this time as a young teenage girl in ancient Egypt:

"It's a very hot day and I'm walking in the desert with some others, whilst some men are riding on camels. I can smell the camels and hear the flies buzzing. I've been taken away from my family and I feel uneasy, tired and a bit faint as I've had nothing to eat or drink. There are blisters on my feet and I'm not sure where we're going, although I can see pyramids in the distance. We're slaves and we've been walking for hours, some are crying and we're all thirsty. Men are shouting at us from the camels and we're taken into a market town where they start pushing us around and they split us up to take us to different places. I go to some sort of palace where I'm going to be a servant to the lady of the house, but it's very brutal and people there are unkind to me. I have to help her to dress, she hasn't got much hair and she puts a wig on and lots of make-up. She's very spiteful and treats me badly. Now I'm watching something going on in the courtyard. Some slaves have been caught stealing and soldiers come and kill them by beheading them. I'm horrified. The mistress becomes more and more nasty to me, in fact I think she's mentally ill, and one day she's so unwell that she

takes to her bed. I wonder if she's been poisoned as she's foaming at the mouth, and when I serve her some food she throws it on the floor and slaps me across the face. She's raging, in a fever and screaming with pain whilst a doctor tries to give her some herbs. I think she'll die. In the confusion that night I steal some jewels and escape so I can get back home, but I get lost in the town and I end up sleeping in a doorway where someone attacks me and steals the jewels. It's daylight now and soldiers see me and take me back to the house where I'm locked in a dark room, like a cell. I'm frightened because I don't know what's going to happen. I hear footsteps and three men come in and push me about, saying that I'm going to die. One of them tears my dress off, and kicks and punches me. I'm trying to fight but they drag me down into a dark cellar and I'm really scared. No one can hear me screaming and they pin me down."

By this stage, as she experienced the unspeakable horrors that were perpetrated upon her, Barbara was crying, squirming and shaking. Her whole body was tense and she was moaning and gasping loudly. *"They lock me in a coffin or a small wooden box. They're all laughing as they push me in and seal the lid and walk off, still laughing. I can't breathe and I'm trying to get out. I'm shouting and screaming, running out of air. It's so dark and I can't get out. I've been in here for hours and I'm suffocating."*

As she was gasping out the words she was taking big gulps of air as if trying to keep herself alive, and her face was filled with terror as she slowly suffocated. Eventually she grew calmer and at last she began breathing normally as she relaxed. The ordeal was over and she had died a death that once more mirrored the claustrophobia in this lifetime and her need to take large breaths all the time. She surfaced from trance, and although she was shocked by her experience she felt quite calm and peaceful. No wonder, she mused, that she had had such a serious anxiety state for such a long time. I knew that it was only a matter of time before she would be completely free of it.

Barbara returned for her final regression session declaring

herself to be approximately 90% better than when we had started her therapy. She felt more at ease in herself, the claustrophobia was much improved (on a trip to London she had been on the Underground and in lifts and had noticed hardly any anxiety), and the need to take deep breaths and yawns had rarely troubled her. All that remained now was to work on and release the final past life, and once she was in trance she slipped easily into it, seeing herself as a young girl (around eight or nine years old) in a Victorian school classroom:

"We're a lot of girls and boys, standing, chanting our times-tables and then doing sums which I find difficult. I feel frightened because I'm new here and the teacher's not nice, she keeps walking around and when I can't do it she shouts at me and hits me on the knuckles. I feel pressurised, I can't think straight and I just want the class to be finished. The bell rings and we go out to play, and I stand in the corner of the playground watching the other children skipping and singing. It's cold but I can't join in because I don't know anyone and I feel scared and lonely. It's a gloomy and cold school in a city somewhere in England. At the end of the day someone collects a group of us and we go back into an orphanage. My mum and dad were killed a few months ago. It's not nice here as they make us eat all the food they give us and I don't like it so they make me stay at the table until I eat it. The dormitory's cold and we don't have enough blankets. Some of the older girls jeer and make fun of me, and one of them steals my book which has a photo of my parents in it and when I try to get it back she pushes me over. I'm crying, I don't want to be here. We have to do chores and the matron is sharp-tongued and I just feel on edge all of the time. One night I have to wash up and I drop some glasses and matron is screaming at me and hits me across the face, saying that I'm useless, and I run away, crying. Everyone is frightened of her. One day I'm accused of stealing something but no one believes I haven't done it, and matron drags me by the hair, screaming at me all the time and locks me in a broom cupboard. It's really dark and it smells in here. She keeps me in for a long time even though I'm screaming to get

out and banging on the doors." As she experienced being trapped in the cupboard Barbara was sobbing like a child and shaking with anxiety. *"I want to get out, I can't breathe and I'm frightened she'll leave me here forever. Eventually she lets me out and I'm just shivering, frightened that she'll lock me in again."* She had stopped crying but she continued to whimper and moan and shiver for a while, becoming calmer as she moved on through time to her adolescence.

"I'm about 15, I've been at the school for those few years and although I still feel lonely as I don't fit in I'm starting to train to be a teacher. I pass my teacher-training and go into an inner city school to teach but I don't like it as it's in a rough area and the children are difficult. I'm not sure I made the right decision, but I didn't really have any options. I get a letter from an aunt, inviting me to join her in Canada, but I'm not sure what to do. However, I decide to go and I'm on the ship now, travelling there. I don't like deep water and I'm seasick and really tense. One night it's really stormy, there are waves crashing on to the deck and I'm worried we'll capsize. Finally it calms down but it's a long voyage. When I get to Canada I stay with my aunt but she's not very friendly; in fact she's quite austere. It's cold here and at first I feel homesick. I teach in a country school which is better than in England and the children are nicer and I feel more relaxed. I'm more relaxed now and after a few years I meet a man at a dance and eventually we get married. He works in a bank and I get pregnant, but he starts being cold towards me, going out a lot. He becomes critical of me and he's not as attentive as he used to be. One night he comes home drunk, starts arguing and pushes me over. I get a bad pain and I think I've gone into labour. I manage to get to the bedroom whilst he goes for a doctor. I feel a lot of pain in my abdomen and it's a long labour. A nurse is with the doctor, holding me down. I'm in a lot of pain and I've lost a lot of blood." Once more Barbara was breathing heavily, her body tense whilst she moaned and shook throughout the experience: *"The baby's alright and they take it away to look after it but I'm really not well, really feverish. I'm drifting in and out of*

consciousness, they think I'm dying. I'm weak and the doctor is trying to revive me. They take me to the hospital where I'm ill for several weeks, but finally I go home and I start to recover. My husband's nicer to me now." Once more she was calm. *"I've moved on now and my little girl is eight. I have another row with my husband when he tells me he's found someone else and he's leaving me. He was nice at first but then he went back to his old ways. I feel lonely and isolated so I decide to go back to England and try to erase all the bad memories. I get another teaching job, meet a man who's kinder and have another child. I feel more settled now, even though I sometimes look at my old photo album and realise I miss my mum and dad. Finally, around the age of 60 I get an infection and I'm not in a good way. I'm lying in bed and my husband's there. I can't get my breath."* Again she became tense, her body stiff and her breathing forced, as if wheezing. The harshness of her strained breath was broken by a sad whimpering, and she started to twist in the chair, her head up and her mouth wide open as if gasping for air. After a short time, she began to soften and finally she slumped down, her body limp and her breathing slow and deep again. *"I couldn't get my breath but I'm floating above myself now, watching my husband crying. I feel light, calm, at ease."*

Once more, we had released the traumas of the past life and she came back to full consciousness. Her journey into previous lives was over and her lifelong anxiety was healed. She contacted me some weeks later to say that everything was going well for her, and that as well as a new-found calmness in herself she was beginning to feel more creative, and she had started sketching pictures and doing a course in creative writing. The breathing problem was a thing of the past, and she said that she was much more confident. She was reacting positively to the things that used to make her feel stressed, and her final words to me were: "You've been a great help in many different areas. You seem to have cleared a lot of rubbish from my head."

Chapter 12

Flying Phobia: Yvonne's, Janet's and Gemma's Stories

Flying phobia is something that most Hypnotherapists treat regularly and I have successfully worked many times with clients who have this fear. Sometimes the cause of the phobia is connected to claustrophobia (or a fear of being trapped), sometimes it's a fear of not being in control, other times it can be a fear of dying. On occasions it can be all three of these and I often find that flying phobia comes from past lifetimes. Here are three successful treatments from my casebook.

Yvonne's Story

In her late twenties, Yvonne was soon to fly to Canada and was already getting sleepless nights as she worried about the flight. She explained to me that she thought it was caused by her need to be in control, although she couldn't think of any reasons why she should be frightened of flying as she'd never had a bad flight in her life. She vividly remembered her first flight when she was only three, and she knew that she found it exciting and not at all scary. She couldn't understand why she felt so frightened when she had to fly anywhere, particularly as she had a fascination with military aeroplanes and air shows. This last fact had me immediately suspecting that this could be from a past life, and sure enough, once she was in trance her subconscious took her into one. What surprised me was that she began to speak in an American accent, and she became extremely tense as she saw herself as a soldier in the Vietnam War:

"It's daytime and I'm with a group of soldiers moving through water in a jungle. I'm frightened, there are explosions going off around us, guns and mortar fire. There are six or seven of us running and

shouting, trying to get away. We're desperately trying to get away from the mortars. We get to a clearing in the jungle and a helicopter is coming towards us. The chopper's coming down now. We climb in and it takes off, flying above the trees. I think we're all OK, but one of us is unconscious. The sound of the chopper is so loud, but we get back to base and he's taken to the infirmary. Someone offers me a cigarette. I feel better now, but I was so scared."

Yvonne began to breathe gently again as she calmed down, but after a few moments she stiffened again as she remembered a previous incident:

"I'm in a big troop transporter. There are no windows and we're hanging on to the walls inside of the aircraft. I'm being drafted to 'Nam and I feel nervous and scared as I don't want to go. My buddy Steve's here and he's scared too. We're so many guys sitting on this fucking plane all so damned scared. We're too young." Suddenly she jumped and started to breathe heavily. Her voice was full of panic: *"There's a loud bang and the aircraft's shaking. We're starting to go down. We're almost there but we've been hit by something. The sergeant's coming out of the cockpit, says we're gonna land here as one of the engines has been taken out. We'll have to go through the jungle to base camp. We're being shaken and we're holding on to our seats. I'm praying it's gonna be OK. We have a rough landing but we're on the ground. My ass hurts; these damned seats are so hard. I'm so scared I almost pissed myself. We run out of the back of the aircraft and head for cover. I can hear guns firing. I'm with our platoon of eight guys. The sergeant gets out the map and we move out slowly. I can see other guys from the aircraft milling around – they're doing the same. It's really hot and the forest is wet. My boots are squelching through the leaves. I'm not looking forward to having to shoot anybody. We follow the sergeant down a dirt road, but I don't know where the hell we are. We fall up and march double time. Steve starts singing dumb, fucking military songs supposed to keep us in rhythm but it really pisses me off. There's jungle on either side and it seems like we walk for miles*

before we see a guy on a jeep. He talks to the sergeant and eventually a bus comes out of the camp to pick us up. I feel safe now."

Yvonne became calm again and I brought her back to full awareness. She was shocked at how clear it had all been and how intense the feelings were, but she no longer was afraid of flying, and she contacted me a few months later to tell me that she had experienced no problems before or during her flights to and from Canada, and she had enjoyed a fantastic holiday in Vancouver.

Janet's Story

Janet had never liked flying and had two difficult flights in the past which had compounded her fear of flying, and as she was about to undertake an eight-hour flight she was feeling uncomfortable whenever she thought about her forthcoming holiday. Her subconscious indicated that there were two past lives causing the phobia, and she was soon reliving the first of them, as a six-year-old girl:

"It's dark and I'm frightened. Where has everybody gone? I can't get out and the floor's dirty. A woman has locked me in the cellar for being naughty; I dropped milk and made a mess on the floor, but a boy had pushed me and I dropped the jug. It made Matron cross. I live where the orphans live – Mummy went away and never came back. I want my mummy back. People said that she'd gone to join Daddy but I don't understand. Why doesn't she come back? She left me here all by myself and that nasty lady locks me in the Naughty Room. It's all quiet and I think they've forgotten I'm here. It's dark and cold and my dress is dirty. The walls are slimy and I'm worried about spiders. They've all gone to church; I can hear the bells and the sound of people outside in the street, and I can smell the dinner cooking in the house. I want to bang on the door but that'll make her cross. I broke the milk so there's no milk. I want a drink, I'm thirsty."

Much of this had been delivered in an infantile voice and manner, her head sometimes at an angle as she spoke and her fingers twisting round each other. Suddenly she began to cry vehemently, shouting out:

"I want to get out – let me out – let me out – let me out – I want my mummy – Mummy, don't leave me here – Mummy, I don't like it here, I don't like the dark, I don't like spiders, I don't like that boy – why doesn't she come and let me out?" This sobbing and shouting lasted for some time, and it was heartbreaking to witness, almost as if I was watching the agony of an actual child. However, I knew that we had to release the emotional pain, and after a while the emotions began to subside. She spoke more softly, rubbing and stroking her stomach as she did so:

"It smells in here and there's something sticky on the floor; it's all over my shoes. I'll get told off for having dirty shoes now. I want a drink. Why does my mummy let them put me in here? Eleanore is my friend and she's there, I can just touch her fingers under the door, but she's got to go now. Don't go and leave me by myself." She started to cry again. *"I can hear the children upstairs. I'm cold and there's something sticky on my shoe and my dress is all dirty. I'm waiting and waiting and waiting and waiting. When are they going to let me out? That nasty, horrid boy always picks on me. He's got a nasty, scabby face and he smells horrible. I want Eleanore to come back. I'm so hungry and thirsty. I've been locked in before and I waited all day for somebody to come and she didn't let me have any dinner. I'm waiting for George; he'll let me out when he comes back with the horses. I don't like being in here, I want my mummy. I can hear the sound of horses, and then George opens the door and it's all light. I have to go upstairs and change before she comes back. Oh go away. It's that boy, it's all his fault anyway. He's in Eleanore's box."* She started to shout. *"No you can't go in there, go away, this is girls only and you're not supposed to be in here; your room's across the way."*

She was quiet for a while so I asked her if she knew what her name was in that life, and if she knew the place where she lived. Without hesitation she replied:

"I'm called Sophie Dent and this place is in Liverpool. It's called

after a bird, it's hard to say but it's Curlew House. We go across the road to school. I want to go to the school that I went to before. I wanted to go and live with an auntie but she brought me here." Once more she began to cry, and throughout all of the following she was sobbing and moaning. As before, at times she was speaking directly to people in that life, at other times sharing her narrative with me:

"They won't let me in the room. Everybody's standing outside and they won't let me in. Why are they all so mean and horrid? Somebody keeps going in and out and I can hear shouting. I can hear Mummy shouting and I don't like it. Someone says, 'The baby's got stuck,' and, 'The baby won't come out.' No, I don't want to go upstairs, I want to stay here; I want to be with my mummy. They lock me in my room and I can't hear the noises downstairs. I want Mummy. I don't want them to take Mummy away like they took Daddy away. I don't know where they took him but he's gone and he never came back. Why has Mummy forgotten me? Auntie Victoria comes into my bedroom crying. She says that Mummy's gone to sleep and she's not coming back. I don't understand and I want to see her. Why is Auntie Victoria crying? The baby doesn't look nice, not like my dollies. Why doesn't he look like my dollies? I can't understand why Mummy won't wake up and her face feels funny. Wake up, Mummy. Who's going to look after me? Auntie Victoria's putting my things in a bag. Where are we going? Don't pull my arm; you'll make me fall over. Where are we going? No, I don't want to go with you. I want to go back with Mummy. I go in a coach and horses to her house but I don't like it there. She's got horrible pussy cats that scratch. It's not nice here. She takes me to the other place. It's horrible."

Jane had finally become calm again, and she now had an understanding of how she had come to end up in the orphanage, so we finished the session. Although she tried to logically make sense of what she had experienced (she was a very analytical person) as she had no knowledge of the concept of reincarnation, I asked her just to accept what had happened and to allow any shifts to take place in her feelings about flying over the coming days. There really is very little need to analyse a past life session, only to experience it.

She returned a couple of weeks later and told me that she was certainly feeling easier in herself and less anxious about flying, and also that her sleep had improved in that she was getting to sleep much faster than usual. We had obviously done some good work and had released some of her pressure in her emotional 'pressure cooker'. In this session, she went deeply into trance and began to experience a more modern past life, I would guess from the 1950s or 1960s. This time she was a man, waiting for his flight at an airport:

"It's late and it's raining heavily outside. The airport's quite empty at this time of night and the plane's been delayed because of the weather. I think it's coming in from Chicago. The one time I need to be there on time and it's late. Wait, wait, wait." She was shaking her head and sighing frustratingly. *"I just want to get back for Christmas, to see Judy and the kids."* Just out of curiosity I asked Janet to give me an idea of the names of her family, and she readily obliged: *"My name's George Hunter and my wife's called Judy. My children are Daniel who's just a couple of months old and Alex who's nearly six. I work in a paper or stationery business, involved in printing. It's only four days to go before Christmas and I still haven't got any presents sorted out. We live in the outskirts of Philadelphia."* She sighed and became frustrated again: *"I've been waiting for six hours and I just want to get home. I'm tired and hungry. I'm on the plane now and it's cold as the heating's not working."* She began to shift around in the chair and breathe heavily. *"It's bloody rough tonight. I've flown this route countless times and it's never been like this. It's a wild night. This is not right. It's too rough. Good God, I now wish I'd waited till tomorrow. Everybody looks scared and even the stewardess looks anxious. The lady sitting next to me is very frightened."* Suddenly she became very agitated, crying and her words came jerkily: *"Lights, I can see lights. Christ almighty. We're coming in to land*

but it's too fast, we're going too fast. Oh no! We've crashed as we landed. There are people running up and down, and there's a mess everywhere. They can't get the door open. There's a terrible smell. There's something wrong with the woman next to me. My foot's stuck under the seat in front. I can't get anyone's attention." She began to squirm around, moving her leg as if trying to dislodge her foot. She started to shout: *"Get me out, my foot's stuck. Everyone's getting off. Get me out. I'm stuck, I can't move."* She became calmer. *"They're trying to get me out first so they can get to the lady next to me but the seat in front won't budge. I can't feel my leg at all. It's still bloody raining. God, I thought we were a goner there. Oh, my foot, what a mess. I won't be playing golf for a time. I'm sitting in the back of an ambulance and I can see that we've overshot the runway. The belly's all crushed and the wheels are all messed up underneath. It's chaos with people everywhere. There are bits of plane and luggage all over the place. My case, I've left my bloody case on board. I just want someone to ring my wife."* She was quiet for a while as time moved on in the experience, then she continued: *"I'm at the hospital now, stuck in a corridor waiting for a theatre. I feel tired. I just want my wife. I can see my leg, looks like it's been broken in two places. They say they can't just pin it because the bones are too smashed. I can see the X-rays and it looks strange. It doesn't look good, it's a mess. I can't feel my foot. My wife's here."* She started to cry and she became very emotional: *"Where are the boys, I just wanna see the kids. They're asking my wife for consent to take the leg off. I was in a bloody hurry to get home, I wish I'd waited."* After a while she quietened, and after a pause she went on: *"It's really strange, it's been several months now and I can still feel toes that are no longer there. They amputated just below the knee and I just have an ugly stump now. The kids think it's funny, but at least I get to spend more time with them, even though I'm not so good at football."*

There was no more to experience so Janet came out of trance, relieved to find that her legs were still both there and intact. No wonder she had a fear of flying, having had such a horrendous experience of air travel in the past life. That, combined with being trapped in the cellar in the first past life, were the reasons why she had always been frightened of flying. She was now feeling perfectly comfortable about flying, and indeed her long-haul flights passed off without a hitch.

Gemma's Story

Gemma came to me for help with her phobia of flying. A 25-year-old assistant manager in a bank, she had always enjoyed flying as a child but over the previous few years she had become increasingly anxious whenever she went on holiday by air. It had become so bad that her last flight had been an extremely unpleasant experience for her because of the panics and nervous feelings that she had endured both before and during the flights. She loved being abroad but the phobia was stopping her from looking forward to her holiday. She told me that she had not had any traumatic flights in the past with any scary incidents that could have caused the phobia to start in the first place. Initially she had just found herself feeling more and more anxious whenever she flew, and this had now developed into a fully-blown state of intense fear before and during a flight.

Once she was in trance her Ideo-Motor Response indicated that there were two past lives causing the fear, and she was soon in the first of them, at sea as a man aged about 34 years old:

"I'm wearing brown lace-up shoes, brown trousers and a brown jumper, standing on the deck of a ship looking up at the blue, night sky. I feel tense, like I'm waiting for something to appear in the sky. I look down at a photograph I have in my hand of a woman and I'm scared I won't see her again. I see a black thing in the sky. It's a plane coming towards us, I think it's a war plane and people are shouting around me. It's got a red top and propellers, and it's heading towards us. I can see people dropping explosives out of the plane and things are hitting the water near us. I'm too scared to move. A bomb's landed on the ship and part of the boat's on fire. They give the order to evacuate. I need to get

off. I must jump and swim for it. The plane's circling back." Suddenly Gemma jumped as she lay in the chair and started to gasp and cry, her hands grasping at her chest. *"There's been a big explosion and I can feel pain in my chest as I fall into the water. I can't hang on, and I'm sad because I know I'm not going to see her again. I think she's my sister."* She became calm again. *"Everything's alright now, I've died and I'm just floating in the water."*

I was curious so I asked her subconscious to indicate which war this had taken place in, and as I recited a list of possible wars the finger raised to signal the First World War. Fairly soon she had moved into the second of the lives:

"I'm an old lady, sitting in a room looking at my necklace as I see myself in a mirror. I'm wearing black shoes and a dress with an apron over it and a white cap on my head. Two men are in the room wearing dark hats. They've come to take away my things and they want the necklace. I've got to pay debts that my husband left but I have no money and nothing of value apart from this necklace. I feel really scared as they're threatening me. I don't want to give it to them as it's the only thing I've got left to remind me of my husband. One of them has a bat in his hand and he's threatening me with it." All of a sudden she jerked and cried out, her right hand over her face as if trying to protect herself: *"He hits me with it and they grab the necklace. Then he hits me across the back and arms, it really hurts and I think my arm's broken. They're laughing at me now."* She started to cry and again her hand was held over her face: *"Don't hit me. Oh, they hit me on the head and I can feel blood. They leave and I'm just left lying on the floor with my face on the floor. I can't hold on and I see a blinding, white light and it's all over."* She was calm again for a short time, before she continued:

"I'm back at an earlier time in that life, a lot younger and looking and holding a photo of my husband. He's wearing a long, white scarf and a policeman's there telling me that he's gone missing. He was away on a trip and they haven't found him but there's nothing they can

do. I feel confused and scared that I'll never see him again. I start to age very quickly, and in the space of about ten years I'm feeling really old. They never find him and life's tough without him. I have no money and have to rent a room in a boarding house and wash my own clothes. He left gambling debts that I try to pay off, desperately scraping money together but they keep harassing me for more. I'm constantly scared." She began to cry and wring her hands together. *"I wanted to see my husband again. I told him not to go on that trip. It was like a journey to a new world which was quite undiscovered, and I'm so angry that he went anyway and left me in this state."*

Gemma spoke no more but continued to sob for a while, eventually easing and calming down again. She came out of trance and when I asked her how she felt about flying she told me that she felt quite calm about it.

It doesn't take a genius to work out that the first past life was causing the phobia because it was an aeroplane that had led to her death. I guessed that the reason the second past life was related to the phobia was not so much because of any connection to aeroplanes but because of the association between travelling and trauma, i.e. her husband had gone travelling and as a result she had endured a difficult life without him and then an unpleasant death.

I spoke to Gemma a year after our sessions to find that the flying phobia had completely gone, and since I had seen her she had enjoyed flying to Tenerife, Morocco, the Caribbean and Portugal without any problems. Not a bad result, eh?

Chapter 13

Jackie's Story

Jackie's phobia was one of the more common ones that we work with as therapists, that of emetophobia. This is a fear of vomit, either characterised as a fear of oneself vomiting or seeing someone else being sick. In more severe cases, as with all phobias, it can totally dominate the sufferer's life, being on their mind all the time and stopping them from living their life freely. It can manifest itself in many different ways. Often they cannot go out in case they see anyone being sick, they cannot go for a meal in case the food makes them vomit, if their children have a sickness bug they are unable to look after their children. Jackie had suffered from the phobia all of her life, and she had experienced an extremely stressful time nursing her mother through her final illness before she died, as her mother had vomited constantly, and she told me that she had often passed out when she handed her mother a bowl in which to be sick.

She was soon to be going on a cruise and she was very anxious whenever she thought about it, as she was doubly worried both about becoming seasick and also eating food on board the ship. Once she was in trance, her subconscious indicated that three past lives were causing the phobia, and she was soon reliving the first of them. Her initial state of relaxation evaporated away as her body stiffened and she started to cry:

"They're chasing me. I'm a young boy, around ten years old and I'm frightened. The men have caught me and they take me to a ship with tall masts. They tie me up and hit me with sticks and kick me and throw me in the bottom of the ship with some other boys. It's dark and horrible and there are rats everywhere. I want to get off but they won't let me go back. After a while they untie us and they're shouting at us and pushing us all on deck. We've got to work on the ship, and the men

are horrible and they're shouting and pushing me around. We're out at sea and the boat's rocking and I feel sick. It's going up and down really fast and I keep falling over. I'm lying down but a man kicks me to get up. I'm being sick and crying, there's vomit everywhere. Everything's rocking and dirty and smelly. I'm scrubbing the deck and it's hard work, and they keep shouting at me. The boat's going up and down and I'm crying and vomiting and being made to wash the sick off the deck. Later I'm lying down but I'm poked out of my bed and pushed into the galley to peel potatoes, there's a fire there and the smell of rotting meat." She began to squirm. *"They're putting slops on to tin plates. I've got to eat it but I don't want to. It's got things in it, things that are moving. He's hitting me now. I don't want to eat it so he's pushed my face in it. He's shoved me down into the hold and it's dark and there are rats. The men are coming down now and they're all drunk and shouting and laughing and singing. They throw me around and one of them hurts me so my arm's bleeding. The next day it's decking time again and I'm scrubbing it. It's really rough and cold, the waves are really high and it's horrible. I'm hanging on to things and scared so the man starts kicking me. My arm's bleeding again. I'm crying now, in a corner, being sick into a bucket. Oh, he's shoved my head into the bucket."* Again she reacted in a troubled way, her head and body moving from side to side as if she was trying to fight someone off. *"Now I'm sweeping all the horrible, disgusting food up and putting it into a bucket and chucking it into the sea. It's horrible, stinking and I don't like it. I sweep the deck and the men are horrible and nasty to me."*

She softened and her distress began to ease, and she moved out of the past life into calmness. She lay like this for a while, and then suddenly her arms began to move and shake violently, and her breathing was rapid and panicky. She spoke in jerks:

"It's a different life. Someone's chasing me. I'm in Scotland and a horrible, hairy man wearing a kilt is chasing me down to the water. He's carrying a weapon covered in spikes and I want to get away from him. He's been showing me how to swing the weapon in order to use it

but I don't want to do it. I'm just a boy but he says I won't be a man if I won't do it. He hits me with his hand so I take the thing and pull it around. It's got a ball covered in spikes on a chain. He's killed a rabbit and is cooking it over a fire. He's got horrible, yellow teeth and is cruel. The poor rabbit. If he thinks I'm eating that he can think again. Oh, oh no. He's making me eat it." Jackie's hands came up to her face and her head moved from side to side, as if to stop herself from being force-fed. She started to retch and choke, at the same time sobbing. *"He's making me swallow it. I don't want to. I run away down to the water and he's shouting as he chases me. The water's cold but I've got to get away. There's a type of boat there, it's a coracle and I get in it and float away. It's rocking and I'm frightened it might tip up but I can't get off it. There's water coming into it now and I'm sinking. It's cold. I sink into the water and drown."*

By this stage Jackie was shivering, but she spoke no more, and after a couple of minutes she relaxed again. I allowed her to go deeper into trance and then asked her to move to the final past life. Once more, as she accessed the life her arms began to move and shake and her body gave out little jerks of anxiety. Once more she was a young boy, this time a black child in a jungle:

"I'm very scared as there are some big, black men cooking something over a fire. It's hot and I don't like it. I run up a tree to try to get away from them but they pull me down and throw me to the ground. They've got spears. They're all dancing around the fire, singing and shouting as they burn the animal. I hide in a hut but some boys come and get me. They're sitting and eating but I don't want it." She started to retch and heave. *"A big black man's pushing it into my mouth. I just want to die. He makes me eat it but I just feel sick. I crawl away and lie on the floor in the hut. My tummy hurts. Eventually they all go except for the big man. I pretend to be asleep but he drags me out of the hut and starts kicking me around. He throws me on to the ashes and I'm all burned. I just fall on to the ground but I can't move. A woman comes and puts some leaves on my body and pours something into my*

mouth. It doesn't taste nice." She was coughing as she said this. *"She covers me over and some boys pick me up and carry me into the jungle. They dump me somewhere and I'm just left there, laid on the ground, waiting to die. I drift off and feel peaceful."*

Jackie was calm again as she felt herself leave the body and move into spirit. The horrors of the past lifetimes, all of which had similarities, were over so she came out of trance, feeling at ease. She had really relived the lives, talking and moving as if she were actually in the events as they happened (as opposed to merely seeing them from a distance and recounting them as a narrative), so she had felt all of the terror in the events and the abhorrence of eating disgusting food and being sick. I asked her to think about being sick or someone else being sick and she didn't react, so I expected that the emetophobia had been cured.

Sure enough, a couple of months later she contacted me and told me that after the session she had not had any panicky reactions whenever the subject of sickness and vomiting came up, but more than that she had been on the cruise and had enjoyed every minute of it. Even though there were two days when the sea was very rough she had not been bothered at all, and the thought of being sick had not triggered her in any way. Her phobia was completely gone.

Chapter 14

Tom's Story

When Tom's mother rang me, she told me that her son was 16 years old and that he had a phobia of needles. This was such a strong fear that whenever he was at the dentist receiving treatment he had to be held down by the dental nurses as he would try to fight the dentist to stop him from giving him an injection. The fear response was now so strong that during a recent visit to the dentist he had actually panicked so much that he had punched the dentist in the face and stormed out of the clinic. Unfortunately, he still needed to have some major dental treatment and the thought of it was causing him to have panic attacks, and he was refusing to go back to the dentist's. This was indeed a severe phobia.

However, when Tom came to see me I found that he didn't have a phobia of needles at all. He explained that he had a massive fear of having his neck touched, which had now also developed into a fear of having his wrists and the inside of his arms touched. He didn't even like anyone talking about their neck or wrists as it made him feel very uncomfortable. As he sat in front of me I tested the depth of his fear by asking him if I touched my neck or wrists how would he respond. As I did this I touched my throat and wrists and he screamed at me, "Don't do that, don't do that!" He sat up sharply and was extremely agitated. He told me whenever he was laid in the dentist's chair he felt incredibly vulnerable, and that as the dentist came towards him with the needle it triggered feelings that he was about to touch his throat and that was what caused the fear response in him, not the needle itself. He knew that the problem was getting worse as not only were his feelings becoming more intense, but also he had recently developed an anxiety about knives. If the blade of the knife was pointing towards him he felt frightened, and he said that he got feelings in his body "as if my belly has been split open."

Initially he was quite uptight as I guided him into hypnosis, but soon he began to relax and once his subconscious had created the IMR finger signal it indicated that there were two past lives causing the phobia, and he was soon reliving the trauma from the first of these. He saw himself as a man in his twenties wearing purple-coloured Arab robes:

"I'm outdoors walking alone between some houses. I feel quite confident but suddenly some people come out from another road and grab me and take me away into another building. I don't know why they're doing this and I feel afraid. There are too many of them for me to fight and I give up." He was becoming increasingly tense and upset as he experienced this, and suddenly he jerked and writhed as he lay in the chair, and his hand went up to his neck. His whole body started to shake and his breathing was rapid and panicky. He started to shout: *"They've pinned me down on a table and I'm laid facing upwards. I can't move. They're chopping my head off. They cut my head off. They don't care about me. I don't know why they do this."*

Slowly his agitation subsided, and he became calm again. I asked him to relax and took him into the other past life, and once more he started to tremble and shake. His voice quivered and he started to cry: *"I'm in another place, in the body of a woman. I'm kneeling in front of a circle of people sitting around me. I feel prepared but afraid. I cut my own throat with a knife. They've made me do it because I've done something wrong and embarrassed some people. I feel horrible and sad, and I try to push my arm away from my neck but I know I have to do it. I can see the people are upset but they're smiling too. My neck opens up in a bad way but I'm still kneeling so I do it a second time and I fall over. I'm looking down at my body from above – it's over."* Once more, the shaking and agitation took a few minutes to soften, before Tom lay calmly in the chair. He surfaced from trance looking very peaceful.

As a test to make sure we had released the negative emotions from those events I asked him to think about going to the dentist for treatment and he told me that he just felt relaxed. I asked him if it would be OK for me to touch his neck and wrists and he said, "No problems," and as I put one of my hands around his neck and on his wrists he lay serenely and didn't react. Remember, just a short time before this he couldn't even cope with me touching my own neck, let alone go anywhere near his. His mother rang me a few weeks later to inform me that he'd gone to the dentist and had all of the dental surgery without any problems at all. The dentist was amazed at the incredible difference in him, and was obviously pleased that he didn't have to fight with his patient anymore.

Chapter 15

Beth's Story

Something that I have successfully treated often over the years has been fear of surgery (I'm also, by the way, one of the few hypnotherapists in the world who has undertaken hypnosurgery, helping a client to have a major operation without any anaesthetic whilst in a hypnotic trance). Most people who are about to undergo surgical procedures are understandably anxious, but for some people their anxiety and fear about having an operation is so great that they find it difficult to function in the weeks (sometimes months) leading up to the operation. Beth was in this category. She was about to undergo a routine cataract operation but she was terrified of the prospect of going into hospital and being operated on. A charity worker from Merseyside, she was constantly experiencing a feeling of anxiety in her chest whenever she thought of the forthcoming surgery. She told me that the fear was so great that she was finding it difficult to keep thoughts of the operation out of her mind, and it was affecting her ability to sleep, work or live a normal life. She had always had a fear of hospitals and she worried about her health even though she was a fit and healthy person, but as the day of the operation grew closer she was becoming more and more panicky and her usually calm mind was increasingly obsessed about the possibility of dying if things went wrong.

I had done some therapy with Beth some years previously when we were both on a charity trek in Peru on the Inca Trail. At that time she was suffering from a phobia of heights and we did some work on it which cured the phobia so she was able to complete and enjoy the trek to Machu Picchu without any anxieties. Beth also mentioned in passing as we started the hypnotherapy session that she had always felt responsible for her parents. Although at first this didn't appear to be connected to the fear of surgery, as you will see it was a significant feature of the problem.

Beth was soon in trance and once her subconscious mind had created an Ideo-Motor Response it signalled that there were three past lives causing the fear, and she went rapidly into the first of them. Breathlessly she spoke about the images she was seeing in her mind's eye:

"I'm outside in a busy marketplace. It's daytime and there are hundreds of people around. It's like a scene from a Brueghel painting. I'm a young man and I think I work here. I feel anxious as the whole place seems mad, as if the people are not in control. It's mayhem. Someone's having their head ducked into a barrel of water. I don't feel safe. I can see oranges on a stall, but I feel really on edge. I'm remembering another time, earlier in that life, when I was younger. It's night-time and I'm in the middle of some woods and I'm sleeping under a tree when some men come on horses. They've got swords and they're angry. They're looking for someone but they can't see me as I'm hiding. I feel scared and lonely. Now I'm remembering when I was a young boy, running in some fields near to a castle. I'm about eight years old and I feel free as I run in the sunshine around the cornfields."

Beth then became quiet, as she gathered her thoughts after the somewhat frenetic nature of the past life memories that had rushed into her mind. After a couple of minutes of silence her face stiffened and she began to breathe anxiously. Her arms started to shake and her body jerked as she spoke hoarsely:

"I'm lying down. My legs and arms feel heavy and I feel sick. I'm thirsty. I can't get up, it's as though I'm paralysed. I feel trapped because I can't move. I'm inside a building, in a bed and someone's watching me. I think there are monks or nuns looking down at me. There's a tight feeling around my heart and pressure in my head. I feel really heavy but I can't move my arms and legs. There's a little window in the wall. Days and nights go past. I feel depressed because

there's no way out of this. I'm tired but I don't want to sleep in case I don't wake up. No one talks to me, I think they speak a different language. I've been a soldier and I'm remembering a battle with cannon balls and explosions. Lots of people have been injured in the fighting, but I'm not wounded. I have a sickness and I was carried here. I feel so alone. There are pains in my legs now." She started to cry as she continued: *"I want to go home. This is a slow, long drawn-out experience. I can't move, I'm so thirsty and I'm starving to death too."* Her body began to shake and she breathed feverishly for a while, before the spasms eased and her breathing began to slow down. She whispered: *"I'm not scared anymore. I feel happy. It doesn't matter anymore. I feel free now."*

The life was over and I brought Beth gently out of trance. She was surprised at how calm she felt after the past life experience, and she explained that she thought she had died of some sort of illness in a primitive hospital. The worst part of it was feeling completely trapped by the paralysis, unable to move for several days and just waiting for death to eventually occur.

Beth returned a few days later and she told me that as a result of the past life session she was feeling much calmer about the cataract operation. It had hardly come into her mind and she felt more distanced from it. She also felt much more at ease in herself generally.

As she went into hypnosis her subconscious took us into the second past life, and this time she spoke quite loudly and sharply. Her brow knitted and her voice had a tone of anger in it:

"It's wartime and I'm in an army barracks-type room. I'm a man, aged around 35 and I'm looking at a big white board. I'm wearing a petrol-blue uniform and a hat with a peak, and I'm carrying a stick. I'm showing something on the board to some other men but I'm very angry. In fact I'm furious. People have died and it was my fault. There have been mistakes made and I'm angry with myself as it's all my responsibility. My name's Gerry and a flying operation has gone

wrong. Men under my command have died. It's my fault and I feel I've let everyone down. I leave the room but I'm still really angry and I get into a plane and take off. I'm so furious that I'm not in control of myself. I feel that I should die because everyone else has. I fly into a cliff-face and there's a huge explosion. It's all white and I feel calm and light." Beth was quiet for a few seconds before she began to sob. She spoke as she wept: *"I've always felt responsible for everyone in my present life, and that something bad's going to happen and it's my fault. I sense that my mother, my sister and my partner were all men who died in the past life because of me. This all makes so much sense to me now."*

I gave her time to release the emotions, and when she stopped crying and had relaxed again, we moved into the third previous life. This one was short but dramatic. She became tense and she started to arch her back and thrash her arms around, as if trying to push someone off her. Her breathing quickened and she gasped out her words in short bursts:

"I'm outside, standing in water, in a lake. It's very sunny. I'm a young black-skinned boy, maybe 15 years old. Someone's pushing my head under the water. It's my sister. I'm fighting but she's stronger than me. It's my sister. She's drowning me. I can't breathe. I'm trapped." Beth continued to writhe and gasp for breath for a few moments, then she became limp and her breathing returned to normal. The life was over. So, for that matter, was Beth's fear of her impending surgery.

Once she was out of trance she was unable to find any remaining fear in her body when she thought about the operation, and several weeks later she called me a few days after the surgery to tell me that the whole procedure had been a complete success. She had not experienced any fear or anxiety both before and during her time in hospital, and she was amazed at just how calm she had been throughout the operation. In some way the past lives had been causing the fear, and once we had released the negative emotions locked within them the fear had dissipated completely, leaving her free and at ease. Beth was incredibly grateful that what would have been a severe ordeal for her had turned into a neutral experience, which had not caused her any stress at all.

Section Four

Emotional Imbalances

Chapter 16

Angie's Story

Angie was in her mid-forties and, as she put it, was "stuck in a rut". She felt blocked in her life and unable to move forward or change her life in any way. A lady with a deeply spiritual outlook on life, she had tried a number of different therapies over the years to help her cope with the traumas from her childhood, and although she felt that some of the psychotherapy she had experienced had helped, she still had a number of issues which held her back from feeling a sense of freedom. She had been bulimic for years, had strong fears of abandonment and was sexually repressed. Whenever she became stressed she would experience a lot of anger and dramatic mood swings, which made her relationship with her partner Dan quite unstable. Having said that, she felt frustrated that Dan was always quite controlling and rigid towards her, which made her feel at times that he was treating her like a child.

As part of the therapeutic process we spent some time healing the wounds of her childhood as she came from dysfunctional, emotionally-repressed parents, who at the age of 12 had sent her to boarding school, the experience of which had scarred her for life. I usually find that being sent to boarding school tends to cause two types of reactions: a minority of people thrive as children in that environment, whereas the majority of people are damaged by it in a variety of ways. As a child Angie, like so many boarding school survivors I have seen over the years, felt abandoned by her parents, confused and unable to understand why they had sent her away from home. In so many cases where this happens, the child simply believes that, "Mummy and Daddy don't love me – if they loved me they would want me to be with them but as they've sent me away they obviously don't want me to be with them." As well as having a lot of negative feelings towards her parents she also had a very poor relationship with her brother. Although the therapy sessions we spent on her childhood helped her to feel much less insecure, it was the past life work we did that had the biggest impact on her and which moved her on so effectively, partly because we released a massive amount of trauma from some extremely unpleasant past lives, but also because she became aware of the connections between those lives and this present one. These understandings were particularly around Dan and her brother who appeared in several of them in different guises.

Her first past life was very clear to her, as she was an extremely visual person. She saw herself as a man in his late teens or early twenties, standing on a long, hot beach looking out at the waves as they came into the shore:

"I feel lost, and although this is a beautiful place it feels hostile too. My family is here and we're all hungry. It's as if we've been plonked down in this strange world without any proper tools to live in it. Here we have to learn how to survive. I've been brought here as a criminal on a prison ship but my family has been brought here too, but I don't know why. Being sent here was a mistake, it was the wrong family that was sent here. I wonder if we'll survive. I feel anxious and sad. I have little memory of the journey here as I wasn't well but I feel clear-headed now. I don't feel useful here and everything is unknown. We all feel lost and we don't even have a shelter." Angie started to tremble as she lay in the chair. *"We have to survive but I feel cold and shivery with fear as there is so much danger here. There's no one else around. I just see acres of sand and the sea. I've moved on in time now, and I'm older and only some of us have survived. I feel angry that they shipped us here as it was a mistake and we lost everything we had. It's a full-time job just getting food. Oh, we're being attacked. A small, dark-skinned man with a stone club chases me and hits me on the head. Ouch! It's damaged my skull but I don't die immediately. I hang on for some time, drifting in and out of the body before I go. As I leave the*

body I see myself, with my body really broken."

Angie softened down again into a deeper trance for a few moments, before she moved into another lifetime, the first of several in which people in her present life played significant roles in her previous lives:

"I feel anxious and there's a tingling feeling in my feet. I'm on a cross, being crucified. My chest feels hot and I'm struggling to breathe; my wrists are tied. I'm puzzled as to why this has happened, although I feel angry with Dan – he's in the life too in some way. Ah, he betrayed me. I'm a man and he was my best friend and I loved him like a brother. I remember earlier in the life that we grew up together and played together. We always looked out for each other. He got married to a lovely woman and I felt jealous of him as I never married. I didn't tell him though. It didn't seem fair as he was so happy and I never met a woman like that, but we were still close friends though and spent a lot of time together. Then his wife miscarries and he's devastated. We don't see much of each other after that and I feel excluded, but he wasn't the same person after they lost the baby. She didn't get pregnant again and he was hard to be around but I couldn't help him. He had so much pain and I could feel it in my heart. He became angry and jealous of me as I still had sunshine in my heart. I made money, and he didn't and he needed money. Soldiers come to him, they're looking for me and they threaten him. There's a reward for me. He tells them where I am. He sold me to them. At first I can't believe it, but when it's proven to me I feel broken-hearted." Angie became silent and her breathing became forced, as if she was struggling to breathe, and her arms slowly moved upwards and then outwards until she lay in the chair as if she was being crucified. She spoke in a hoarse whisper:

"My wrists are sore and I'm so tired. I have cramps in my stomach and pain in my jaw. I'm so angry with him, so angry that I could kill him for what he's done to me. He doesn't come to see me on the cross, he's just a coward. I want revenge." After a short time, during which her body writhed in the chair and she groaned and cried,

she relaxed and breathed normally. In a softer voice she went on: *"I'm looking down at my body. I want to go and find him. In spirit I go to his home and I send nasty, dark thoughts at him. He's sitting with his head in his hands and I'm hitting him with bolts of energy but I don't feel any better. I feel so sad and I've just realised that my brother in this present life is the Roman soldier who pays out the money for the information about me. We all three played as children together but he was always a bully. I feel myself becoming a ball of energy, and I start to leave that life."*

Angie came out of trance and, as well as feeling exhausted, was amazed at what she'd experienced, saying that it all made so much sense in terms of the energies that she'd so often felt when she was in a rage with Dan, and how hard she'd always found it to have a heart connection with her brother. She knew that she'd had a profound experience and that it would help her to shift some of her 'stuff'.

When Angie came for her next session she reported that she'd done lots of processing since I'd seen her and that the two past lives had brought up a lot of emotions, both good and bad, but the main feeling that she had been left with was of depression. Fortunately she had sufficient understanding that this emotional roller coaster can occur when one is 'in therapy' and she was OK with it, but the fact that she had felt generally depressed as a result of opening up the past lives showed both the power of the things she had experienced and also that the therapy process was working. I reassured her that it was just a matter of time, combined with releasing the negative emotions locked in the other past lives that we were yet to go into, before she would start feeling better. The next past life was short but its brutality had a lot of impact on her:

"I'm a little girl, maybe eight–ten years old and I'm sitting in a cornfield in bright sunshine. I'm alone, wearing a brightly-coloured linen smock over petticoats with black woollen tights and I feel gloriously happy. It's wonderful to be alone in the sunshine as I have

a lot of brothers and sisters so I'm never on my own." Angie wore a blissful smile as she said this, which suddenly disappeared as she jumped and yelped: *"Oh, why? I don't understand. I've been killed. A soldier wearing red has just killed me with his sword. I can feel the shock of it in my back; he's almost sliced me in two. There's no pain, just sudden death but how dare he do that? I'm suddenly out of my body, there was no warning. It's as if the soldier has a right to kill me. As if everybody has a right to do hurtful things to me. I feel totally disempowered, as if I have less right to live than everyone else. Why did he do that? I was happy in the sun on my own and he just sliced me in two. Oh, I understand. He's my brother in this life. That makes so much sense. No wonder we've always been so separate and he's always bullied me. It's a pattern he's following from other lives. My father and brother still have power over me. That's why he's always been so angry towards me. Wow! I suddenly feel so much lighter."*

Although she was smiling, Angie was a little emotional for a while as she processed these new learnings, but soon she regained her composure and she moved into a life in France at the time of the French Revolution:

"I'm walking through beautiful gardens in front of a huge chateau, wearing a wig and an amazingly beautiful dress of embroidered silk which is pinched at the waist and I'm carrying a fan. I'm talking to my dressmaker. There are lots of people around, not friends but acquaintances. This is where I live. I have no parents or siblings and I'm looked after by lots of servants. It's sunny and light and I'm walking around the edge of a huge park. The men are in satin breeches and embroidered waistcoats and wigs. I'm around 20 years of age and although beautiful I'm lonely. Suddenly there are chills running up my back as I'm grabbed by some common men. They actually touch me. They have no respect and put me in the back of a cart. I've no idea what to do. How dare they? They're jeering loudly and being disrespectful. I've got a very bad feeling about this. Nothing has prepared me for this, and I didn't realise the common people were so unhappy. The cart takes several of us through the grounds. I'm not going to let them see

me cry. The cart jerks and I have to hold on to the side. There's mud on my beautiful dress. I know some of the others in the cart, including an older man who used to be kind to me when I was young. He looks white but he's trying to be brave. They've knocked his hat off and his clothes look rumpled. There's a woman I know who's very high-born and she's crying. I wish she'd stop – she needs to keep her dignity but she's hysterical. Two other men are in the cart, standing silently. How did it come to this? Why is no one stopping it? The world is not a safe place and I'm powerless. I'm numb and cold and finding it hard to breathe." Throughout this Angie was becoming increasingly tense, and as she went on she began to breathe anxiously and shake. *"I've moved forward in time and I'm in another cart with several people and we're on our way to be beheaded. I can't breathe. I feel sick with terror. We're moving through a crowd of people who have no compassion for us. A lake of people, as far as the eye can see, moving past the carts like water. They're all shouting. I've got to keep my dignity; I will not let them see me cry. There's a pain in my stomach from the fear. It's taking forever to get there and they're spinning it out to make it more cruel. I feel so alone. My beautiful dress is all muddy and I'm bruised. I'm rigid with horror and trying to shut my thoughts down. I'm not looking at the people but they're so loud. I'm not used to this; I'm used to a cultured, quiet life. This is not right. We finally reach the platform. The poor hysterical woman won't let go of the cart so they drag her away screaming. I'm shaking but I hope it doesn't show. I'm going to be first and they'll make the others watch. They force me to kneel and put my head on a block. I can't breathe, I'm gasping and shaking and hoping that the peasants can't see me. I will be dignified and I will not give them the satisfaction of seeing me break down. The noise is so loud. I clamp my teeth together and I'm praying it will be over quickly. They fasten my head in and I can feel boards beneath my knees. Time seems like it's stretched and we're just waiting. Why don't they get on with it? My legs and back ache. I feel the wood that my neck's resting on. I'm shaking and my jaw is clenched so tight that my teeth hurt. Suddenly there's a shock and my head's severed. I can feel the shock waves pulsing through my body, but then it eases and I've left my body and I'm looking down at myself. I still feel connected to the executioner though. Ah, it's my brother. That explains a lot. Also, the older man in the cart who was kind to me is Dan. I look back on the life and realise that although I've got a title and a lot of money I was always alone and lonely. I spent a lot of time walking in the gardens on my own. There's no sense of parents or family, I was brought up by servants. I was too young to die. It's as if I never started living. I float away into the clouds and feel peaceful now."*

Angie lay calmly in the chair and we finished the session. Once more she had a lot of processing to do, particularly regarding the relationship with her brother. When she returned a week later she said that she'd felt very calm since the session, and a sense of peace had been with her at all times. It was obvious that we were succeeding in our goal of helping her to feel freer inside. This time, once she was in trance she went back to a past life in ancient Egypt:

"It's bright and hot and I'm a little boy, living in a poor family amongst very rich families who wear lots of gold on their clothing. I just wear a white cloth wrapped around my waist. Father works for the Pharaoh, building things. I help too even though I'm only seven or eight. My sister is older than me, about 12, and Mother cooks for lots of people. I feel happy by nature. My name sounds like it's something like Leemar." Suddenly Angie jerked violently and she began to gasp and writhe around: *"I've been attacked. My penis has been chopped off. I feel faint and there's blood everywhere, soaking into the sand. Why? Who did it? I screamed and screamed but they did it anyway. Where are my family? They've been attacked too. Where is my sister? The pain is so great my body shuts down and goes into shock. There was a big man with a huge mane of dark, curly hair and he leads the men who attacked us. I think it's because they believe in different gods to us. The pain is too much so I keep leaving my body. I can hear myself screaming. Oh god! They cut my sister and mother all over really bad*

and then kill them. They cut off my father's hands and take him with them. They kill some of our animals too. Father was very gentle, a very loving father. They leave me lying on the ground and I can't move because it's too painful and I bleed when I move. I manage to get to the river and slide in and I black out with the pain. When I come round there's a lot of red in the water around me. I'm screaming again and I just want to die. I didn't know people could do this to each other. Men are not to be trusted. I feel resentment that [Father] failed to protect me but also guilt that I couldn't help anyone. I feel ashamed that I just wanted to run. It should have been me who died. I failed. I deserved not to breed as I would only have had cowardly children." By this stage she was sobbing helplessly, which continued as she gained other realisations: *"The leader of them is smiling while they do it. I know that he's my brother in this life. My father too is Dan now."* The crying continued for some time before it slowly abated and she moved on in time:

"I'm older now and living with different people. I'll never be normal. I'm an outsider in so many ways. I don't feel close to anybody. What must it be like to make love to girls? They've been good to me – they fed me when they found me, gave me new clothes and somewhere to live. I wonder why I carried on living. I feel sad a lot of the time. I work with animals, looking after the cows. I think often of my family. Everything seems pointless. Why didn't I die? I drag myself through the days and the sadness just goes on and on. I feel so alone. Eventually I grow old and die. I feel released now."

She was calm and she said that she could feel some sort of healing energy moving through her body. After a while this ceased, and she told me that she'd moved into another life:

"I'm a young woman wearing a lot of skin and fur clothes. It's Mongolia or Siberia. The people have Inuit-type features. We're a small tribe and at times it's very cold weather and lots of snow. We live in a series of Mongolian yurts in the summer and igloos in the winter. I don't feel close to anyone. I'm not originally from this tribe. They found me as a baby after my parents were killed in a fight, and a woman with

a baby fed me. I'm deaf so I never learnt to speak. I never felt part of the group and no one protected me. I always knew I wasn't a part of them. I'm the property of a man who uses me sexually whenever he wants. I fight but he just hurts me. There's nowhere I can run to and I can't tell anyone. He lends me out to other men too. He hits me but he's never squashed my spark of defiance. I walk by the stream during the day and it's where I feel safe, as if it shelters me from the rest of my life. I care for my clothes made of animal skins because it's all I have. I dread the sun going down. The sex is horrendous. It all started when I was quite young. When my periods started he claimed me. I leave my body while it happens. It's disgusting what he does to me. I've thought about killing him but they'd kill me. He sees me as an object, not a person. I feel ashamed. Going walking by the stream keeps me sane. I'm raped every night. As night approaches at the end of each day I start to feel fear. Sometimes I can't walk very well and my back hurts. Sometimes my vagina bleeds from what he's doing to me but it doesn't stop the pig having a go the next night. Sometimes he puts his hand over my mouth so I must be making a noise. He hits me across the face when I struggle. I can't stop him invading me. I survive because I'm good at surviving. Sometimes he lays me down on a prickly surface – I think they're seed cases from bushes – it feels like a bed of nails. Then he gets on top of me and he's turned on when every movement he makes gives me pain. It's all about power. I'm his property and he gets turned on because he can do what he likes to me. Anal sex hurts and with oral sex I can't breathe when he's in my mouth. I can smell him. I realise that he's my father in this lifetime. I feel hopeless knowing that no one can save me. I have no protection and there's no end in sight, just routine violence night after night." Once more Angie was squirming in the chair, crying and moaning and wringing her hands.

"One night he's punching me in the stomach and I hit him and he loses his temper. I'm fighting him but he hits me really hard. Something's happened to my neck and I can't move. He's gone too far, and he's got his hands over my nose and mouth and I can't breathe. I've died and been released. I'm looking down at my body and he's still

holding my nose and mouth. It's over."

Angie slumped down in the chair and sighed. I brought her out of trance and, as you can imagine, she felt shattered by the hideousness of what she'd relived. However, she was also very calm. Again, we had released a substantial heap of negative energy which had been inside her all of her life. As well as this she had further knowledge of the connections between her family in this lifetime and in previous ones. This dual aspect of the therapy was vitally important to her healing.

She returned a few weeks later and told me she'd realised that she was childless in both the previous lives and in her present life. More than this, though, she was feeling a lot stronger and because of this had instigated several deep and meaningful talks with Dan about their relationship. Although nothing had been resolved she felt better for taking a degree of control, something which she hadn't been able to do in the past. She was also starting to wonder if the relationship was over. She'd also successfully achieved another milestone, that of spending time with her parents and siblings, and surviving it without being triggered too much by being in their presence. She had been much more at ease with them than she had ever been before and they seemed to be less controlling with her, probably because she found it possible to stand in her own power as a woman and not as the bullied child, the energy of which she used to embody whenever she visited them.

This time, as she went into a life from more recent times, her face became serious and body rigid:

"I'm a man, experiencing some violence towards me. It's dark and another man has flung me up against the side of a motor vehicle, a clean white van, and he's got his arm across my windpipe. Something's happened and he's really angry with me. I feel really scared. We're both wearing workmen's clothes and are quite dirty, as if we've been working. A child of his has died, his son, and it's my fault. He's married to my sister. I feel that I messed up. Nothing will ever be the

same again. I was looking after his son and he drowned. I couldn't help him. I panicked and I didn't jump in to try and save him. We're near a bridge over a wide and deep river. The boy was about 12 years old and he could swim but he got into difficulties and started yelling. I'm on the riverbank and I can't move, as if I'm paralysed. He's screaming and yelling and it all goes into slow motion. My body's gone into freeze-mode. There's no one else around and his head goes under the water then he comes up gasping and yelling. I don't know what to do; all I feel is panic, fear, horror and disbelief. The boy's name is Kieran and he's my nephew. I crumple up and fall over; I've shut down and I lose consciousness. I lie in a heap next to the river. When I come to, I can't think of anything but my brokenness. I can smell cooking so I think there's a café nearby. I feel detached as if I've left my body in some way. Some ambulance people arrive and I'm panicking and so ashamed that I'm tempted to cover it up and not tell them what happened, but I manage to tell them. They put me in an ambulance and take me to hospital. I don't even ask if he's alive. What have I done? Although I have huge guilt I also feel as if I've lost my life too because of what's happened, and I know that's selfish but I can never make it right. I'll always be the bad guy. I've wrecked my life and I don't want to carry on; eventually my mind fractures and I have a breakdown. I know I'm a coward but I take a full bottle of tablets and kill myself. What a sense of relief."

Angie relaxed again and was quiet, but the relief she was feeling didn't last for long as quite soon she stiffened and began to cry. She had moved into another lifetime:

"Oh no, more violence. I'm lying on the ground with a long spear with feathers on it sticking out of my chest. I'm a Native American man, looking back on a difficult life as I'm dying. I've lost so many people. My brother died in battle. My wife died when she was young when we'd barely begun our lives together and the child she was carrying died too. I've never known such sorrow. I didn't marry again, I felt as if I'd had my heart ripped out. I've never got over all the pain and life's been a heavy burden, and I'm not sorry I'm dying."

After a couple of minutes of silence she smiled and started speaking again.

"I feel blissfully perfect. I'm on a beach with white sand and lush growth beyond the beach. We're living off things that we don't need to cultivate. I'm a young woman wearing a skirt woven from grasses and flowers in my long, black hair. I feel so relaxed and contented. It's a carefree life and we don't need to work or do anything. We fish and there's lots of laughter. I marry a young man and I'm even happier; I become pregnant and give birth to a beautiful girl. As I get older, I get visions of the future and of previous generations. My husband and I die close together and I leave my body easily. It was a good life."

Angie's subconscious had taken her into a positive past life in order to give her some healing after the rigours of the past lives she'd experienced. This had happened quite spontaneously and shows that her subconscious knew exactly what she needed at that time. It gave her a positive past life which could act like a soothing ointment after we'd dug out the pain of the traumas of the negative lives. She came out of trance feeling happy and light, with a real sense of release.

It was a few months later before she came for another session, and a lot had happened to her in that time. She told me that she'd felt several big shifts had taken place inside her, and in many respects she felt empowered and much stronger in herself. However, one major crisis that she'd endured was the ending of her relationship with Dan. It had been a mutual decision and although obviously painful she had handled the break-up well and in a mature fashion. Rather than just going to pieces over it (which, she readily admitted, is what she would have done had she not changed so much as a result of the therapy) she had been able to deal with the situation by talking things through with Dan as an adult rather than feeling like an insecure child. She even said that she felt like a spiritual warrior, able to overcome the hurdles that life was presenting to her and being totally honest with herself and with Dan. Having said all that, she had noticed that for no apparent reason she had been feeling a lot of guilt, and she thought that this was because our work together had been peeling off layers of issues and this was the next layer that needed dealing with. Her subconscious, when she was in hypnosis, indicated that there was one past life at the heart of the guilt. At first she felt a lot of resistance as she moved into it, as if she didn't want to go there, but soon she saw herself as a man dressed in the uniform of a Nazi officer:

"I'm standing in a barn, holding a whip and I'm whipping people who are standing in a pit. I'm thinking about how good I look in my uniform and I'm getting pleasure from inflicting pain; it's my idea of fun. I know that four of the people in the pit are from this present life; my brother, sister and Dan and another previous partner. I feel strong and in control of these people. I like the power and I come alive when I'm doing this. I enjoy hurting people using a variety of methods, whether it's a whip or a knife or a bayonet. I'm a totally heartless, vicious individual, and I feel very disconnected from my own feelings and the feelings of others. I had a difficult childhood with no affection from my parents and a controlling father. I remember being a young boy, crouching down in a hole in the ground hiding from my father. I hear a scream behind me and I put my hands over my ears to block out the sounds of him hitting my mother. He hits her very hard in the tummy and her head is bleeding. It's always been like this. He's a bastard to her and I feel guilty because if I hadn't been born he may not have behaved like that towards her, and also she only stayed with him because of me. Later, in my teens she dies after he hits her in the kidneys and ruptures something. It was all hushed up. He killed her and I didn't stop him as I was too scared, but she loved me. I had a sister and something happened to her too, but I closed it down." Angie was a little emotional at this point, and I waited for the crying to subside. When it did she continued: *"I'm back in uniform again, remembering a particular girl who I had a fancy for. She's in a camp and she's a bit cheeky so I keep looking out for her. Then I have her and she cries out so I bayonet her, but I feel bad about it as it feels like*

losing my mother again. I feel sick and remember thinking that my mother abandoned me and I cried when she was dead but Father says I must never tell anyone. I'm so angry with her for leaving me, it's like she betrayed me. I'm now whipping Jews as they come off the train carriages into the camp but I have a bad feeling inside and I feel shaky, as if I'm frightened. Something's changed and it's not bringing me the joy that it used to. But life carries on as usual for a while, until – oh, I've been shot! Who could have done that? I can suddenly feel my body and as I'm dying I start to doubt that the way I've lived my life has been the right way. I'm full of regrets and it's as if I have a complete re-evaluation of my life as I'm dying. I feel terror because I can't put it right and I'm scared I'll burn in hell. As I pass into spirit I feel stuck, as if I'm in a prison cell just with my thoughts. I can't see any way out. It wasn't my fault but it was. I'm so sorry. I start to feel lighter and I'm reunited with my mother, realising that she watched over me after she died. I feel myself releasing all the pain and upset from my stomach."

Angie's body started to jerk and shake as she released the trauma from the past life. This kinaesthetic releasing continued for some time, and I simply sat patiently whilst it took place. Eventually the shaking and jerking died down, and she told me that she felt light and free, so I asked her to come back out of hypnosis.

What Angie had experienced was actually quite unusual in past life therapy, in that she had lived a life as an aggressor rather than a victim. My experience is that at least 95% of past life therapy is about working through previous lifetimes where we have been traumatised as a result of negative things happening to us, so for her to have relived this particular life was atypical. My take on this is that although we have lived many lifetimes we have done everything and been everything (e.g. we have killed and been killed; raped and been raped; been poor and been rich etc.), the subconscious normally doesn't want us to know about the lives in which we have been very bad because there is a chance that we couldn't cope with the knowledge. However, because Angie was an extremely self-aware woman who, as a result of a good deal of therapy, was able to be ruthlessly honest about herself, her subconscious knew that she could come to terms with the nastiness she had dished out as the Nazi officer. This is exactly what happened. Obviously she was surprised at her experience but much of it made sense to her as many of the feelings she had experienced in trance she could recognise as connecting with this life. As a result of the sessions she was able to let go of the guilt that had been gnawing away at her, and any residual feelings of betrayal that she had lain at the feet of Dan dissolved away too. She was able to start to live her life as a single woman, unencumbered by her old feelings of insecurity that would have inhibited her from feeling free, and standing in her own power as a strong individual. As so often with Past Life Therapy, the regression sessions had completely changed her life.

Chapter 17

Mark's Story

Mark was a classic case of a one session cure (a.k.a. a 'one-hit wonder'), which all therapists get every once in a while. This means that a client will come in to the consulting room with a serious issue and after a single session they walk out completely cured! It doesn't happen very often but when it does it's amazing and incredibly gratifying. He was also an interesting case for me because he was disgusted that he had experienced a past life as he thought the concept of previous lives was baloney, and in the hypnosis session he kept fighting against reliving the past life. However, his resistance was fruitless, as his subconscious knew what had to be done to fix his problem.

Mark was an 18-year-old office clerk, utterly lacking in self-confidence and feeling anxious in most social situations. He'd always been shy, but he'd enjoyed a loving childhood and he was not bullied at school. However, since he'd started work he was experiencing shyness to the 'nth degree. As he spoke to me he avoided eye contact and there was sadness in his voice as he explained how everyone at his office thought he was weird and ignorant because he just sat in the corner at his desk not speaking to anyone. He wouldn't look at them and if he answered a question he would just give one word answers. As he did this he would feel tense and anxious, his throat dry and his shoulders tight. His bottom lip quivered and there was a tremor in his voice as he said to me, "But I'm not weird, I just feel so scared when they look at me and ask something of me." Mark sat blinking, trying to hold back the tears.

Once he had composed himself, I took him into trance and asked his subconscious what was causing this massive lack of confidence. His IMR indicated just one past life. I could see from the look on his face that he was shocked by this, as his brow furrowed and he started to nibble his bottom lip. However, having got permission from his subconscious, I continued to regress him into the life. For a while he was silent, and then he started to talk with a degree of hesitation in his voice about the images he was seeing:

"I'm in a prison-type cell, with stone walls and a dirty, sandy floor. It's very quiet and I feel as if I don't want to be there. I'm alone." Mark had a quizzical look on his face as he was silent for a couple of minutes. Then he spoke directly to me: *"Steve, I don't think this is real, I think I'm imagining it. I don't believe in past lives."*

This reaction is quite common in past life therapy, as most people wonder if they are making the images up. I reassured Mark, as I do all of my clients, that such a reaction is quite normal but to just go on with the experience anyway to see what happens. I asked him what he was feeling. He was a bit disgruntled but he continued: *"I'm starting to feel quite tense. At first I felt very alone, as if beaten and completely without hope. Now I'm starting to feel frightened. I don't know what's happening. Steve, I don't think I want to do this. Can we stop now please?"* Calmly and quietly, though with a degree of firmness in my voice, I told him that it was most important that we continued otherwise he might feel worse if he came out of the experience without seeing it through. I asked him to describe what was happening. His body started to tremble and his voice shook. *"I'm walking across a small yard and stepping up on to something like a stage. There are people in front looking up at me and people behind me pushing me up there. My hands are tied. Steve, I'm feeling really scared, I don't think I want to do this. I can see a man and a woman kneeling on the stage with their hands tied behind their backs, facing towards a large group of people who are watching from below. The man has his hair tied up in a bun and the woman is wailing. She's very upset. I've got to watch them being put to death. The three of us have done something and we're being executed. We don't think that what we've done is bad or wrong.*

Steve, this is horrible, tell me I'm imagining it all."

Once more I calmly but firmly reassured him that it was OK to relive it as if it were really happening right now as this would help him to feel so much better in this present life. Grudgingly, he continued: *"There's a man there, holding a big black axe. The man who's kneeling bends and puts his head on to a block and..."* Mark didn't have to say anything, the grimace on his face told me what had happened. *"Now it's the woman's turn... she's crying and then she dies too, the same way. They're making me watch because they think I'm the ringleader, so it's punishing me more to see my friends put to death like this. It's horrible. Now it's my turn."* Mark's body was rigid, his face set and his breathing panicky. He held on to the tension for a few seconds and then he flopped down and began breathing deeply. *"It's over, I'm peaceful now."*

I asked him to re-experience the life again, which he reluctantly did, but this time he felt no tension or fear. We finished the session, and once he was out of trance he told me that he was most unhappy with what had happened, as he didn't believe in past lives and he thought that he was just making it all up. I didn't want to upset him so I told him that some people think that the past life experiences are metaphors created by their subconscious, but all he had to do was see how he felt after he had processed the session for a day or two. He wasn't convinced and left my office with a bit of a scowl, but he agreed to come back for another session the following week. I was a bit peeved that he had had such a reaction but I knew that it had been a good therapy session, so when he came back a week later I was hoping for some improvement in his low feelings of confidence. However, I was shocked when he walked into my office with something approaching a swagger and a big smile on his face. He was standing tall with his shoulders back, a picture of self-assurance. He was feeling, he told me, totally transformed: *"I don't know what you've done* (they always say that, by the way!) *but I feel completely and utterly different. All of the anxieties have vanished and I feel free. I'm like a different person. I can sit in the office chatting to the others there without a care in the world. It's as though a weight has been lifted off my shoulders. I can't thank you enough for what you've done for me. I'm so sorry I was so angry with you last week, but I think I was a bit shocked. I still don't believe in past lives by the way, but for some reason what you did has worked."*

I allowed myself a wry smile, but it didn't matter what I believed or what Mark believed. He was completely better, and able to live the rest of his life with self-reliance and fearlessness.

Chapter 18

Colin's Story

Colin was an interesting character. In his early 40s, he had lived a colourful life and was now trying to settle into a more stable way of living. He had married a counsellor who loved him to bits but who was aware of his emotional imbalances and particularly of his anger issues. His interactions with his wife were generally good, with his wonderful sense of humour bringing a lot of fun to the relationship, but at times he would fly off the handle easily and his wife found herself walking on eggshells at times in case his anger flared up. As is usual in these cases, Colin at first denied that he had a problem. He was a typical working man (a builder) who didn't go near his emotions, preferring (as most men do) to ignore his inner state and pretend that everything was OK in his world. Fortunately, as a counsellor his wife knew that we are all driven by underlying emotional states, and over time her patience helped him to understand that he didn't need to live with his irrational anger outbursts and that something could be done to change his inner workings. At first he reluctantly agreed to do therapy with me but once we began the process of opening up his 'stuff' he embraced the opportunity to heal his negative emotions and he looked forward eagerly to each regression.

When I first met him he explained that he felt his anger problems were connected to a lack of self-confidence and self-esteem as a result of what he described as a "tricky" childhood. I fully expected to spend time in our sessions working to heal his childhood wounds, but once he was in trance his subconscious indicated using the IMR that the root causes of his emotional imbalances were several past lives. The first of them was over fairly quickly, as a soldier speared through the chest in battle and he died on the battlefield. Soon, however, he moved into another life as a young man aged around 20. He saw himself outdoors, standing near some fields in a town square close to a well. He had bare legs and was wearing sandals. I asked him what was happening:

"I'm helping a woman to fill a jug with water. I think she's my mother. There are some soldiers coming into the square, watching us. They're dressed like Romans. I feel frightened, they're burning the houses. People are screaming, some running and some fighting them. I'm running with the people through the fields to the woods. Soldiers on horseback are following us, swinging their swords and killing people. An older man is shouting to us not to run but to stop and fight. We stop and we run forwards towards them. I have a sword. I see men on the horses with their red capes flapping. A horse pushes me to the ground. I'm looking up at the sky, shocked. A soldier thrusts a sword into my chest. I can hear the sound of horses moving off into the distance. Now there are people from the village standing around me. My mother is holding me in her arms." Colin was quiet for a few seconds, experiencing the passing of time, before he went on:

"It's night-time and I'm in a hut, laid next to a crackling fire. I feel scared and sad. I should have done better; I let the village down. The man who gave us instructions to stand and fight is angry with me. When I was at the fountain helping the woman I should have been on lookout. I should have seen them coming. They trusted me and I let them down." As he said this he started to sob, and I allowed him to release the sadness for a few minutes before he calmed down again and the tears stopped flowing. Quietly he whispered, *"It's gone dark. It's over."*

Soon Colin had moved into another lifetime, and he began to explain in hushed tones what he was experiencing:

"We're in a forest. There's a group of us, all soldiers. We're talking to some Native Americans. I'm dressed in a green uniform with a triangular hat, carrying a musket with a bayonet on it. I feel tense, because beyond the forest is a fort with red uniforms. The Indians are our guides. They're telling us how best to approach it; a soldier is

translating. They have strange hair – they're bald but with a patch of long hair hanging at the back. There are a lot of us waiting, ready to attack the fort. They don't know we're here. I can see people moving around outside the fort." He was quiet for a few moments, then his body stiffened as he spoke excitedly: *"We're bringing the horses forward and we mount them. I feel scared. A man in a dark uniform carrying a sword on a white horse is in command and he gives the order to charge. We charge forward, we're killing people outside the fort with our swords. We head towards a bridge and a spiked wall. I dismount and try to cut the ropes. Lots of Indians are fighting with us. We're at the wall of the fort, trying to cut it down. There are bodies everywhere; we're being fired on from the fort. The officer in charge has been killed. The black uniform is on the floor. We're firing and charging. We take shelter behind the spiked wall. There are loud bangs and explosions, we're under fire now. I feel frightened. We're debating what to do as we can't run back. Anyone who runs out gets killed. We're trapped."* He continued after a short pause. *"We surrender to the soldiers in red and they take us into the fort. An officer is talking to me as the rest of our soldiers stand behind me. He's wearing a strange hat with a plume and fur on it. I feel proud and scared. They're going to hang us. I can see them putting ropes up. They march me to a platform with my hands tied behind my back. They put the rope around my neck and I shout, 'Vive la France,' and then I'm hung. I feel light now."* Once more Colin relaxed, but very quickly became emotional. Through his tears he told me that he was remembering an earlier incident in that lifetime.

"It's dark and I'm in a street outside a pub or an inn. An ugly woman's trying to stop me fighting her husband. He has a sword and I'm goading him to fight me. She's protecting him but he pushes her away. I stab him in the neck and kill him. As I get on my horse the ugly woman is pulling on me, trying to get me off the horse. I slash her across the throat with my sword and she dies too. I ride off and just carry on as if nothing has happened."

Again I waited until the tears had subsided and once he

relaxed I asked him to come out of trance. Colin was shocked by his experiences, but accepted that they had felt intensely real and he felt a lot easier now that he had moved through them.

When he came for our next session, Colin told me that in the intervening weeks he had been feeling much calmer on a day-to-day basis, and his wife had noticed a positive change in his attitude in that she felt he was happier in himself. Once in hypnosis, he moved into another military past life, which this time was in WWII. In fact, this was a factor in all of the past lives that we explored, and I feel that much of the therapy process for him was releasing battle trauma and death trauma. Initially he was relaxed as he recounted his experience, with a smile on his face at times.

"I'm outdoors and it's daytime. There is a big group of us, all laughing. I'm wearing leather boots with fur at the top of them and grey-blue trousers and jacket. I'm a man, about 20 years old and I feel excited and nervous at the same time. There's a plane behind us and someone's taking a photo of us. I can see other planes and life jackets around. It's a big plane, a bomber. Everyone's laughing and joking as we take our positions on the plane. Two of us are pilots. They call me Group Captain Gibson. There are a lot of planes in the bright, sunny sky. We wave to the others and take off."

Colin was quiet for a few moments as the smile on his face wore off and became a frown. His jaw was set and he began to breathe quickly. His hands and arms became stiff and his body stiffened. Through gritted teeth he went on:

"We're flying low through clouds and snow. Everybody's nervous. I can see reflections of the planes as we fly over water. There's firing and banging and rattling. We're bombing a castle on top of a mountain; that's the target. We're under fire, the noise is horrendous. No one's laughing anymore. I feel scared. The plane's tossing around, we've been hit and I can't control the plane. There's fire and smoke. I'm trying to keep the plane straight. My co-pilot's dead, he's covered in blood but his eyes are open. I'm trying to move him off the stick. I can't

control it; we're going down towards the mountain. I can't keep hold of it." He started shouting: *"I can't keep hold of it, we're going down."* Suddenly he slumped in the chair and was calm and quiet for a few seconds. He spoke softly: *"We've crashed. It's all light now. I feel guilty, as if I killed everybody. But it was nobody's fault."* Once more he paused before he continued: *"From being a boy I was taught never to show fear. Never fear. My father's strict and he shouts a lot. He's in uniform too. I don't like him, he's a horrible man. He tells me I'm a failure and I've let him down and he's shouting all the time. I feel sorry for my mum 'cos he's a bully. I'm older now and I've hit him for beating my mum. He's shocked but he can't do anything. I had to wait until I was old enough to hit him and he's scared now. He knows I'm better than him."* Once more he was silent for a while, and then he told me about the final past life connected to causing his anger issues:

"It's daytime and I'm inside a minimalistic-type building. It's China or Japan. I'm a man about 30 and I'm wearing sandals and a silk gown. I feel good. As I stand, women are bowing and moving around slowly. They're dressing me in a beautifully embroidered gold and black suit of armour. It's all done very gracefully and slowly, as in a ceremony. I have a long black and gold sword with a red handle. They open the doors and I step out and see water fountains and gardens. Everything looks simple, and restrained. A servant is holding a horse covered in armour and as I mount it they all bow. They give me a helmet with a visor on it. I feel proud, but even though I'm outwardly relaxed I feel nervous. There are six or eight other men on horseback, dressed in a similar way to me, carrying a flag. I take a drink from a servant and then we ride off. We're going to war. We've arrived and I'm looking down at a big army. There are soldiers as far as the eye can see. We ride to the front. The whole army is on horseback, and I'm one of the leaders in front with the others. We're ready to fight and we're looking down at the opposition, it's a big army dressed in orange with orange flags. I feel nervous and excited. I keep getting flashes of a Japanese or Chinese girl in my mind. We draw swords

and we're charging fast at the enemy. We smash straight into them and there's a great thud of steel. We're fighting hand to hand with swords against people on horseback. It's very bloody, lots of bodies and I can hear crying and shouting and moaning. Everything's a blur; it's happening so quickly. We're cutting legs and arms and heads, there's blood everywhere. We're moving through, causing devastation and they're running. We're cheering. I've been caught on the arm and I fall to the ground. I feel cold and someone's holding me whilst someone else takes my armour off. I see faces looking down at me. They prop me up and I'm looking at the hills. I'm saying goodbye to people but I don't feel scared as I've accepted my fate. I feel proud. It's quiet now, and I see nothing other than light."

Colin relaxed and I asked him, whilst he was in the Spirit, to become aware of anything else that may be of significance. He pondered for a few minutes and then said:

"The whole way of life is very simple and slow paced, there's no rushing and everyone is polite and courteous. I think the woman who I kept thinking about was my wife. She was very obedient and always smiling. I think she was raped and murdered by those other people and the battle was to avenge her death. I felt angry and I fought wildly, killing as many men as I could. They have no army now. I feel angry with myself for not protecting her. I feel guilty that I wasn't there and it was my fault there was no security for her. I feel better for taking so many lives in revenge."

Colin's voice was full of passion as he spoke these last words, and I could see his bottom lip quivering with emotion. After a while it passed and he softened again, so I asked him to move once more into Spirit. He sighed and smiled gently. *"She's waiting for me. It feels good."* He spoke no more, but just lay basking in the warmth of love and looking deeply happy. I asked him to come out of trance and bring the good feelings back with him. He felt very strongly that his wife in this present lifetime was the same person as his wife in the past life, and the knowledge of that created a very special connection between them. He realised that his feelings for her were very deep and that made their relationship very meaningful to him. He felt that a real healing had taken place inside him as a result of the session. He felt lighter and he was aware that something had shifted in him, as if he had let go of some negative energies that had been holding him back for a long time.

Colin arrived for our next session looking happy, and he told me that he had continued to feel more positive and brighter since I had seen him. He still felt that there was some work to do on his low self-esteem, and it was with this in mind that we regressed back into a further three former lives. After a few minutes in hypnosis, in which he drifted back through time in his mind, his face took on a sad expression and a tear rolled down his cheek as he explained what was happening:

"I'm wearing shoes with buckles on them, white tights and a long dark coat. I'm a boy, about 13 years of age and I'm standing outside on a dockside looking at big sailing ships. I'm walking with a crutch. I've only got one leg and it's a struggle to walk. I used to be on board a ship and I miss the work. I feel like a freak or a cripple. Everyone laughs at me and makes fun of me. They call me 'peg-leg'. I feel really sad and inadequate. I remember that a mast fell on my leg and crushed it. They cut my leg off. I can't get a job now as nobody wants a cripple. I wander the dockside with no focus every day, feeling lost. I can only work chopping up buckets full of fish and I feel frustrated. I've lost my spark and people treat me like a retard. I start to drink in the taverns, often getting into fights. I'm surrounded by horrible people, dirty and smelly and living in squalor. I feel anger and resentment, it's too much for me to bear. I hang myself in a dark room with dirty walls and a flea-ridden bed. I feel relieved now." Once more Colin relaxed for a short time before he went into another lifetime and he smiled as he recounted his impressions:

"I'm in some gardens and there's a man, a member of royalty like a King being jovial with a group of us. There are about four or five of us and we're all laughing. I'm a man, between 30–40 years old. The King's

a big man, wearing shoes with buckles on them and stocking breeches, and he's carrying an eagle on his arm. I think we're his advisors. He's flying the eagle. Suddenly he turns serious and he says that he wants to know where the gold has gone. He's looking at us and we've all stopped laughing. I feel frightened. The gold was being transported and it's gone missing. He's blaming us for not taking better care of it. It was a payment for something to do with Scotland. I think that the gold is for Scotland to become allies with us against the King of England. We're paying money towards the war with England. The word Battenberg comes to mind but I don't know why. England would then be divided between Scotland and Germany. We're arrested and escorted away into a dungeon. We have to confess we know where it's gone. I don't believe him; I think he's betrayed us. He's got the gold and he's using us as an excuse. We're all loyal to him but this is injustice. I'm angry he has this control over us and my loyalty to him has gone. Our fate is decided without a hearing and a priest tells us we'll be executed in the morning for treason. I feel angry as nobody listens to us. We're all to be beheaded. We're taken out individually on to a scaffold in a courtyard in front of a few priests. I'm scared but angry that I've been betrayed." As he was reliving the execution Colin's body was stiff with tension and he became anxious, then he suddenly softened and breathed a big sigh. *"It's over, I feel calm and relaxed now."* Once more Colin became quiet whilst he moved to his final past life. Then he began again:

"I'm outside in a cobbled street at night-time, talking to a woman. I'm a man, aged between 40 and 50. I'm richly dressed, in smart shoes and a long cape with gloves and a tall hat, carrying a walking stick. I'm asking the woman about a girl – 'When was the last time you saw her?' A carriage is close by waiting for me. I give the woman some money and thank her, get in the carriage and pull away. I can smell the leather upholstery and hear the clop of the horses' hooves. I've got a London accent. I'm frantically trying to find my sister. Our father has kicked her out of the house for bringing disgrace on the family. She's young and vulnerable, and he's disowned her for having a child out of

wedlock. He's also threatened me, if I have anything to do with her I'll be removed from the will. Father is a horrible man. I'm trawling the streets to find her. I try everywhere – hospitals, pubs, friends."

Colin's agitation throughout all of this was palpable, his head moving from side to side as if looking around for his sister, and his hands clasping and unclasping as a sign of his desperation. After a few seconds he continued:

"I've found her. She's sitting near the riverbank, distressed. She won't tell me who she's protecting as he's somebody I know. She's going up North to have the child and she'll write to me but I'm not to tell Father. She has some money. I plead with her to tell me who the baby's father is and finally she relents. It's our father's friend and as he's married already there'll be a scandal. She swears me to secrecy but I can't promise it. Father should know; how can he be so blind? He should protect her. She goes and I give her some money. I feel angry both with Father and the man who's got her pregnant. I want revenge. Firstly I tell Father but he has none of it. He's saying that I'm no son of his and I'm just as unworthy as she is. My allowances are to be stopped. He says my sister is a common, spiteful whore and it's preposterous accusing his friend. I hit him, hard. He tells me to get out and never come back. I tell him I'm going to his friend's house – I want to spoil his life as he's ruined mine and my sister's. He's a rich man. A butler greets me at his door and tells me to wait in a room. He comes in and I tell him what I know. We're shouting and arguing. He has no remorse and says it's all lies. I'm incensed and want to kill him. I challenge him to settle it with a duel but he won't as he's a coward. Then his wife comes in, she's heard it all. He accepts the duel." Colin paused again as time moved on, and then he jumped sharply, as if being hit by something. He began to speak more hoarsely:

"It's a warm, sunny morning. We both fire the guns and hit each other. He's fallen to his knees. I'm standing but I feel warmth seeping through the shirt. I'm fighting it, holding on to see if he's dead. They tell me he's dead, so now I can accept my fate. It all goes white and I feel released, although I'm sorry I don't see my sister. A part of me

wants forgiveness for killing the child's father." He breathed deeply and began to come back to awareness. His therapy sessions were over, and the journey he had taken in them had a profound effect upon him. Months later I saw him and he was brimming with confidence, full of good humour and joie de vivre. He had closed down his building business and was doing a job which he felt was much more rewarding, working with underprivileged people and helping them to get their lives together. As with so many of my clients, the past life therapy had transformed his life.

Chapter 19

Sally's Story

Sally came to me for help with her anger issue. A highly efficient and intelligent 30-year-old account manager with a multinational company, she was struggling both with her relationship with her boyfriend and with her stressful job. She told me that she was working long hours because she had a need to succeed in everything she did, caused by a fear of failure. However, the pressure of her workload meant that she constantly felt uptight and overwhelmed, and as a result her sleep was suffering and she felt tired most of the time. Sally's reaction to this was to go home at the end of a long working day and take her feelings out on her partner Dave, who was constantly on the receiving end of her anger. She would find herself regularly screaming at him and starting verbal fights, which she knew was beginning to destroy their relationship. Indeed, at that time she was staying at her parents' home in order to give Dave a break from her hostility. As we talked, however, I found that her issues were much deeper than a simple anger problem. She said that at times in the past she had felt so unhappy that she had even contemplated suicide. Some years before she had been anorexic and nowadays she was obsessively tidy and clean. These last facts indicated that she was carrying a serious amount of emotional wounding, as I always find that anorexia is a deeply significant issue which is a person's response to a substantial load of inner pain. The chances are that although the anorexia had stopped occurring she was now reacting to her emotional pain by using a form of Obsessive Compulsive Disorder (OCD) to try to anaesthetise it, and to try to remain in control of her life.

Once in trance her subconscious indicated that several past lives were causing her problems, and she was soon experiencing the first of them, as a frightened little seven-year-old girl, locked in a dark room:

"I'm all alone, sitting on the floor with my head resting on my knees. My feet are bare and my legs are dirty. I feel confused because I've been locked away and I don't know why. I don't like it, the floor's hard and my hair's all knotted. A lady has taken me out now and she's putting me in a tin bath and then she starts dragging a brush through my hair. It's really hurting and I'm crying, but she tells me to stop crying. I feel frightened and cold and I know that the people here don't love me. They shout at me a lot and keep putting me in the dark room." A tear silently ran down Sally's cheek and she sighed. *"I'm older now and she doesn't like it because she can't boss me around anymore like she used to. They don't put me in the room anymore but I'm not allowed to go out. I don't know why they keep me in; maybe they're ashamed of me. I feel so isolated and I want to run away but I have nowhere to go. Nobody else ever comes to see us and I'm made to clean all the time. They just shout at me and my face is bruised where she hits me. A man shouts and throws things at me and says I'm stupid, but I'm not because I can read. I wish they'd leave me alone. I just can't cry anymore and eventually I run away. I'm cold but a nice lady finds me and takes me to her house where she looks after me. It's a big house where I have my own bed and I laugh now each day, and she says she'll never let them find me. The lady is not very well and she doesn't breathe well, and I'm worried if anything happens to her that I'll be on my own again. She gets worse and I try not to let her see me crying, but she dies. Her friends come and at the funeral I put daisies on her grave. I'm exhausted with crying. I stay with her friends but I don't have a home anymore and I just want to be settled and have someone to look after me like she did. After a while a man from another house says that he'll look after me. He laughs a lot and he's older than me, around 25 I guess. He says that he wants to marry me but I'm only 17 so I don't feel old enough. He's bought me new shoes as a present. I feel happy but bewildered with all this attention. We have walks in the countryside together. I won't go this time as it's raining and I don't*

want to ruin my shoes. We get married on a really hot day and we're both really happy. After a while he comes home drunk sometimes and I'm angry because we don't have much money and he's spending what we have. He wants us to have children but I'm happy as we are, but we have two babies, a boy and a girl. He's not interested in the girl. I'm having another baby now and this one hurts. It's not time for it to be born but there's a lot of pain and lots of blood. Everyone's crying and shouting at me but everything's becoming muffled. It's stopped hurting now, I've died and they bury me next to the lady. He's got to look after both of the children now and it's the first time he's been close to our daughter."

Sally was quiet for a while and the tension which she had been exhibiting eased away. After a few minutes of silence she began to speak about another past life which she had moved into in a voice that had a childlike quality to it:

"I'm outside on a sunny day and I can see grass and trees. I'm a little boy, around three years old, wearing little sandals, shorts and a little T-shirt. I'm happy, playing with other children. When I go home there's something not quite right, nobody's smiling but somebody's gone missing. I feel confused as I don't understand what's happened. People are coming to the house and I'm not allowed to go out and play anymore. It's my big sister. I'm sick of being inside, I'm only allowed in the back garden. After a few days my mum and dad sit me down and tell me that a man took my sister and murdered her and that she's not coming back anymore. Mum's crying and she says she needs me to be there all of the time. As I get older she still doesn't let me out of her sight and she doesn't even want me to go to school. She's smothering me and she keeps crying. She's told me she's going to have another baby. She has a baby boy and I feel jealous. Lots of people come to visit to see the new baby and they're either talking about the baby or my sister, and I feel as if I've been pushed out. Mum doesn't cry as much now the new baby's here – I couldn't stop her crying but the baby has. The baby sleeps in my parents' room but I have to sleep on my own. They still don't let me play outside and I feel they don't want me

there but I'm not allowed to go anywhere else. Hmm, they're not happy with me because they've caught me nipping the baby but I don't care and I've got some attention for a change." Sally paused for a few moments before she continued:

"Mum's having another baby and we visit my sister's grave to tell her about it. I keep getting told off and they say I'm the eldest but I'm not really. I'm about 11 now and the children are getting bigger and they're driving me mad. Everything I've got they want. There's no peace. I feel more like a grown-up and I'm let out on my own more. I still visit my sister's grave, but it's strange that the children know who she is but they never saw her. Mum's upset now, it's something to do with the man who took my sister but nobody'll tell me what it is. At school I'm known as the kid whose sister died but it doesn't upset me. I feel more responsible now and my mum gets me to look after the other two." Sally stopped talking and then told me that the life had slipped away, so we finished the session at that point. She told me about the unease she had felt in that past life, especially around the time that her sister was murdered. It was a feeling that she had known and felt regularly throughout her present life.

When Sally returned for her next session, she told me that she had felt a marked improvement in many ways since she had seen me. She was much calmer (her boyfriend Dave had noticed a big difference in her) and she felt she could cope much more easily at work. She was more tolerant of the people around her, and because she was doing so well she had moved back in with her boyfriend and they were getting on much better than before. She had noticed that he was more loving and attentive towards her, and I explained that this was because she was no longer attacking him all the time, and he was able to show her love again. As well as this, the unease that she had commented on at the end of our previous session was not inside her anymore. She was looking forward to exploring the other past lives because she had felt so good and she wanted to see if she could improve even more. I guided her into hypnosis and quite soon she was back in another lifetime. This time, her voice was harsh and at times slurred:

"I'm a lady in my forties in a room in my home, arguing with my husband. I'm holding a tumbler of whisky and I'm drunk and feeling very angry. This happens a lot. We're all dressed up and supposed to be going out somewhere but it's only 7pm and I'm drunk. He's shouting at me and I'm shouting back at him very aggressively, and our two children come in the room all upset because we're arguing. I throw my glass into the fireplace and swipe everything off the table on to the floor. I feel so angry and he just puts his head in his hands whilst I go up to bed. The next morning I feel ill and ashamed. I don't want breakfast, just want headache tablets. He didn't sleep with me last night and he comes in and tells me I'm a disgrace. The children were frightened and I need to get some help. He's called Charles and he can't put up with it for much longer. I feel upset as he's not a bad husband and I don't know why I'm so unhappy. Later that day I get drunk again and Charles is shouting at me, he can't put up with it anymore. He says that we can't spend time with friends anymore and I shout that he can go and take his stinking friends with him. He says he doesn't love me anymore, I'm not the person he married and he's put up with it for 20 years and he can't anymore. He starts packing and says he's leaving me. I'm in our bedroom crying and as I go out the door I'm not steady on my feet and I fall down the stairs. He tries to catch me but he can't. I'm laid at the bottom of the stairs and my son wants to send for the doctor but Charles says it's too late, and he's just lying on top of me, holding me and crying. He tells me he didn't mean the things he said and I can see blood on his hands. I'm outside my body, watching everybody. They're all sad – I didn't think that they were bothered about me. The doctor tells Charles that he's not to blame. As time moves on I stay around them, feeling unhappy. I want to help them. Sometimes I stroke his hair when he's asleep."

Sally lay quietly for a couple of minutes, and when she began to speak her voice had lost its drunken quality and was more normal:

"I'm in another lifetime, working as a schoolmistress in a classroom. I'm in my early forties and I'm trying to control the children. I'm quite stern and I'm shouting at them. They don't like me but they know I'm in charge. I feel powerful and I smack their fingers if they don't do things right, and I set them targets which are too high so they won't achieve them and I can shout at them. One boy is always naughty and in a fit of temper I hit him and make him sit on the floor in the corner. He tells his parents and I'm in trouble; there's talk about me being suspended or sent to another school as it's not the first time it's happened. However, time goes by and I'm still there. Today that boy's really pushing me all the time so I take him out of the classroom. He's gone too far and I feel so angry I want to burst. I want to shake him I'm so annoyed." At this point Sally's hands were clasping and unclasping, and her breathing was rapid. Suddenly her hands and arms pushed forward, as if throwing something away from her. *"I'm shaking him but as I push him he falls and bangs his head. He doesn't get up. I didn't mean to do it but he was goading me all the time. He's taken away to hospital with a fractured skull but he doesn't regain consciousness and I know it's all my fault. I didn't mean for this to happen. I'm in big trouble and they sack me. I'm able to get a job in an office for low pay but it's not a very good job and no one comes near me because they know what I've done. I feel down and depressed, I'm full of self-pity but no remorse for what I've done. I lose pride in my appearance and stop eating properly. After a while my health worsens and I can't go to work anymore. I feel and look awful but I can't be bothered to do anything about it. I haven't got any friends and nobody wants to know me. I don't need to be here."* Tears began to stream down her cheeks as she said this, but after a few minutes finally she became calm again and sighed. *"I feel sleepy, I just die alone. I have nobody to say goodbye to. I'm calm now."*

The life was over, but rather than press Sally to give me information on how she died (afterwards she told me that she felt she'd starved herself to death, which possibly had connections to causing the anorexia in this present lifetime) I asked her to move away from the life into the final one that we had to work through. This proved to be a very unpleasant death experience but which was mercifully quite short. She became very tense, and she began to shake and cry as she explained to me what she was reliving:

"I'm in a dark room and I'm feeling very afraid. I'm a girl, in my twenties and I have bare feet and I'm wearing a nightdress. I'm being held here against my will and I feel so afraid. A man says I can't leave here and he won't let me go. He's making me get into a bath of warm water and forcing me to lie down. I'm begging him to let me go. I can feel him cutting me with a knife. I'm starting to feel cold and I can hear him talking to me, saying some strange things. I think he's mad. He's trying to lift me out of the bath but I'm too slippery so he just lets the water out. I can't fight him. I can feel my life fading away. I just see myself in the bath now, it's over."

Once more she heaved a big sigh of relief and she came back to full awareness feeling very calm. The therapy sessions were over and she knew that she would enjoy a vast improvement in herself as a result of them.

I caught up with Sally a year or so later to find that her life had been transformed by the past life therapy. The anger outbursts had completely gone, she felt much easier in herself all the time and she felt much less stressed at work. However, more than this she told me that because she had let go of so much of her neediness and insecurities as a result of our sessions she had come to realise that the relationship with Dave was not right for her so she had finished the relationship. She was now pregnant, living with a man a few years younger than her (she jokingly called him her "toy boy"!) and really enjoying their life together. For the first time in her life she felt very settled and she was also looking forward to being a mother. The process of releasing the locked-in emotions from the past lifetimes had enabled her to become much more balanced and she was able to be in a relationship in a mature way, without running her old patterns of self-sabotage and anger.

Section Five

Unusual Cases

Chapter 20

Christine's Story

Over the years working as a regression therapist I have heard quite a lot of stories about so-called 'Past Life Therapists' and the appalling way that they have gone about their work, either making a mess of the process of handling clients once they were in a previous life, or even causing their clients more problems than they started with because they have done such a bad job in the regression sessions. To someone like myself who thinks of himself as a well-trained, highly experienced professional, such stories anger me because they detract from the reputation that Past Life Therapy deserves to hold. As I said at the start of this book, I think that Past Life Therapy should be accepted as a credible, psychotherapeutic discipline, and I have spent over 27 years working in this field as a passionate advocate of the healing power of this process. Anyone working as a hypnotherapist should undertake credible training in past life work or they should not touch upon it at all with their clients. Past Life Therapy is very deep therapy, and if it isn't done properly it can leave people feeling worse than when they started. Also, if a client doesn't get improvements in their issues then they tend to think that Past Life Therapy doesn't work, which (and I hope you'll agree if you've read this far) it patently does.

Christine was one such person, who had experienced some past life regression with an inexperienced hypnotherapist and as a result had been left in a very bad state indeed. For several months since her regressions she had been feeling deeply depressed and unhappy. Whereas prior to the regressions she had been an outgoing, happy-go-lucky person, afterwards she was unable to get on with her life and she felt stuck in a spiral of misery and anxiety. She had started comfort eating, turning to food and sweets as a source of solace, and had put on a lot of weight, making her feel even more depressed. In fact it was one of Christine's friends who phoned me to ask for my advice as she was so concerned about her welfare and the big, negative changes that she had seen in her since she had been regressed. It appeared that the hypnotherapist had opened up some past lives but had not cleared them of their negative emotions, and as Christine was a very good trance 'subject' the past lives had stayed open, in her mind, after her session, leaching their negative energies into her daily life. As a result of the telephone conversation her friend convinced Christine to come and see me, in order to release the past lives that were causing the problems. Once she was in hypnosis, her subconscious indicated that there were four past lives that needed working on. Quite quickly, she went back into the first of them:

"I'm a soldier, carrying a short sword and wearing a leather tunic and sandals. I'm wearing a breastplate and a helmet with a fluffy, red plume. I have very brown skin and I'm standing on the side of a dock looking at a big ship. There are a lot of other soldiers around me. I think I'm in ancient Egypt. I feel very thoughtful about something."

Christine paused for a while and then continued: *"I've moved on in time. I'm inside a bricked-up space. I'm a member of the King's Imperial Guard and this is his tomb. He's died so we all have to take poison and be entombed with him. I feel claustrophobic but the death itself is not traumatic. As we die there's a procession of us moving into Spirit, going into a massive golden hall. I feel at peace now."* She was silent for a couple of minutes, and when she spoke again she had moved into another lifetime. This time her body had stiffened as she lay in the chair and her face was tense. Her voice sounded tremulous and scared:

"I'm in a forest, hiding from some other people. I'm a woman and I've been making things; ointments and medicines. They say that I'm

a witch. I'm shocked because this is what my family did before me and it's been passed down. I feel angry too because I've been curing them of their illnesses. They catch me and drag me by my hair to a dungeon. It's filthy and there are lots of others here. There's nothing to eat. I know that there's no hope. They try to get me to confess. They say they're from God but I think they're from the devil." Christine started to cry and shake; her arms and legs jerking as she relived the torture. *"They're using thumbscrews and they stick a big metal stake through my hand. They try to get me to swallow something. Then they put me in a metal coffin with spikes in the top and shut the lid. The spikes go right through me and I move out of my body straight away. As I die I vow to get even with them one way or another. I leave my body but I don't pass over, I stay earthbound for a long time. I'm angry and I do my best to hurt them. I scare them, particularly the ringleader. I don't forgive him until he dies, then I move on fully into Spirit. I've gone now."*

We did a bit of work rescinding the vow that she had made in that life to hurt her killers and to forgive them for the hurt they had caused her, and then she moved into the next of the four lives:

"I'm standing on the top of a cliff looking out to sea. I'm a man wearing leggings and boots with brown laces around them, and a tunic and a heavy cape. There's a crown on my head; I've just looked at it and put it back on. It's golden and heavy, finely woven with stones on it. There are a lot of other men around and we're all armed with swords and big, round, leather shields with bronze medallions in the middle. We're on the attack and we've been fighting for months. I'm looking out at a ship and I'm puzzled whether it's one of ours, but no – it's a Viking ship. They're the enemy and they're very fierce. I'm tired. We keep having battles and I know it's just a question of time before they invade us and take over. Sooner or later I'm going to die."

Christine sighed a big sigh and her face was drawn, mirroring the gravity and the hopelessness of the situation. Suddenly her arms began to jerk and her breathing came in short, sharp bursts. Her head turned from side to side before her back arched upwards and she let out a gasp. Through gritted teeth she spoke: *"It's a battlefield and a big sword goes into my chest. I can feel the pain in my chest. I go down on to my knees and I've been beheaded. I have no anger; it's a soldier's life."* Her body relaxed in the chair and she breathed deeply and calmly again. I allowed her to relax for a few minutes to make sure that she had fully released the tensions of that lifetime, before she moved into the next past life that we had to work on. As I've said before, sometimes the subconscious saves the best (i.e. the most intense) till last and it was the case here, as this final life was the most traumatic of them all. Christine's brow was knitted and her lower lip trembled as she relived a life during WWII, probably as a young Jewess who was a victim of the Holocaust. She spoke in a voice tinged with sadness:

"Me and my family have been captured and we've been taken on a train. I'm a girl, 15 years old and I have a little brother and sister. We had a nice house and beautiful things. I'm seeing it all quite rapidly. We've been put on to a cattle truck to be taken away. I feel helpless; complete despair. I'm taken to a camp and separated from my siblings. I see a pretty girl being raped by a soldier. I have to decide what to do. Some people cooperate and become prostitutes. I know that we're all going to die. I disassociate from my feelings. I decide that if I kill them then they'll kill me and it will be over." A tear rolled down her cheek and her voice kept breaking with sadness as she continued: *"I'm in a room with a young soldier. He's quite handsome. He has a dagger. We have sex and when he's asleep I stab him. I wait for them to come and take me."* Through her tears she started to cough and her body jerked as her hands tightened into fists. *"I'm waiting in the dark with hundreds of naked people. It's cold. I still don't feel any emotions. We're packed in really close. There's no light and I can hear people crying. I just want them to get it over with. There's a bitter smell, a bit like bleach. I can't catch my breath."* Her coughing intensified and her breathing came quickly, in short bursts: *"I'm*

suffocating. I see things from my life flash before my eyes; I think I was a ballet dancer. I feel sorrow for my family and my nation."

Christine continued to cough and shake for a few moments before she relaxed and her body softened. The life was over, as was her ordeal in releasing the traumas from the past. She came out of trance and breathed deeply. Her face looked so different to how she had looked at the start of our session. When I first met her she had looked drawn as if she had a black cloud hanging over her. Now she looked brighter and happier. "Gosh, I feel so light and free," she said, a big smile on her face, "like something's been lifted from me." All of the bad feelings that she'd been carrying for months had evaporated away, and she told me that she felt "normal" again. I was so pleased to have helped her, because it restored her faith in the healing powers of Past Life Therapy and it meant that I was able to help to undo the damage that had been done by an inadequate therapist. Like I said at the start, this is powerful stuff and needs to be done correctly.

Chapter 21

Gerry's Story

Gerry was a therapist and healer who was very interested in spiritual matters, and he wanted to use past life regression in order to enhance his spiritual connection with the Almighty. A practising Christian, he had something of a monastic energy about him, and he had never married and was living a quiet life relatively separated from other people. He wondered where his interest in spirituality had come from.

I guided him into trance and asked his subconscious to take him back into the past, to wherever he needed to go in order to reconnect with his interest in spiritual issues. After a short pause he began to tell me what he was seeing:

"I'm standing on top of a hillside in blazing hot sunshine. I'm dressed in Arab garb with a hood on protecting me against the sun. My feet are bare. I'm looking down across the sea – the Sea of Galilee comes to mind. I'm coming towards the end of my life and I'm reflecting on things. I wonder did I do a good job, the job that the Divine had sent me to do. Did I achieve what I was sent to achieve?

I'm alone and I feel worn out. I'm about 60 years of age. It's all over bar the shouting. Everyone I know has gone, maybe to foreign parts. I regret I didn't go with them."

SB: "Move to another significant experience."

"I'm about 13, and I'm at home, enjoying life with my parents (I feel like they're my parents in this present life too). I've got to go away from home, never to see it again. I've got to go to a spiritual establishment to start my training, maybe as a monk. I feel sad. I can see a donkey with all my worldly goods on it, my clothes etc. I go with someone else, a boy, and I think he's from the establishment I'm going to. I see my parents in the distance, waving to me, tearful. It was a happy childhood, but it's over now.

I can see a sort of monastery. Mount Carmel comes to mind. It's built like a castle, with a big door. Everything's stone and solid. It feels unfriendly, with people there being a bit callous. There are no females. They're here to do a job, to convert me into a spiritual being, focussing totally on working for God. From day one it's as though yesterday never existed. As if you're here now, this is what you've come to do – prayer, meditation. A 5am start, then breakfast, then teaching, then lunch, then more teaching, then practical work (maybe in the fields), then evening meal and then prayers and then bed. It goes on like this day after day, week after week, until you totally forget about life outside. I just live the life of the monastery.

After a time I start feeling energies. It's almost as if I know what to do without anyone telling me. We're doing tests in tunnels. We start in pitch darkness with someone holding your hand. We go down the tunnels, there are lots of blind alleys but I feel safe because I'm with someone who knows the way out. My throat feels really tense and [I'm] worried about doing it on my own, knowing that no one will rescue me. I feel a block around trusting, so my teachers are encouraging me to trust, especially in my intuition. I feel I can't do it. The teachers are working on me to trust myself. They do this day after day, year after year. I see a vision of light around me growing in intensity throughout all this training, until one day they say it's time for me to do it on my own.

They open a trapdoor, I descend and they close it after me. I feel panic-stricken. It's pitch blackness. Will I ever find my way out? I sit for about half an hour waiting for the panic to subside, then I realise it's as if I can see in the dark. There are three tunnels, and I go into the one directly in front. I begin to feel easier, now I'm on my way. I crawl through it – it's about three feet high. I come to another junction, and I take the right tunnel, like it's a crossroads. It's so dark as I go down the tunnel. Then I turn left at another junction. I can see the light at the end of the tunnel. It comes out into an olive plantation. I sit down. I've done it. I go back into the monastery with a broad smile on my face. Everyone is there congratulating me. It was an initiation and I feel a huge feeling of relief."

Gerry sighed deeply and smiled. After being silent for a couple of minutes he continued his narrative:

"Then the teaching changes and I become one of the few, it's like I've graduated. Now they're showing me healing methods, how to heal by focussing on people's chakras and channelling energy into them. It's a long period of training. I'm also shown various herbs to help with different illnesses, and crystals. I'm being shown how to use crystals and what they do. It takes about 3–4 years. I'm about 19 now and I'm told it's time for me to leave the monastery and start travelling, healing. I go with another monk and work as an apprentice, and we go around the villages doing almost like clinics. People are queuing up for our services. We do healings and walk from village to village collecting herbs. It's a poverty-stricken area. Most nights we sleep under the stars. In the morning we meditate and then go on to the next village. When we eat our evening meal we either stay where we are or go on to the next village. I'm being marked as an apprentice, and this goes on for ten years, with just me and this fellow monk. We go from village to village, healing. I get a deep sense of fulfilment and people are so grateful as there's no other form of medical care for them. People treat us like a god, but I'd rather they didn't. I don't like the adulation. I wish they'd get in touch with themselves more. They could do it themselves and I don't like them relying on us. We sometimes get runners coming for us, 'please come quick', and it takes us off our schedule."

He paused again so I asked him to move to another significant part of that lifetime.

"It's about ten years later. We're called back to the monastery as a great event has happened. There's a great new teacher – the Master Jesus. He has a new way of working, and the focus is on raising consciousness. We're all going to work in a group. The figure 120 is quite important. A group of 120 people will create its own consciousness, to raise consciousness wherever we go to help the people become more positive. As a result of my healing experience I am also to become a confidante of the Master Jesus because I've become a good healer. We

have a feeling of brotherhood and we aim to create new possibilities for the people. We come with a message of hope but everywhere people have a feeling of hopelessness so they distrust us. Some of what we do helps them to feel more hopeful."

SB: "How is this done?"

"People are drawn to us when we go somewhere, 120 of us all together and we leave some energy there. Then, as we go back to each place several times, people start to listen. I can see Master Jesus teaching and people listening, and then we ask people who are sick to come forward for healing. We try to help them find out why they created the illness – do they have a grudge against someone or have they been short-changed? Forgiveness is important. They need to understand that there is a reason for their illness and that it's all to do with negativity. I'm starting to think about skin problems, lesions and warts – leprosy is important but it's not incurable as they believe. There are lots of growths on people and it seems that leprosy is the number one illness. We heal the causes of it and it's a great success. There are such a lot of lepers, often in the marketplace. The less experienced healers work on the easy cases whilst the more experienced like me heal the more serious cases. I feel that this is my life's work, being an itinerant healer, moving from town to town. We sometimes stay in places run by the Essenes. It feels like we're doing good and it feels that the happiness of the people has gone up, giving them more potentiality."

Once more Gerry paused, and after a long silence of several minutes he began talking again. It was obvious that he had moved on in time:

"I've stepped into bright sunshine and I'm dressed in Arab garb with a hood over my head to keep the sun off. I'm alone and I can see green grass as it's peak growing season. It's possibly winter because in the summer it's so dry and hot. There's greenness everywhere, everything's alive and vibrant. I feel it too. I'm making my way back to the monastery to learn more skills, to learn the next level of healing. I think I'm about 45. I've been working on my own and I got

a message from Spirit to come back, for an initiation into a higher level of consciousness that will improve my healing skills. There are a lot of us there, and it's like a seminar. We've all used our higher selves to connect with the Divine and now we're going to dispense with the higher self so we connect directly with God and the God-given energy. It's all about releasing your own negativity so you're a totally clear channel. It's like releasing your ego and surrendering your whole self to a life of service. Surrendering your individuality, the illusion of an individual self. It makes you a much more powerful healer. We're releasing our anger – I'm showing severe anger – it's quite traumatic. Being in that amount of light energy it brings up a lot of emotional stuff. We're very fractious in the seminar, almost wanting to punch people. The tutor tells us to express it and not to punch each other. We do it and I feel weak afterwards, as if the anger is completely gone. I realise the anger has driven me on. At the end of the seminar there's no anger left in us. We're told that we're ready to go out and continue healing and raise consciousness more. We go out in a group, about 20 of us. We have to be seen to be living the higher life. There's a spring in our step, it feels as if we've got a rise in consciousness and a love for all. We're living examples of living happily and thinking abundantly. People are sceptical of our message at first but it starts to work for them and they're able to change.

The group broke up once we believed in ourselves. We were given areas to work in, working in ones or twos. It's not so much fun on my own and doubts start to creep in. We'd expected things to improve dramatically but there isn't a huge difference. We couldn't lift people out of their consciousness. The happiness we hoped would lift the world didn't materialise and I'm disappointed that things haven't lifted. We had all lived in Atlantis in previous lives and we thought that things would get better but it was not to be."

SB: "Tell me more about your connection to Jesus."

"It was before this time when he was introduced to me. I was a lot older than him. He was about 20 and about to start teaching. He accompanied me and we struck up a friendship as we'd been friends

in past lives. We both had a burning passion to lift people out of their squalor. We spend a lot of time talking, including about sex. We remembered Atlantean past lives where the population was naturally curtailed. When we went to places where there was a lot of starving children we wondered why they had been born. We talked endlessly about it, about what could be done to change the consciousness to create a better society, but whether we were doing as much good as we would like. I'm together with him for approximately ten years. We felt that we were changing things but were we doing enough? We wanted to create a Utopian world but things were not changing much. We stressed the importance of prayer and meditation to the people. After his crucifixion a huge depression settled on us all and there was a sense of it all being over. What was the point, as we hadn't created a Utopia. We split up. I decide to stay and carry on the healing of the lepers. Others go to France. I carried on developing my expertise and it made me feel good helping to heal people, helping lepers to get back into society once they were healed. They were ostracised by society and they were angry about being outcasts. I'd counsel them to see the anger inside them, and when they saw it they began to heal. I got a kick out of this. The people felt that they had been cursed by someone and they wanted me to take away the evil spell. I looked into their energy fields and there were no curses. They didn't want to know they had created the illness themselves. I'd spend a lot of time with them explaining this, but most of them didn't want to listen – they just wanted me to fix them."

I asked Gerry to go to the end of the life:

"I'm worn out with all the walking. I have very little money and I'm so poor I'm almost living like the people I'm helping. I have a sense of disappointment that we hadn't changed things very much despite all our efforts to raise consciousness. People are still oppressed by the Romans. I've had enough and I just feel spent. I'm too old to go back to the monastery and live that sort of life. They don't really want me back because my energy is depleted. I feel a bit hurt by that.

I'm dying now, lying on a bench in the middle of the night. I just ask God to take me, 'please embrace me with your love'. It's a very peaceful end; I rise up out of the body and look down. I see myself worn out. I feel free, elated and I'm welcomed with open arms by the Hierarchy. They embrace me and tell me it's been a job well done. I'm being shown a movie of my life, a life of service. I feel I've paid back Karma somehow. I feel complete."

Gerry stopped talking and lay with a big smile on his lips. As the life was over I asked him to come out of trance and return to normal conscious awareness. He opened his eyes and his face looked serene, as if the divine energies he had spent that past life connecting to had been opened up once more. He felt satisfied that his quest for spirituality in this present lifetime was the right one.

Do I believe that he had spent time with Jesus? I don't know, and obviously there was no way I could get any evidence to prove it. However, all I can say is that everything he said whilst in hypnosis was congruent with what we know of life 2,000 years ago in the Middle East and it is certainly within the bounds of possibility that a spiritual community like the one he described actually existed. Such ancient communities are well-documented and his descriptions of the work he undertook in that life certainly connect to the work of those groups in trying (and failing) to raise the consciousness of the people by using spiritual energies and practices. Gerry's regression certainly shines an interesting new light on the life of Jesus as a spiritual leader trying to create a higher vibrational state of the ordinary people.

My feeling is that the picture of Jesus which we have in the Bible is a highly distorted one, an image created to promote certain beliefs and support a religion aimed at controlling the masses rather than fostering individual enlightenment. As such, Gerry's visions of Jesus as a Spiritual Master rather than a proto-god sit comfortably with the hidden teachings of Jesus which were excised from the 'official' teachings as the Bible changed and was rewritten over the centuries. I can certainly believe that what he experienced in our sessions was highly likely to have been true.

Section Six

Depression

Chapter 22

Holly's Story

Holly was training to be a counsellor and she attended an evening lecture I gave to her group of trainees on hypnotherapy. Afterwards, she pulled me aside and asked if I could help her, using hypnotherapy and regression therapy, with her depression. I explained that if we could regress back into the negative emotions causing the depression, and release them, then she would get better. Also, it wouldn't take lots of therapy sessions to find if she could be helped or not. She had had counselling but it hadn't helped her, and she was now taking antidepressants prescribed by her GP.

Forgive my rant at this stage of her story, but the medical myth that depression is caused by a 'chemical imbalance in the brain' is simply a lie. In March 2008 *What Doctors Don't Tell You* magazine published an excellent article highlighting the fact that there is no independent scientific evidence to support the theory that a chemical imbalance in the brain causes depression. It is a theory that is not backed up by any neuroscience research, and quite simply it is a lie that allows drug companies to sell antidepressants. Depression *can* be caused by certain physical problems such as underactive thyroid or candida. However, my experience is that depression is usually an emotional state caused by locked-in anger. The anger comes from Significant Emotional Events in which a person is wounded emotionally and the negative emotions are stored inside the subconscious. Anger is also a composite emotion, which means that there is usually another emotion underneath it. In the case of depression the negative emotion is sadness. This is why depression is characterised by melancholy.

All of this means that if antidepressants work at all, they do so via the placebo effect, although they often cause side effects which make a person feel worse than they did before taking them.

I think Holly was impressed by my approach (or she was simply desperate to get better!) so she booked in for a session. A 39-year-old nursery worker, she arrived at my office looking miserable and dejected. She explained that the depression had been with her for several years, and despite trying many approaches to get well, the only thing that really helped her to stop going deeper down into desolate bleakness was the martial arts classes she attended a couple of times each week. This obviously made sense, as depression is characterised by feelings of dejection and doing forceful physical action helps to break out of the feelings of dolour and sadness. However, it was only acting like a sticking plaster over a gaping wound, and within a day of her martial arts class the misery would return. In desperation she had gone to her doctor, who prescribed tablets.

Holly settled nicely into hypnosis and her subconscious indicated that there were five previous lives causing the depression. Not surprisingly, to me at least, all of the past lives involved death trauma. The first one was particularly poignant. I asked her to tell me what she was seeing and what she was wearing:

"I'm outside, standing on a busy street and it's daytime. I'm a woman, I guess around 36 years old, and I'm wearing a big, long dress and a bonnet on my head. I've got posh shoes on my feet. I'm shopping. I go into a shop and buy some bread. I have a little boy with me and he stays outside. He's about six years old and called Thomas. I'm starting to feel really tense now, my chest feels heavy. I've left the shop and see him lying in the road, sweating. He's all limp. I'm really worried and I start crying and shouting for help. I pick him up and start running with him, carrying him in my arms. I run to the doctor's with him and he lays him on the bed and starts checking his heart. He shows me his stomach – it's all swollen. The doctor looks worried. Thomas has

stopped breathing. He's dead."

Throughout all of this Holly was breathing quickly and shaking. She paused for a few moments and, although she was more relaxed, her face was contorted with anguish. Tears ran down her cheeks as she described his funeral, and how she put bluebells on his grave but she didn't want to leave the graveside. She then went on: *"I'm back in my house now, alone. I'm drinking alcohol in the kitchen. I'm overwhelmed by my grief and I just want to be with him. I feel empty; like I want to die. I start taking some tablets. I'm doing it deliberately. I leave my body and feel the release. I'm walking through fields of poppies with Thomas, holding hands. It feels nice."*

Holly had obviously passed away in that life, and as she was now calm after the rigours of the experience I brought her gently back to full awareness. She told me that she felt easier inside herself, and surprised at how light she felt. This is quite usual after such a session, but I knew that we still had more work to do to fully heal her depression.

She returned a couple of weeks later, telling me that she had felt much better for a few days after the regression but then the feelings of woefulness and anxiety had returned. I explained to her that this was normal, as we had released some of the 'pressure' from her 'emotional pressure cooker' and she would naturally feel some freedom for a while, but then the next bit of pressure would bubble up to the top of the pressure cooker causing the bad feelings. When she was ready, I guided her into trance and into the next of the past lives:

"I'm standing on a cobbled street and it's daytime. I'm a young woman, maybe around 26 years old, and I'm wearing a long dress and holding some flowers. It's very busy, and I'm trying to sell the flowers to passers-by. I think it's Victorian London. I'm poor and very thin and my stomach hurts very badly. I go home and go to bed to rest. I don't live in a very nice place. I'm alone, laid in a dirty bed, sweating. I feel very ill." As she relived this Holly was holding her stomach and

her legs were shaking. After a short pause she went on: *"I get better and I'm back selling flowers on the streets. But after a while the stomach pains come back. I'm crouched down, holding my stomach. I feel scared. I go up some steps to a big house and I'm knocking on the door. An old man opens the door; I think he's a doctor. I hope he can give me some tablets or something. The pain's really bad. I don't feel comfortable with him; it's as if he's a bit dodgy. My legs feel stiff and they're aching."* She started to breathe rapidly, and her legs and arms started to shake violently. Her head moved from side to side as if trying to get away from something and her voice was close to a shout: *"I sit in a chair but I don't feel safe. I feel scared. He's struggling with me. I'm on the floor. I don't like this, he's raping me. I struggle but can't get away. I'm too weak. I keep looking at a tea cup on a table and then I see a knife. I think he's cut my throat. There's blood on my hands. He stabs me in the stomach. As I'm dying he kisses me on the head. He's dragging my body out now. It's over."*

As she said this Holly began to relax again, and when I asked her how she felt she told me that she was at ease and peaceful. Just before we left that lifetime she got a strong sense that the man who had killed her in the past life was her ex-husband in this present lifetime. This didn't surprise me because in our first session she had told me that her ex-husband had been very difficult to live with and had caused her a lot of problems once she had left him. I gave Holly a couple of minutes to regain her composure, and once she had relaxed more deeply she moved into another lifetime. This time her voice was faster and staccato: *"I can feel tightness in my stomach and I can't breathe. I'm a man in a village in a desert, running from something. There are shacks which are made from some sort of material, and they're burning. I see a man on a chariot going really fast. I'm panicking. I'm looking for someone. There's an attack and fighting all around me. I'm trying to find a woman and a baby. I find them but they're dead. I feel very angry. I'm angry with myself for letting them down, and angry with the people who have done this."* Suddenly, she held her stomach and her head bent forward as her body jerked uncontrollably. Her breathing was rapid and she spoke: *"They've got me. I'm tied up and they're dragging me along by my feet from the back of the chariot. It's a relief to know that I'm going to die as I'm disappointed with myself that I didn't save my family."*

She stopped speaking for a couple of minutes as she experienced the death in that life, during which her body continued to jerk and shake, until finally she relaxed again as she left the life and moved into spirit. Once more Holly came out of trance feeling a sense of relief, a feeling which stayed with her for some time after the session, although she still experienced some days in which she felt down and sometimes angry for no reason. We then spent a few sessions over the next few weeks regressing back into the lives of some of her ancestors from whom she had inherited trauma. As with the past lives, this trauma was successfully released so she continued to feel a major improvement in herself, and all the time the depression was getting weaker, and less and less of an issue. Her final past lives were just as powerful as the earlier ones, although they were over quicker and had less narrative content in them.

In one of them she was a young boy hiding in a forest at night, trying not to get caught by someone. She was very scared throughout this experience, which ended with her dying once she was found and punished. In another she was a woman who was murdered by her lover, who she felt had been around her in this lifetime in the form of an ex-boyfriend (another man with whom she'd had a difficult relationship).

The final two lives that we worked through also contained traumatic deaths. In the first one she started to feel very frightened as she began to access the life, and then the images came into her mind:

"I'm a woman, in prison. I'm looking out through the bars, waiting for something. Someone's coming with the keys and he's leading me out. I'm wearing really nice clothes so I think I'm well-to-do. I'm led

into a courtyard in a village. There are lots of people there, looking at me." She started to shake violently. *"I'm really scared. They're putting a rope around my neck. I can see my children in the crowd, watching with everyone else. I don't want to leave my children; I haven't done anything really bad. They say that I'm a witch. I can't believe it's happening. I'm begging them not to do it. I'm hung from a big, wooden gallows."* Holly continued to shake for a minute or so before she relaxed, a sign that the life was over. I asked her to move into the next (and last) past life. Quite soon she was breathing quickly and her whole body shaking vigorously:

"I'm in a battle. There are loads of horses and lots of fighting with swords. It's chaotic; there are men falling off horses and being trampled. I'm a man, in the middle of it all, on a horse. I'm out of breath and my throat hurts and I'm terrified. I have to get away; I'm riding very fast off the battlefield. I get to the top of some cliffs and can't get any further. There's no other way to go. I don't know what to do. I'm alone, scared and out of breath and the horse is just going round and round at the top of the cliffs. I think we've been defeated and they're chasing me. I feel guilty because I should have stayed and fought. I've been a coward and let everyone down." Suddenly she started to moan and her body twisted in the chair so that she lay in an awkward position. Her voice was softer as she spoke through a clenched jaw: *"I'm going down, it's a long way. Not on the horse. I'm laid at the bottom of the cliffs. The horse threw me off and then fell on to me. My eyes are open but I'm not moving. It's all peaceful now."*

Holly's shaking eased and she sighed deeply and relaxed. Her final past life experience was over and she came out of trance, surprised but at ease. She called me a few weeks later to tell me how well she was feeling. The depression had gone and she felt much happier in herself. She said that she was now able to live a normal life, feeling freer inside than she'd ever felt in her life before. I've bumped into her once or twice over the years since then and can confirm that she still is doing really well without a trace of depression to pull her down.

Chapter 23

John's Story

I find John's past life sessions with me to be particularly interesting because one of the lives he relived would have fitted very nicely into my previous book *Famous Past Lives*. A sprightly, intelligent 70 year old (who felt more like a 50 year old as a result of his outgoing personality) John had enjoyed a successful career in business and was married to Jenny, who like him belied her advancing years with her youthful character and looks (probably due to the yoga that she practised and taught regularly). However, despite of all the positive things in his life (a lovely house in the countryside, a closeness to his children and grandchildren, regular travels abroad, for example) John had been plagued by a form of depression for most of his adult life. Like Churchill he called it his 'Black Dog' feeling, and he explained to me that it came on him virtually every morning upon waking, and it could take most of the rest of the morning before it began to fade away. Only then did he feel that he could face the rest of the day with any sense of cheerfulness.

So, unlike many people suffering from depression he was able to live a normal life (and being a wise man he refused to take antidepressants) but he just felt that he was held back from feeling he could live his life freely and naturally. He couldn't understand why he had this problem as he had enjoyed most of his life, and his childhood did not contain any significant traumas. He was happy to experience regression to work on the emotional root causes of the problem, and although sceptical about the concept of previous lives he admitted he was fascinated by the idea that he could have lived before.

Once I had taken John into trance and his subconscious had created an Ideo-Motor Response signal using one of his fingers, his subconscious indicated that there were three past lives causing the 'Black Dog' feeling and I guided him back into the first of them. Within a short time John's body started to twitch and his face carried a serious frown. I asked him how he was feeling:

"I feel concerned. I'm flying in the cockpit of an aeroplane and we're lost. The instruments are damaged. I'm the only person in the cockpit but there should be someone else there. I can't control the plane. It's cold. We need to get back from a mission but we've been damaged by anti-aircraft fire. I can't do it, it's too damaged." Throughout all of this John was jerking and breathing hard as his body relived and released the anxiety and fear from the incident. Suddenly though it stopped moving and he slumped down in the chair, breathing a long sigh of relief. *"It's the end. It's light now, it's gone."* Shocked by what had happened John opened his eyes as if wanting to come out of hypnosis, but I asked him to close his eyes and gently took him back into trance so he could experience everything that had happened on this fateful mission which had taken place (as we found) during World War II. After a few seconds he regressed swiftly back and he began filling in the details:

"It's a war plane, a Lancaster Bomber. I'm checking the aeroplane before we go off. It's an evening; we're going on a night raid to Germany. We're flying from Lincolnshire. The plane's not right and I don't think she'll make it. One of the engines isn't good but we're made to go anyway. We just have to try it. I feel resigned to whatever's going to happen. We take off and fly over water. The others call me 'Skipper'. Engine No. 3 won't go. Number Two's gone to check. It's not running properly, we can't get enough height. It was OK last time, it wasn't right but we flew through it last time and we had a good run and we were the first home last time – we got the drinks in for the others. We just made it, but not this time. It's very dark and hard to find the target, there are no lights anywhere. We can't climb. We're being shot at. There are sudden explosions. We've been hit." Once more, John's

body was twitching with fear and his speech and breathing were rapid. *"I'm scared. We're breaking up. I'm trying to keep going but nothing works. We can't get back. There's a big explosion and then just a tremendous light. We're all gone, none of the crew got out."*

With these last words he softened again and his breathing slowed down as his face showed great calmness upon it. In order to fully clear the life of its negative effects I had John go back through it again a couple of times, but the second time there was no tension left in it so we had obviously released the trauma from his subconscious. I brought him back to full awareness, and John was flabbergasted by what had happened. He was amazed at how frightened he'd been, declaring (as so many people do in regression) that the feelings had overwhelmed him. The thing he found particularly significant was that he has always had a keen interest in flying, so much so that in his forties he had taken flying lessons and even owned a single-seater plane for a while. As it turned out this interest with flying was to become a particular theme in our past life sessions.

One curious aspect of John's past life was that it had taken place in the 1940s, which was strange as he was born into his current life in 1938. He questioned that the past life couldn't therefore be true, as how could he be alive as a small boy in this lifetime and also alive in another body in the 1940s? This has happened several times before in my career as a therapist, and I admit that it used to concern me whenever a client relived a life which had taken place at the same time as they had been alive in this present life.

However, upon reading Michael Newton's book *Journey of Souls* I found that some of Newton's clients had experienced the same thing. Whilst they were in Spirit between lives they were informed by their Spirit Guides that our soul is so large that it is possible to live on earth in two different bodies at the same time. This 'splitting' of the soul allows the soul to experience more learnings to help them grow at a faster rate towards enlightenment. So although it appears to be unusual and it has only happened a few times in the thousands of regression sessions that I've facilitated, John was fascinated to learn a little-known feature of the journey of our souls over many lifetimes.

John came back for another session a few weeks later, telling me that he was feeling some improvement with the 'Black Dog Feeling'. Although it hadn't gone completely, he felt that it had less of a tight grip on him and it didn't last so long in a morning or feel as heavy as it used to do. He also informed me that he had started woodturning for the first time in years. He had always wanted to do it and many years ago spent a lot of money on a range of equipment, but after a short trial had never returned to it, and the tools and machinery had just been gathering dust in his workshop. This might not seem like a tremendous change, but it was indicative of the lightening of his depression and the shifts that had started to take place inside him as a result of the release of the first past life. He was eagerly awaiting the next instalment of his regression experiences and within a few minutes of going into trance was once more in another former existence, which displayed certain similarities with his last life:

"It's night-time. I'm a man standing in a workshop surrounded by wooden aircraft frames. I'm inspecting them and I feel apprehensive because I know we're going to be flying them later on. It's World War I and I'm an English pilot in France. We're going to spot the guns, fly very low over the enemy trenches keeping the plane still while another chap takes pictures. It's very hard to keep it still with big guns going off rocking us all over the sky. But these planes are no good. They're poor quality and too slow, leaving you vulnerable to everything, ground fire and enemy aircraft. They shoot at you as soon as they see you. If anybody gets back it'll be a miracle. The Hun outguns us in every way. There are only three of us left. I got away with it the first time, but it was a long walk back. He got me from behind; the observer who was with me didn't make it. It was a long walk back, and no sympathy from the poor bastards in the trenches – 'get on with it,' they shout at

me. The second plane was no better than the first, really crap and no protection at all. Tony didn't come back; he'd gone before he hit the ground. I think he jumped but they never found him. They're just too slow. We just can't get the good stuff. What we want are those new SE5s. These are awful. We've lost some good men and there aren't many of us left. It'd be alright if we had the right gear. We've got to go again though so it's no good moaning about it. Got to find out where those guns are and get some pictures back. We go at first light." John paused and sighed, his voice soft with a touch of resignation in its tone. His face was set as he continued:

"Six a.m.; got to go. I've no options, there's no way out. It'd be better going over the top when they blow the whistle than this. It's poor light. We head north over Ypres, towards the guns and the light. The guns are causing a lot of turbulence, chucking us all over the place. I've got to look out for the other two so they can get some good shots." He started to breathe heavily, his body tense and his hands clenched hard into fists. He began to talk jerkily and loudly, obviously experiencing a great deal of fear and anxiety: *"Been spotted by them. Enemy aircraft coming, there are too many of them. I've got to cover for the others. There's a lot of the Bosch. They haven't seen me but they've got the other two. I've got to try to get out of it. They're coming at me now from all sides."* John slumped down into the chair and was silent for a minute before he continued quietly: *"It's alright now. It's all gone green and I feel totally at peace. The other planes were in danger, but I can't help them now. It doesn't matter now."*

As the life was over and there was no more for John to experience, I asked him if he could remember his name or serial number. He thought for a few moments and told me that the name Pilot Officer Andrew Evans with a serial number of 96713 felt right. He also felt that he'd learnt to fly in Hampshire and was a very new pilot who'd recently arrived at the front with little experience.

We finished the session and once more John was confounded

by the experience, although he felt lighter at the end of it, probably as a result of letting go of a lot of tension from the life. A couple of days afterwards he emailed me with the following, which verifies the information he came up with in the session:

> *I was telling my son James about my last session with you & he just did a website trace on pilot Evans – he was found to be a pilot with 64 Squadron RAF in October 1917 flying Farman FE.2BS pusher Biplane.*
>
> *His squadron was issued with the latest SE5 Fighter aircraft just a month after he was killed in 1917.*
>
> *Just food for thought??*

Food for thought indeed! I was thrilled that he had tracked down his former self and found proof that Pilot Officer Evans really did exist. He now had proof that past lives are not an imaginary phenomenon. This helped him to embrace completely the therapy process without any scepticism holding him back. Although there is plenty of evidence that the concept of reincarnation is a reality (witness the many books and articles in which people have researched their former lives which either came spontaneously to them or via hypnotic regression) very few people after experiencing past life therapy bother to find evidence for their former selves. I think that there are two reasons for this: firstly, the aim of the regression session is usually to release traumas from the past and so we do not go looking for specific information. The most important thing is to go into a previous life and neutralise it. This is usually done emotionally or kinaesthetically so particular details about the life are generally unimportant.

Secondly, after clients explore past lives and their issues get better, they don't feel they need to prove the validity of the past lives to anyone. They know that they have got better and that is enough for them. So, for John to check up the information from the past life is rare. However, the checking that he did after his next and final session was quite incredible and yielded some even more amazing information.

John arrived for his next session and told me that although the depressive feelings hadn't gone altogether, he was feeling less bleak in a morning and that both his son and daughter-in-law had noticed that he was much brighter in himself generally. After expressing pleasure at the subtle changes he was experiencing John settled down in my recliner and began the process of going into trance once more. Within a few minutes of me asking his subconscious to take him back into another lifetime, he began to shift around in the chair and breathe heavily in an agitated way. I asked him to share with me whatever he was experiencing, and to my surprise he began to speak with a very strong Yorkshire accent, quite unlike his usual somewhat refined Northern tones:

"I'm a farmer. I've nowt to do with my time as I've inherited too many people who do everything for me. T' farm runs itself, business is good and it doesn't need me. I feel frustrated; I want to make something happen. It's just a hobby, but I'm sure we can fly, or I'll bugger meself. We're building it out back on t' farm, making this flying machine. Everyone thinks I'm mad, but it can be done. I'll do it. It's gonna work. I keep taking people off farm work that has to be done and they don't like it. They say they've more important things to do, but I'm gonna bloody do it. Carpenter thinks he's making a cart – I want a flying machine. It's too heavy, I keep showing him pictures. I can't get carpenter to stop thinking about making wagons. It needs to be light. I'll do the bugger meself, we don't want bloody cartwheels. I feel annoyed that nobody can see what I can see. I can't make bloody joiner understand – I want it my way. They'll have it right, it can be done."

After all this ranting John was quiet for a few minutes so I asked him if he could tell me his name and where he lived in that life. Without a moment's hesitation he replied, again in a thick Yorkshire accent:

"Me name's George Cayley. I live at Old Brompton, North

Yorkshire. I think it's around the 1850s. I've learnt from books, including pictures by da Vinci. They all think I'm mad, but it can be done. It's going to float off the side of a hill. Get a windy day and it'll be alright. We need someone light to ride in it. I'm too heavy else I'd do it meself. Young Thomas'll do. He doesn't like the idea, but he'll do."

John was quiet for a while and his head moved from left to right as if he was watching something move across in front of him. A big smile appeared on his face:

"It didn't go far but it were good, but Thomas didn't like it. It were a bit of a crash-landing but it were alright. We got it to work, but Thomas said he'll stick to driving t' carriage in future. He's said he'll bugger off if I make him do it again. He only got in it 'cos I made him do it. It's just a hobby but I feel a sense of achievement and I know it works and that's good enough for me."

By this time the agitation and frustration that John had been feeling had calmed right down and he felt himself float through to the end of George Cayley's life and die of "old age and boredom". He came out of trance and was amazed at the things he had remembered. No wonder he had always been interested in flying! A few days afterwards John emailed me with the following incredible information:

Hello Steve,

Lots of food for thought this time?

Accurate date too! I couldn't possibly have known about the date, the name of Thomas, or the London involvement?? I obviously did not pick up on either his knighthood or the fact that he was a sitting MP.

Interesting though & quite intriguing?

Many thanks – John

Sir George Cayley, 6th Baronet of Brompton (27 December 1773–15 December 1857) was a prolific English engineer and one of the most important people in the history of aeronautics.

Many consider him the first true scientific aerial investigator and the first person to understand the underlying principles and forces of flight. In 1799 he set forth the concept of the modern aeroplane as a fixed-wing flying machine with separate systems for lift, propulsion, and control. He was a pioneer of aeronautical engineering and is sometimes referred to as 'the father of aerodynamics'. Designer of the first successful glider to carry a human being aloft, he discovered and identified the four aerodynamic forces of flight: weight, lift, drag, and thrust, which act on any flying vehicle. Modern aeroplane design is based on those discoveries including cambered wings. He is credited with the first major breakthrough in heavier-than-air flight and he worked over half a century before the development of powered flight, being acknowledged by the Wright brothers. He designed the first actual model of an aeroplane and also diagrammed the elements of vertical flight.

Cayley served for the Whig party as Member of Parliament for Scarborough from 1832 to 1835, and in 1838 helped found the UK's first Polytechnic Institute: the Royal Polytechnic Institution (now University of Westminster), serving as its chairman for many years. He was a founding member of the British Association for the Advancement of Science and was a distant cousin of the mathematician Arthur Cayley.

Cayley, from Brompton-by-Sawdon, near Scarborough in Yorkshire, inherited Brompton Hall and its estates on the death of his father, the 5th baronet. Captured by the optimism of the times, he engaged in a wide variety of engineering projects. Among the many things that he developed are self-righting lifeboats, tension-spoke wheels, the "Universal Railway" (his term for caterpillar tractors), automatic signals for railway crossings, seat belts, small-scale helicopters, and a kind of prototypical internal combustion engine fuelled by gunpowder. He also contributed in the fields of prosthetics, air engines, electricity, theatre architecture, ballistics, optics and land reclamation, and held the belief that these advancements should be freely available.

Around 1843, he was the first to suggest the idea for a convertiplane, an idea which was published in a paper written that same year. During some point prior to 1849 he designed and built a biplane in which an unknown ten-year-old boy flew. Later, with the continued assistance of his grandson George John Cayley and his resident engineer Thomas Vick, he developed a larger scale glider (also probably fitted with 'flappers') which flew across Brompton Dale in 1853. The first adult aviator has been claimed to be either Cayley's coachman, footman or butler: one source (Gibbs-Smith) has suggested that it was John Appleby, a Cayley employee—however, there is no definitive evidence to fully identify the pilot. An obscure entry in volume IX of the 8th Encyclopædia Britannica of 1855 is the most contemporaneous account with any authority regarding the event. A 2007 biography of Cayley (Richard Dee's *The Man Who Discovered Flight: George Cayley and the First Airplane*) claims the first pilot was Cayley's grandson George John Cayley (1826–1878). Dee's book also reports the rediscovery of a series of sketches from Cayley's school exercise book which suggest that Cayley's first designs concerning a lift-generating inclined plane may have been made as early as 1793.

Source: Wikipedia contributors. (2019, January 13.) George Cayley. In *Wikipedia, The Free Encyclopedia*. Retrieved 19:27, January 21, 2019, from https://en.wikipedia.org/w/index.php?title=George_Cayley&oldid=878210824

I think that's pretty impressive, don't you? There is no way that John could have known any of this as he hadn't studied the history of flight, and Sir George Cayley is not well-known in standard academic circles or to the general public. Not only did John get the date right, but he got the place where he had lived as well as the fact that he was fascinated with aeronautics. As well as this he knew about designing and flying a plane with a young boy ('Thomas') as a pilot. How could John have known all of this unless he actually was the reincarnation of Sir George Cayley? Oh, and by the way, as well as all of this, his depression was reduced too.

Chapter 24

Andrea's Story

Andrea initially came to me when she was pregnant for help to give birth more easily. She was expecting her second child and she was fearful that both carrying the baby and giving birth would be a painful process, as her first pregnancy had been extremely uncomfortable. This was because she had previously had a lot of gynaecological surgery which left her with a lot of adhesions (old scar tissue) around her bladder, and now she was pregnant again she was starting to feel a lot of pain as her bladder was stuck to the front of her uterus. She was concerned that her bladder could be permanently damaged and she was worried that later she might need to have some form of surgery as a result of the birth.

We worked in hypnosis using a combination of visualisations and affirmations to firstly allow the body to start healing itself. It may surprise some people to know that many changes can be made to happen in the physical body using the power of the mind. For example, a hypnotherapist friend told me recently about the work she did with one of her clients which created an amazing physical healing. She had been doing a therapy session with an elderly client and at the end of the session she remembered that the lady had told her that in a week's time she was due to have surgery on some polyps in her nose. Whilst the lady was in trance, my friend asked her to imagine the polyps dissolving away and healing. For a few minutes she did this and then just before she was brought out of trance she was told to expect being sent home by her specialist because he wouldn't be able to find any polyps. A few days later she was admitted to hospital for the surgery, and then discharged almost immediately because when the surgeon examined her there was no trace of any polyps to be seen!

Andrea was asked to continue giving herself affirmations and doing the visualisations in the run-up to giving birth, and I asked her to let me know how things had gone once she had given birth. A few months later she came back to tell me that after our session everything had gone incredibly well, the intestinal pain that she had been getting before she saw me had disappeared a few days after the session and the birth had been very easy, with no problems at all from adhesions. It had, she said, been a much easier delivery than her first child was, and she was now the proud mother of a bouncing baby boy. However, and this was why she was sitting in front of me again, she had developed a bad case of post-natal depression and was struggling to cope with the new child. She felt continually tired and stressed, she was sleeping badly and as well as being regularly tearful she felt very aggressive to both her husband and her two children. She had no tolerance towards her baby, and she was constantly irritable and felt very angry about everything for no reason. As you can imagine, she was worried about the effect that this would have upon the baby, and especially worried that she could become so angry that she could hurt him.

As usual, once Andrea was in trance I asked her subconscious to take control of a finger so it could signal to me the causes of the anger and irritability, and we found that there were four past lifetimes at the heart of the problem. Three of the past lives were over quite quickly; the last one, however, was particularly unpleasant (remember, the subconscious sometimes keeps the 'best' – i.e. the worst – till last). The first past life was quite short and consisted of being killed by having her head crushed (she couldn't see what was happening but she felt a lot of pressure in her head and a lot of fear), and the second life also was short and brutal. In this she experienced being a child who had her hand chopped off for stealing some bread. She felt as if she was starving and had been caught stealing in a marketplace.

Although she didn't die as a result of being maimed, the horror of the mutilation was the source of the trauma. The third life was as an old Native American man who had fallen off his horse and as a result of badly damaging his leg was left to die by the rest of his tribe, as they continued on their journey without him. Andrea became emotional as she explained the sadness and loneliness of the dying old man.

These three past lives were worked on and cleared over a few sessions although as these were mainly relived kinaesthetically there was little narrative to report. As a result she was feeling a lot easier with her role as a mother, and most of the angry outbursts had eased right down. She was not 100% better though, as she still occasionally felt a bit uptight and although she could control her anger she knew there was still something under the surface bubbling away inside her. She especially felt this whenever she was in contact with her mother, with whom she'd always had a difficult relationship. It was the final past life that held the key to clearing the problem completely.

Once she was in hypnosis, she moved into the life and she saw herself in Victorian London as a young girl aged about thirteen. She became very tense and as her body began to shake with fear she started to cry as she explained what was happening:

"I'm running away, someone's chasing me. I'm trying to escape from a woman who owns me. I belong to her. Oh, they've caught me and they're taking me back. I'm terrified they'll hurt me. They punish me by beating me. A man ties me up and whips me and rapes me. She tells me that if I run away again she'll kill me. I work for her in a brothel and I ran away because it's horrible and rape is a regular occurrence, sometimes with two or three men at a time."

Although she remained tense Andrea relaxed a little and paused for a minute or two before she continued with her story:

"I remember how it all started. My mother's just had a baby and she says I've got to work to earn money to help feed the family. She works as a prostitute. She says she knows someone who will look after me so

I have to go away, but I feel scared and I don't want to go, and even though I beg her not to send me she puts me on a horse and cart driven by a man. He says that he knows where I'm going and what I'm going to do, and that I need teaching. He stops the cart and really hurts me. Then he takes me to a big house and a lady asks him if he's checked the merchandise – they mean me. She locks me in a tiny room and tells me I start work tomorrow. I just want to go home. The next day I have a nice breakfast with five other girls who are all older than me. The lady says that I belong to her now and if I'm a good girl she'll let me go home. She says that men are going to pay to do what the driver did to me. But he hurt me. One of the girls gives me a dress to make me look pretty and she puts make-up on me. I feel really scared and she says that it won't hurt as much, and that if I don't do it the lady will hit me and that's worse. I see the door open and I run out but she chases me and catches me and takes me back. The lady says that naughty girls get extra special surprises and she takes me into a room in which there are three men and tells me that they like little girls. She says that they're allowed to hurt me because I ran away and then they tie me up and take turns. I can't believe that my mother could have done this to me." At this point the tears began to fall and Andrea sobbed, her voice sounding heartbroken: *"I can't believe a mother could do that. She would have known but she still did it. How could she send me here?"*

Andrea continued crying for a while, before finally sighing deeply and becoming quiet. Eventually she spoke again:

"I'm cold and hungry and alone, lying down inside a dark room. I'm locked in so that I can't escape. I've been here for a while now, working as a prostitute. I find that I can get time out if I'm badly behaved or if I fight with the other girls. I get punished by being locked up and not fed but it's worth it. Sometimes I get beaten but I want to make it so difficult so that she sends me home. She won't let me out of the house as she knows I'll run away. I'd rather die than live like this. I've annoyed her again so she sends me with someone I've never seen before. He will teach me how to behave. He doesn't want to have sex with me, but just to hurt me. I feel really scared. He hits me and says that he'll hurt me

so much I'll beg him to kill me." Andrea's whole body began to shake, and her breathing came fast with the horror of what she was experiencing. Her legs and arms jerked violently. *"He ties me up and he whips me at first, before he beats me with a rod. Then he decides I don't scream enough, so he breaks my fingers. I'm screaming, terrified and in agony. He starts to strangle me but he's so enraged that he goes too far and he kills me. Even after I've died he continues to assault me and then he takes a souvenir – he cuts off one of my fingers. I'm glad he's killed me."*

Slowly Andrea started to relax, and once she had regained her composure and a sense of calmness, I asked her to become aware of any other aspects from that experience that might help her in this one. She pondered this for a few seconds and then replied:

"I can see that the mother in that life is also my mother in this present lifetime. Gosh! That makes so much sense. No wonder we've always had such a bad time with each other. I've always felt that she didn't love me and she's always been distant towards me. Now I understand why."

Andrea's past life journey was over, and she surfaced from trance feeling as if a massive weight had been lifted off her shoulders. I spoke to her a few weeks later to be told that the anger issue and post-natal depression was a thing of the past, and that moreover she had been able to spend time with her mother without being 'triggered' by her presence. She now felt able to control herself when she was in contact with her mother, which made her life a lot calmer than ever before.

Section Seven

Sexual Issues

Chapter 25

Lars' Story

One of the most humbling experiences for me as a hypnotherapist is when people travel substantial distances to undergo therapy with me. I have clients who come from all around the UK and around Europe. I really appreciate the effort that they've put in travelling such a long way, and I feel very privileged and honoured that they trust me with their therapy.

Lars was one such client. He flew in from Norway, where he lived and worked in local government. A handsome, highly intelligent man in his mid-30s, he had struggled for most of his adult life with what he described as a sexual blockage. He explained that whenever he was in a passionate, sexual situation, he would suddenly and for no reason lose his desire. His passion and sexual feelings would just turn off, he would lose his erection and he would be unable to continue making love with his partner. He was unable to control this automatic reaction, and whatever he did in order to try and stop it from happening did not work. As you can imagine, he was extremely troubled by this (what man wouldn't be?), and as he had recently separated from his wife and was just starting a new relationship with a very attractive woman who he had fallen in love with, he wanted help so that his new relationship would be a successful one in every respect.

Upon questioning Lars in our first session, he told me that he could think of no embarrassing sexual experiences in his childhood or adolescence that could have caused this blockage. I have found so often when I work with sexual issues that they connect back into earlier experiences in this present lifetime. In some cases it may be that my client has been caught masturbating during their adolescence or that at some time they saw their parents having sex. I have had a lot of clients who were severely traumatised by lying in bed listening to their parents having sex in another room, especially if the mother was being forced to have sex with a bullying father. However, his parents were both mature and sensible when it came to discussing anything sexual with him as a younger man, and furthermore there were no significant traumas in his life that could have caused anxiety that might, perhaps, be feeding into the problem. Apart from this sexual blockage he was a very balanced and happy individual.

I settled Lars down into a comfortably relaxed state, and as he drifted deeper into trance I asked his subconscious where in the past had the events taken place in which anxiety or guilt or fear had been locked in which were causing this sexual 'blockage'. His IMR signalled that as well as events in this present lifetime in his childhood there were also two past lives which needed to be worked on. Within a few moments he had regressed back into his childhood and he began to remember an event which had taken place when he was only five years of age. He felt a lot of tension in his stomach as he relived the time when his friend painted a picture of Lars inside his mother's stomach before he was born. His friend was trying to explain to Lars how the body works but he had painted his mother with no clothes on. Although this was done in childhood innocence, when Lars' parents saw the painting they were very angry and in trance he re-experienced all the upset and fear as if he was five years old again. Once we had released the emotion from that memory, his subconscious then connected it with other early memories. Firstly, of his mother finding photos of women in underwear that he had cut out from magazines and hidden under his pillow. Secondly, she catches him in bed with his younger cousin who was trying to kiss him for a joke. In both cases she was very upset and gave him a good talking to, confirming to his young mind that sex brought him bad feelings of discomfort. As he worked through these 'forgotten' memories his body was uptight and he became extremely anxious. However, fairly quickly he released the tension and he was able to relax again. We had successfully released the negative emotions from those memories and we were ready to begin exploring the past lives that were underpinning his sexual problem. He moved into the first of them, in which he was a monk living in a monastery.

Suddenly, his body became tense and he began to breathe quickly. His arms clamped themselves into his sides and he looked quite rigid. I asked him what he was experiencing. Through a tightly set jaw he answered:

"I can't breathe freely. There's something tight around my chest, as if I'm in a straitjacket. It's uncomfortable; I find it hard to breathe. I think I'm also vomiting. I'm on an earth floor; I can smell the earth, as if I'm in a basement or a cellar. I'm on my knees, crawling around. I'm a man, I'm alone and I feel upset, as if I regret something and I dislike myself. I've had some sexual feelings which are like an animal in my body that shouldn't be there. I'm punishing myself. It's cold, lying on the floor. I don't think my lungs work properly – maybe I've got lung disease. I have to cleanse myself and drive out the sexual feelings. Some other men have been pouring hot and cold water over me to wash the feelings away."

Lars went quiet for a few moments, as he processed the information that his subconscious was bringing through to his conscious awareness. I sat patiently and in silence, awaiting the further unveiling of the life. His head shifted slightly to one side and his brow furrowed as he continued:

"I'm getting an image of a young girl in her late teens, smiling at me, standing in grass. I'm in love with her. She's wearing red and picking flowers. I'm trying to get rid of this feeling of attraction to her. I'm desperately trying to release the feelings; it feels like a snake inside me. I'm a young monk, maybe in my early twenties, and I'm angry with her because I blame her for not being able to get rid of the snake inside me. This is exactly how I feel in this present life when I'm attracted to someone – I feel angry with them – it's the same feeling. In

that life I feel like I'm dirty, sick in my mind. I cry with anguish and frustration but I can't stop thinking about her. I want to feel pain and to punish myself. There's an older monk there. He's fat and bald and in a greyish cloak, and he has a round face and intense eyes. He's my master but he's obsessed with me. Earlier on in that life, when I was around 17 and he's in his thirties he desires me. Maybe he's even done something sexually with me. He tutors me and other boys, there's a lot of praying and sitting around on cold, stone floors. When he finds out I'm in love with the girl he starts punishing me and showing a lot of anger towards me. He wants me to suffer. I want to suffer because I feel I'm bad."

Lars stopped talking again and his body softened as a slight smile crept on to his face when he remembered a happier time. His voice was softer as he went on:

"I'm in a garden with lots of flowers and trees. I'm there with the girl and it feels nice, although I'm afraid I might be seen. We keep looking at each other, gazing into each other's eyes. We sit on a bench and talk. This feeling of attraction is new to me; it's a very light, innocent feeling. I feel empty when she leaves. I'm upset but I smile and feel happy when I think of her. She picks things from the garden and puts them in her basket, and I try to be there when she's doing this. We're chasing each other around a tree and laughing, but I feel that someone is watching us from above, from a window." Suddenly his face became sombre as he sighed. *"Someone interferes and I'm not allowed to go there or to see her anymore. I feel very sad and angry. They keep me inside a lot, making me do chores like scrubbing floors. The older monk is always there, talking harshly to me and treating me badly. I can sense my personality changing as I become more resentful of them so they just punish me even more. I spend a lot of time on my own. I think about ten years go by before they start putting me in the basement. I'm in my early thirties and I feel trapped there as I think about the girl all of the time. I've changed so much and I can't undertake my duties as a monk. I just get angry when I read or pray. I become desperate and I start to rebel, shouting and screaming and knocking*

things over. This is when the 'treatment' starts in the basement. It's as if the inner conflict between my duties as a monk and my love for the girl just erupt. This is the same feeling of conflict I've had throughout my marriage, knowing I have a duty to be there but also wanting to leave and follow my heart. I could have left the monastery to be with the girl but it's safe there. I would have gone out into nothing, no job, no way of earning a living, no safety. I'd been there a long time, since I was a child."

Lars sighed heavily, as he relived the pain of the emotions. He was silent again for a couple of minutes, then his body stiffened again, his arms rigidly clamped by his side and his hands became fists. Once more he began to breathe harshly and he spoke through gritted teeth:

"The brothers tell me I'm infected by the snake and I have to be cleansed. They think they can cure me. They discuss me a lot and come up with a plan. Initially they give me hard work, washing floors etc. They try to love me but I'm always angry. The other monk – my master – is in on the meetings and he wants me to suffer. I entered the monastery when I was very young so a lot of the monks really love me and it's hard for them to punish me. My early years were good there and I had lots of love and safety and happiness. Now I resent everyone so they're afraid of me. They try to be gentle and loving but I'm rebellious. The inner battle inside me is killing me. I don't have the courage to leave but I should have gone when I first fell in love with the girl. It's too late now. In the end it's very quick, only a few weeks before I die. They tie me up and they're putting my head into a bucket of water and alternately pouring warm and then freezing cold water over me. They're trying to wash away the beast inside me. I'm not angry at them as I too want to get rid of the feeling. I'm getting extreme feelings throughout my body. I'm lying on the floor in the cellar. It's dark and cold and I quickly become ill. I have a fever and my chest and lungs are weakening." Lars started to shake, coughing his words out as his body relived the maltreatment in the cellar. *"Some of the monks want to stop it but my master convinces them to*

continue as I'm not cured. They put me in a big wooden tub and push my head under water. It's freezing and I hate it. I feel very tense but my lungs are giving out. I start to drift away. It's the lung problem that kills me." After a short while Lars' body stopped shivering and he began to breathe more easily. *"I'm in the Spirit now and there's someone there like a teacher giving me learnings about the life. I know I can work on those issues again."*

SB: "How do you feel now?"

"A lot calmer, though there's still some tightness in my stomach. There's still some core tension there." I asked his subconscious if this tension was coming from the past life which he'd just experienced and it indicated, "No." I asked if it was coming through from another past life and it indicated, "Yes." Using the tension in his stomach as a means of connecting him quickly into another past life, Lars began to go rigid again and he spoke slowly:

"I can feel my throat tightening. I can feel sadness about losing the person you love. I'm a woman and my husband's been killed. I have to keep going because I've got three children so I have to lock down my feelings. We're in a country house in France and soldiers come in and kill him. He's lying in a pool of blood. I feel so sad and angry, but I tell myself I mustn't feel anything as I have to be strong."

Lars' body began to jerk, a sign that it was releasing kinaesthetically the locked-in emotions. As this releasing took place, I asked Lars if there was anything else that he was aware of. He told me that he realised that in his mind as a result of both of these past lives there was a connection between love and death and anguish which he had subconsciously been holding on to in this present lifetime. I knew that this awareness, combined with the release of the physical and emotional trauma which had occurred during the sessions, would also contribute to a significant healing of his sexual blockage. Finally, he sighed and his body settled down and relaxed. As a tailpiece to the therapy, I used a technique that I rarely use in therapy as I don't always feel that it's appropriate as it creates memories which are not real (as opposed to the past life memories which I usually consider to be very real). Sometimes called 'Change the Events', this allows the client to recreate a more positive outcome in a past life. I asked Lars to think about the past lifetime as a monk, and to imagine that instead of staying in the monastery and suffering he had left when he was young and gone to live with the girl and that he had lived a happy life with her. He felt a strong feeling of spiritual and physical freedom and the tension in his stomach, which was already considerably reduced, dissolved away. This sense of freedom coursed through his body and mind, and he told me he knew that the old, mistaken belief of love equalling death or passion equalling suffering was released. He reframed this by realising that sex meant freedom, and as we finished our session he came out of trance with a big smile on his face. He was amazed at how strong the feelings had been during the regressions, but also at how vividly he had re-experienced the past lives. He was also looking forward to testing the results of the therapy over the next few days as he was about to spend time with his new girlfriend on a short holiday together. I told him that sometimes after therapy of this nature people immediately experience a complete improvement of their old problems, but sometimes the change is a little more gradual and not quite as dramatic. A couple of weeks later I was chuffed to bits when he emailed me:

> *Hello Steve! Now I'm on my way home and Alice has just left on another plane. Thought I may let you know how things have turned out. First evening I thought nothing had changed. I had some great feelings, but things were over pretty quick. Then the next day I felt something had changed inside me (but as you predicted I was still uncertain if it would last). It was a feeling of ease and calmness. Still we needed some time to get to know each other physically and we had lots of talks, fun, massages and hypnotherapy (she had some*

negative feelings for her own body that we worked on).

[These have] been some fantastic days and nights with lots and lots of sex... Sex in a way that is almost completely new to me...

We are very, very happy together and had a fantastic time in Scotland!! Thanks a lot, Steve. Hope to see you again sometime...

Take care!

Good result, eh?

Chapter 26

Mike's Story

Mike was in his late 50s, a senior officer with a city council who had, one year earlier, become divorced from his wife after twenty years of marriage. The separation was quite traumatic for him although the marriage had been on the rocks for many years. One of the major problems was that he had not been sexually attracted to his wife and they had not made love for the last 15 years of the marriage. He had now started a new relationship with a new woman, Sarah, and unlike his ex-wife he found her very attractive and sexy. However, his problem was that whenever they had sex together he was *unable* to climax, something which he found both distressing and embarrassing. It had now got to the stage that whenever they made love he would feel anxious throughout their lovemaking, and as he was worrying whether he would be able to climax he was not totally present with his partner. Of course, as a result the problem was more likely to happen because it was on his mind all the time.

From a therapist's perspective, an inability to orgasm (known as 'anorgasmia') is more usually a female issue, and is an unusual problem for a male (it's more often that we treat the opposite – premature ejaculation). In fact, as Mike himself said jokingly to me during our initial discussion, "I realise most men would give their right arm for this problem." Nevertheless, the anxiety he felt about it was likely to damage his new relationship with Sarah, and making love had become a source of frustration rather than pleasure.

Once in trance Mike's subconscious indicated that as well as two past lives causing the anorgasmia, his birth experience in this present lifetime was also connected to it. Although slightly outside the scope of this book, I'd like to share with you Mike's regression back to birth (something we call 're-birthing') as it highlights a regression process which is very powerful and liberating. I guided him back into his mother's womb before birth and he told me initially that he felt safe and warm. However, after a short time his body began to stiffen and his breathing quickened. He had begun to experience the time pre-birth when he was in the birth canal. I asked him to tell me what he was aware of:

"I feel restricted, claustrophobic. I can hear bubbly noises, like hearing sounds under water. I feel like I'm being moved and a tightness against my body, but I can't move. My shoulders feel stuck. I'm frightened and helpless. It's getting colder and I want to climb back to where I was. I feel like I'm being rejected as I'm being born. I'm coming out." He sighed loudly and began to relax. *"I can smell my mum, she's holding me. It feels wonderful, safe and secure. I can feel the love."* The smile on Mike's face began to fade after a few seconds, however, and he began to cry. *"Somebody else is taking me, I'm on my own. I can hear voices but I can't hear her. I'm being wheeled down a corridor into a darkened room with big windows, I can hear babies crying. Mum's not there. I feel awful, really sad. I'm aware Mum's not coming back."* He continued crying for a few minutes before he became calm again and continued: *"My stepparents are looking after me. I feel that I accept what's had to happen. I feel easier now."*

Our session was finished so I brought Mike back to full awareness, and he told me that he had been adopted as a baby when he was only four weeks old. His real mother had had a brief affair and become pregnant, and her family had forced her to put the baby up for adoption. He felt that he'd experienced a deep form of separation anxiety when he'd been taken away from his mother and that he'd somehow closed his emotions down in order to survive. As we talked and he processed what had happened during the re-birthing, he realised that during his marriage he'd also shut off his emotions from the sexual connection with his wife. Sex therefore brought for him a separation anxiety which had obviously been triggered subconsciously whenever he was making love with his new partner.

I realised that Mike had had a 'double-whammy' as a result of our session, which would make significant inroads into his problem. Firstly, we had released all of the tension from his body which had been locked into his system at a deep level from his birth experience, tension that would have been 'triggered' each time that he had sex. Now, he was free of that tension so his lovemaking would become freer. Secondly, he had some insights as to the nature of his issue (the separation anxiety) and because of this he would be able to cognitively make sense of it and let go of some of its negative effects.

Our next session took place a couple of weeks later, and when he was in hypnosis this time we were able to explore both of the past lives which were also contributing to the anorgasmia. Mike relaxed deeply and was soon regressing back into the first of the lives, a death experience which was over very quickly. Suddenly, his body became stiff and he began breathing quickly. His words were clipped, as if it were an effort to speak:

"I can't move. I'm frightened of falling. I'm hanging on to some grass, over the edge of a cliff. I'm alone and I can feel the fear in my stomach. I think I've slipped. I can't get back up, I feel desperate, hopeless. The grass gives way. I've gone. Blackness." Mike sighed and his body softened. I allowed him to enjoy the relaxation for a short time, before I guided him into the other past life. After a few seconds he started to share it with me:

"I feel happy. I'm a young teenage boy, about 14 years of age, and I'm at a family meal. It's a celebration, it's Christmas. My parents are there with some aunts and uncles. There's a girl there, she's lovely. We dance and I know we love each other. I sense her family don't agree and her brother doesn't want me to be with her because she's my cousin. They're saying that I'm only a kid and she's older than me – she's about 19 I think. She tells me not to worry; it'll be alright because she'll talk to them. Her name's Marie. I'm always on edge though, in case somebody

finds out. The only time I spend time with her is when my family visits hers. It's all hidden. This goes on for a couple of years I think. Time's moved on and I'm about 16 or 17 now. Her brother is mean to her and is suspicious of us. He's threatening to tell my family. I push him up against a wall and make him promise to keep his suspicions to himself. He's weak, but I don't trust him. I feel frustrated that we have to keep our feelings secret. I've decided that I'm going to tell everyone about us, but first I want to tell Marie about my decision so I'm going to her house. I'm walking through a town, feeling anxious. I'm worrying that I'll be attacked so I'm carrying a staff."

Suddenly Mike's body jerked, and he started to shake and writhe about as he lay in the chair. He became emotional and through his tears he spat out the words with difficulty:

"I didn't see them, somebody was waiting for me. They came up behind me out of an alleyway. I reacted too late. It happened so quickly. I feel something cold at my neck. Somebody's cut my throat. It's her brother, he's killed me. He's only a lad like me, and he thinks he's protecting her. It's all going black. I feel calmer now." Mike began to ease down again as his body relaxed and he breathed slowly and deeply. He spoke quietly again, aware of a significant insight: *"I can sense that Marie in that lifetime is Sarah in this one. No wonder I've been so uptight whenever I've been around her."*

I was pleased that he had become aware of this connection between the past life and this one, because once more the combination of the emotional and kinaesthetic release he'd experienced in the regression and the new understanding that Marie was the same soul reincarnated in his present life would make significant inroads into the issue we were working on. As it happened, the anorgasmia was completely released. Mike contacted me a few weeks later and told me that the sexual problem had totally gone, and he was enjoying the pleasures of sex like there was no tomorrow! He was able to orgasm and ejaculate when he was ready to do so, and his partner had noticed that he was much more relaxed during their lovemaking.

Moreover, he was noticing changes in other areas of his life too. He felt calmer inside and his work colleagues had noticed a big difference in him, one of them saying that he was "shining more".

Section Eight

Relationship Issues

Chapter 27

Benji's Story

Benji was an articulate, intelligent and attractive thirty-something year old who was also one of the UK's top complementary therapists and trainers. A published author, she was highly successful in her fields of expertise, running a very busy therapy practice and facilitating courses and seminars around the country. She had done a lot of work on herself over the years, believing that to be a good therapist you should have worked on your personal 'shit' as much as possible so that you present yourself as a balanced personality to your clients (and it's amazing how few therapists have done this!). However, in spite of all of this personal development work that she had done, there was still one issue that she'd never been able to come to terms with, one issue that no other therapy process had managed to heal.

Benji sat weeping as she explained the resentment she felt towards her sister, the vehemence of her words betraying the anger she felt inside towards her younger sibling. She felt that much of her emotional pain stemmed from her own childhood, as when she was about 11 years of age her mother had had a debilitating combination of deep depression coupled with Chronic Fatigue Syndrome. This had left her physically and emotionally unable to contribute to family life, and Benji had been forced at that young age to assume the role of mother to her sister. Benji felt that this had robbed her of her childhood and early teenage years as she was unable to be a normal, free-spirited child due to the responsibilities she had to take on. She knew that as an adult she should not feel so much hatred towards her sister, but she felt a massive amount of conflict inside whenever she had any dealings with her family; on the one hand resenting them bitterly for her hurts, on the other hand feeling guilty because she knew that logically it wasn't the fault of her sister or mother that her childhood was so dysfunctional and damaging.

As a result of this, she knew that she continued to play out the mother role in ways which were not appropriate. For example, in relationships she would 'over-mother' boyfriends, and if her partner or his son became ill she was unable to tolerate their illness and would feel very uptight all the time they were sick. As well as this, she was unable to spend any time with her sister or mother without feeling inside like a smouldering volcano, ready to erupt at the slightest provocation.

Obviously, it goes without saying that the events of her childhood had contributed enormously to her anger issues, but I felt that despite this her response to her family was an over-response to the hurt she was feeling from her early years. Her hatred of her sister was so extreme that I wondered if there were other causes locked in her subconscious creating her severe reactions. I so often find that if there is an over-response to a problem, there usually is more than just the pain of this lifetime's Significant Emotional Events causing the problem. Once she was in trance, sure enough Benji's subconscious indicated that my surmise was correct. It indicated that there were two past lives under the surface which lay at the heart of the matter.

Benji moved swiftly into the first of the lives, and she sighed heavily as she began to share it with me:

"I'm outdoors and it's daytime. I'm a teenage girl wearing a dress and I have bare feet. I'm standing in a field of yellow corn – I just had to get out of the house. I feel like I'm confined there all day long. I feel sad, sad for the way my life is. I'm not appreciated." Benji started to cry, and as the tears rolled down her cheeks she moved into the next scene: *"I'm in the house, all I do is work. I'm overlooked. I'm looking after my mother, it's expected of me. It's my duty and I just accept it. I feel sad that I've settled for so little and I've just not questioned it. She's just slumped in the chair and*

I'm on the floor. It feels relentless, just looking after her all the time. I feel like I hate her, I can't stand it that she's so useless. These are the same feelings I remember from this present life, when my mother was ill and I just spent years looking after everybody else. I'm so angry and frustrated."

As Benji continued to feel the tension in her body, I asked her subconscious some questions using the IMR and it indicated that the mother in the past life was her sister in this present life. No wonder she felt such strong emotions in this lifetime towards her sister, as she was just triggering the feelings from the previous life without realising that this was happening. I took Benji through her death in the past lifetime and the feelings eased. Soon, however, she moved into the other past life, and her body stiffened as she started to recount it:

"I'm in a log cabin and it's night-time. I'm lying alone on a wooden bed. Something's wrong with my legs. I'm a man in my 30s and I feel frustrated. I think I'm a farmer and there's been an accident. I can't use my legs. I've got a wife and children and she has to work because I can't. I feel desperately heavy-hearted as I had a life before this happened and now life's changed and I can't take part in anything with them. It's an injury that's never going to get better so it's always going to be like this. I feel defeated, hopeless and helpless. I feel frightened that life's just going to pass me by. I live a normal lifespan, so it's relentless misery for years and years."

I allowed her to cry softly for a time, and then as the sadness started to ease I took her through the death in that life. After a while she sighed and relaxed. *"I feel easier now, lighter."* The suffering was over, and I guided Benji back to full consciousness.

Although neither of the lives had contained dramatic traumas, they both connected at a deep level with the extreme anger she had felt for such a long time towards her sister. As a result of our session the anger dissipated and Benji was able to spend time around her family in a calm manner, without being 'triggered' by them in any way. I spoke to her some years after we had done this session together and she confirmed to me the enormous benefit she felt the past life therapy had given her.

Chapter 28

Jim's Story

Jim was a psychologist who had come out of a difficult relationship with Alice over three years earlier. However, since then he had been unable to come to terms with the fact that his four-years-long love affair with her had crumbled, and he could not move on with his life. He was obsessing about Alice in that she was on his mind all of the time, and this was despite the fact that Alice had been increasingly difficult to live with, and that during the latter period of their time together she had been constantly unpleasant to him. As he said to me during our first session together, "I just can't get her out of my head. I wake up thinking about her, I drive past her house sometimes hoping to get a glimpse of her, and sometimes I call her on the phone just so I can hear her voice." He knew that he didn't love her anymore as a result of her vindictive behaviour (as a psychologist he analysed her as 'Passive/Aggressive'), but he just could not let go of her, and thoughts of her coloured almost every moment of his waking life.

I was not surprised, when I took Jim into trance, that his IMR finger signalled that there were five previous lives which were causing this obsessive connection to Alice, as I have found so often that relationship issues and jealous or obsessive thoughts about another person frequently come from previous lives. What I was surprised about, however, was the way in which Jim re-experienced the past lives. He was not only very hypnotic but he was also extremely dramatic when he was in some of the past lifetimes. He had the ability to relive events as though they were actually happening, which meant that he would shout, swear or scream and virtually act out the past life events as he lay with his eyes closed. His body would jump around, and I had to make sure all the time that he didn't fall out of the reclining chair and hurt himself! This happens rarely in regression sessions, but when it happens the therapist has to keep their wits about them in order to keep the client safe. It certainly is quite different to most regression sessions in that it is a much bigger experience for both client and therapist.

However, the first past life was over quite quickly and didn't give me any hints as to the dramas to come. Jim started to shake and his body jerked, clear indications that he was in the past life. I asked him what he was experiencing, and through clenched teeth he spoke quietly and with difficulty:

"I'm in a cave, alone. I'm in pain with a wound of some sort in my right side. I'm cold and frightened. I'm a boy, about 12 years old. I think I'm dying. I've been bayoneted. They killed my mother." He started to cry, and then his body softened and he stopped jerking. *"I've gone."* I asked Jim to go back into the life to experience what had happened before he was wounded. Once more, he began to jerk and his face contorted with fear as he started to shout:

"I think it's the American Civil War. What are they doing? They're raping my mother. GET OFF HER, GET OFF HER! I can't stop them. Mother's being raped. GET OFF HER. I've got to run. Agh!" He held his side and his body doubled up as he relived being stabbed. *"Got to hide. I'm frightened... cave."* After a time the shaking subsided and Jim gasped and relaxed. I asked his subconscious if the soul that had been the mother in that life had been or is around him in his present life and the IMR signalled, "Yes." I then asked if the soul who was his mother in that life is Alice in this life and again it indicated, "Yes." This meant that we had already found some 'unfinished business' between he and Alice, which had been causing the ties between the two of them to be so strong. There was more to come, and Jim began to move into

another past life. As before, his body started to jerk but this time his chest puffed out and his shoulders opened up.

"I'm in a boat, like a Viking longboat. I'm a warrior and I feel powerful and strong. It's the calm before the storm – we're going on a raid. I don't understand, I'm remembering being a boy and I feel sad." His face puckered and tears rolled down his cheeks for a few moments and then stopped. *"I'm not allowed to cry, Father says it's weak. Leaders don't cry and I'll be a leader one day. Mother's dead and I'm watching her burn. Hmm. I'm back in the longboat now and I'm a leader. I've had enough of killing but it's kill or be killed. It's time to kill."*

Suddenly, Jim's hands were holding an imaginary sword, and as he lay in the chair he started to fight with it, re-enacting the battle in the past life. His arms were flailing as he swung the sword, and he grunted and shouted as he fought with opponents. At times he swore at his assailants; sometimes he shouted out with relish things like, *"Ha! I've taken somebody's head off."* This was all very dramatic to watch and I had to keep telling him to relive it but to stay in trance in the chair, and also to stay aware of my voice so he could keep a connection to this present life. After he had shouted, *"Grab the girl, take her. Take the bitch,"* and physically pushed a woman to his fighting colleagues, the flailing started to subside as the battle came to a halt. He continued:

"That's done, let's see what we can take. The girl's mine. Let's get home. We're back in the boat. Row, you bastards, row. We're home now. I've brought you a present – a slave. She can help you. No one's touched her. I do love you. You need help, the baby's coming soon." He was obviously talking to his wife in that life, and after a pause he started to cry. His hands were screwed into fists and his face wracked with emotion. *"I must not show emotion. The baby's died and my wife's very ill. I love her so much. I'm fucking angry. I can't do*

anything and I just feel powerless. My wife dies and we burn them both together. I feel like a child again, watching the one I love being burnt. I can't show emotion." Eventually the tears stopped and he became calm. He spoke softly; this time to the female he had captured who had become his wife's slave.

"Thank you for caring for my wife. I will return you to your home. You want to stay here? You should go, my wife kept you safe here. You want to stay with me? I don't know, I need to move on. You can stay if you wish but you're not forced to stay." Once more he was quiet for a while, and then he told me that the woman cared for him and in time loved him. She surrounded him with love and that helped to heal the pain of his loss. There was nothing else to experience in that lifetime, but his subconscious indicated that the baby which he had lost had been reborn in this present life as Alice.

Jim came out of trance and was shocked at the strength of the feelings he had experienced during the regressions. He had taken part in many different types of psychology processes during his career but nothing had been as powerful as this. He was amazed at what had happened, as well as feeling exhausted. He also felt calmer inside, as if he'd let go of something that had been stuck inside of him.

Jim returned for our next session a few days later, and although there had been no change in the intensity of his feelings towards Alice, he had noticed that he was generally feeling less stressed and more at ease in himself. He understood that this was quite normal as we still had more past lives to open up and 'clear' of their negative effects, and once he was in hypnosis he soon moved into the third past life chosen by his subconscious. His face clouded over and his body became tense. He spoke angrily as tears rolled down his cheeks:

"I'm near a lake and a tepee. I'm a man and I know I'm not safe. She's dead. My partner's dead. We were being hunted. Horses and soldiers in blue uniforms. They attacked us for no reason; they killed everyone. She was cut badly; there was nothing I could do. She was pregnant. I had to run, I couldn't stay and fight. Why do they hate us? We just wanted peace. I'm burning her body beside the lake. I try not to feel anything. I walk away without looking back. I've nowhere to go, all of the tribe's dead. I'm just walking; been walking for days."

His voice by this stage was a low monotone, as if he was devoid of energy and feelings. Suddenly, though, he became animated and his speech came quickly as he shouted: *"I see three of them on horseback – I'll give them something to hate. I've no weapons but I don't care. I see a long sword. Aghhhhh!"* He screamed loudly and his body arched in the chair, and he laid with his arms and legs spreadeagled. Finally he drew a long breath and relaxed as he told me that it was over and that he was dead. He had run at the American soldiers hoping to injure one of them before they killed him. As he lay in the chair feeling calmness returning, his subconscious mind (using his Ideo-Motor Response finger) indicated that the unborn child from that life was Alice in this present lifetime. As if we had no more to learn from that life, his subconscious swiftly took him into another one and he started to jerk and breathe quickly:

"I'm a soldier in WWI in the trenches. I can smell the mud. Get down, get down." This was shouted to his companions. *"We're all frightened. In France, there's mud and barbed wire everywhere. Fog, rain, wet, cold and I'm scared to death. I've had enough."* Suddenly he clutched at his chest and jumped, as if hit by something. *"I can't move, just shocked. It's peaceful now, there's no noise. As I'm dying I'm remembering a woman I care about. She brings me feelings of peace and sadness. I'm thinking about being at the railway station as I go off to war. I don't want to go. She doesn't come to see me off,*

she can't face it as it's too painful for her to say goodbye to me. I feel let down but I understand. I get a sense that she's been around me in this present lifetime, I think it's Alice's daughter. I was close to her all the time I was with Alice, and I still miss seeing her. I'm feeling sad now."

As he said this, Jim sighed deeply and he looked intensely upset. Although he didn't cry, he was close to tears and spent some time immersed in the feelings and releasing the energy of the sadness. After a while he began to relax, and when I asked him how he was feeling he told me that he felt calmer and more at ease. He remained in this calm state for a couple of minutes before his subconscious took him into another lifetime, this one though was only a short experience. He began to shake violently and his breath came in gasps. Through a tightly clenched jaw he spoke with difficulty:

"I'm somewhere cold and I'm very young, possible an infant. It's very dark and feels like I'm lying in a cave wrapped in animal fur. I'm alone. My mother's there but she's dead. I'm cold and hungry. I feel angry with her but I know it's not her fault. I can feel myself getting weaker and then I die. It's over now and I can see a blue light as I pass through."

As he said this he gradually relaxed and his breathing slowed down. There was nothing else in that life that we needed to relive so I asked him to come back to full awareness. He told me that he felt that the mother in that lifetime was also his mother in this life. He was surprised at the depth of his feelings in all three of the past lives, but he felt a good deal more at peace about Alice than he had done at the start of the session. Although his psychological training and his work as a psychologist had taught him to be sceptical, he knew that the past life therapy was working and he was grateful too for a new insight that he had gained into psychotherapy processes. He was also grateful for the healings he was experiencing.

Jim's final session of past life therapy was unusual, but in a different way to his other sessions. Before he went into trance he told me that he felt very little towards Alice now, and the obsessive turmoil that had been in his head before he began his therapy had eased right down. He hardly thought about her at all, in fact, and apart from a sense that she had betrayed him he felt that he was now free of her and had almost completely let go of her.

Unlike the other past lives he had relived, this final one appeared to have no direct connection to Alice, and it had a strangely spiritual feel that would not have been out of place in a Dan Brown novel. Once Jim entered the trance state and his subconscious guided him back through time into the past life, he began to speak softly and yet his voice had an air of authority about it:

"I'm a knight on horseback, travelling across a field. I'm in France. I'm not frightened. The knight is there to protect, not just to fight. I feel peaceful and yet at the same time powerful. In my mind I can see a picture of a wolf's head. I'm wearing a big ring and travelling with a big box. I have to protect the box. The ring is a symbol for the keeper. The box is not to be shared, but protected. I'm the last one left, there were six of us protecting it but I'm the only one left. It's so valuable. I can't tell anyone what it is. It came with us from the Holy Land and it's been in Scotland but it's not safe there now so I'm taking it to France. I have to pass it on to the new Keeper. I have travelled much and I feel very spiritual. I'm old and it's time to pass it on to a new Keeper. I know I'm going to die soon but I feel at peace with it."

Suddenly he became tense and he started to relive being in battle. As in our first regression, his hands were holding an imaginary two-handed sword and he was swinging it from side to side as he lay in trance, as if hacking at invisible opponents.

Through clenched teeth he grunted loudly as he fought. After a while the movement subsided and he lay still once more. Quietly he continued his narrative:

"I've been a very strong warrior and although I know that killing is wrong it had to be done to protect the box. The box has much power. I feel a lot of conflict inside me between the soldier and the knight parts of me. The soldier has no purpose and is scared, whereas the knight has purpose and is not frightened. My sword is powerful; it's as if a yellow light emanates from it. I've shed a lot of blood to protect the box; I didn't want to but I had to. The name Saint-Clair keeps coming into my mind. I'm bringing the box back to my home in France. The new Keeper is my son, I can't trust anyone else. I'm dying; I feel a pain inside me. My death has not been in vain, I've passed the box on; I've done my job. As I die I see images of crests, a blue bear's head and a blue owl's head. Now there's just a purple light. I've gone."

Jim sighed deeply and was still, his breathing calm and slow. He came out of trance and he said that he felt a deep sense of peacefulness, as if he'd got closure on something even though he couldn't verbalise exactly what that was. Although we discussed the experience he had just had he was unable to say just what the box was that he had guarded so zealously. Could it have contained some Christian holy relics? It certainly felt like he had remembered a life as a Crusader-type knight. Thoughts of the Ark of the Covenant even came to mind as we pondered its meaning. However, it was to no avail, but whilst Jim couldn't get any specific knowledge as to the true meaning of the box, what did happen was that he felt he had gained closure from his issues with Alice. All of his angst towards her had been completely eradicated as a result of his past life experiences, and he was able to move on with his life. I have bumped into Jim a few times since then and each time he has confirmed to me that his obsessive attachment to Alice had been dissolved away, and he felt happier and lighter because of this.

Chapter 29

Mary's Story

Mary is one the world's leading complementary therapists, a self-aware and spiritual lady who runs therapy and spiritual development courses around the world. I was honoured when she asked me to work on an issue that had bubbled up, as if from nowhere, and surprised her by its intensity. Mary had recently started a new relationship with a man, Paul, who was a very grounded and gentle person (much like herself). Their relationship was progressing very nicely for several weeks when she began to realise that she was having very negative thoughts about Paul's best friend Craig. Whenever Craig appeared at Paul's home she would find herself feeling irrationally angry towards him. The first time that she met Craig she had an immediate dislike of him, and her negative feelings had grown stronger each time she spent any time around him. Mary told me that she felt extremely tense whenever Craig appeared on the scene, and that she also felt jealous of his relationship with her boyfriend. She found herself obsessing about Craig, and she was unable to get him out of her thoughts. As she explained this to me I could hear the malice in her voice as she used some extremely unsavoury adjectives to describe Craig. The most polite was the word "sponger". The least polite words were unprintable! As a spiritually advanced person who tries to see the good in everyone, she was shocked that she could be feeling this way about another human being. She didn't want this to come between her and Paul but she knew that if she didn't do something about it the chances were that it could have caused them to break up. She had done a lot of work on herself over the years, letting go of issues that had caused emotional imbalances, and she had not expected such a basic feeling of jealousy to be worming its way inside her mind, upsetting her usual calm nature and her feelings towards her partner Paul. There was no rational explanation for any of this, and she realised that all of this was an overreaction as Craig had not done anything to cause her bad feelings.

Once in trance Mary's subconscious indicated that the roots of her reactiveness towards Craig were events that had taken place in past lives, and I gently guided her into the first of them. Softly she began to share it with me:

"I'm looking up at a tall man wearing a chain mail hood and jacket and metal gauntlets. I'm a woman wearing a red and yellow dress and gold-coloured slippers. We're in a room in a castle and he's leering at me. I don't like him or the way he looks at me. I know he's a bad person and he's killed people. I'm pregnant and I feel powerless and unsafe. I know that this man is Craig in this present lifetime. My father comes in the room; he's got red hair and is wearing a fur-trimmed hat, a top with puffy sleeves and white tights. I feel more at ease and I'm able to leave the room. The man who is Craig is one of my father's soldiers, he's a senior officer." Mary relaxed again and was silent for a minute or two before she went on:

"I've moved on in time and I've had a baby boy. Craig is supposed to protect me and the boy. In a way that feels OK because he's a strong soldier and I know my son will be safe. The boy grows up and he will be the successor to my father, who's a lord or a baron or something like that. The man who's Craig is in the background all this time, as if he's in the shadows as his bodyguard.

I've moved much further on in time now. My son's around 16 years old now and he's out hunting with Craig. But it's nightfall now and he hasn't returned. I feel as though something has happened. I feel pressure in my stomach and powerless. I have to wait until the morning but he doesn't come back. He doesn't return after a few weeks, and I find out that Craig has kidnapped him and taken him over the border into Scotland. I'm feeling really churned up now. I decide I have to do something as no one else is. I dress as a man and put my hair up inside a cap. I take my maid and we ride to the border. No one stops us. I feel better because I'm doing something now. We meet with some highlanders who tell us they've seen my son and they tell us where he's been taken. I give them some money and we move on. It's night-time now and I'm feeling cold. I see a tower ahead; that's where he's being kept prisoner. It's all in darkness and I can see two sentries outside it. One's asleep. I don't know how I can get in. I feel weak as I can't fight them. The only thing I can do is to use my body. I take off my pants and let my shirt hang down – I'm naked underneath. I beckon to the sentry on guard and lure him away. He starts to touch me but my maid's hiding behind a tree and she jumps out and we both stab him. I then kill the one who's sleeping. I open the door and go inside and quietly ascend a staircase. I open a door at the top and Craig's inside the room. He sees me and I bargain with him. I'm still partly clothed and he agrees to let my son go free if he can sleep with me. I feel disgust and a loathing towards him but I have to do it."

Mary's body was rigid at this point, her face screwed up with tension and her fingers clawed into the arms of the chair in which she was laying. Through gritted teeth she rasped out the words:

"He's on top of me. I just want to get it over with. I disconnect from my body. I'd love to stab him in the back but I'm unarmed. He finishes and rolls over. He gives me the key and I open a door and call for my son. He comes out and sees Craig lying half-naked on the floor and he understands what's happened. We run down and out of the building and ride off. He's on my horse and I'm riding with my maid. We get safely back home, and I bathe and cleanse myself." Mary relaxed again for a few seconds, but almost immediately was tense again. *"In the morning I go to an herbalist for a potion to make sure I don't become pregnant. He brings it the next morning and I drink it. It's a black liquid. Too late I realise that it's poison. I feel myself leaving my body. The herbalist is in the pay of Craig even though everyone trusts him. My son won't realise this and he won't know that he's in danger. I've been doubly betrayed. First he has my body and then he kills me. I'm outside of my body now and I can see the herbalist telling Craig that*

'it's been done'. I stay in spirit for some time, watching over my son. I'm beginning to realise that he's Paul in this present lifetime. He's 20 now and my father's died so it's time for him to take over. There's a big ceremony and a banquet. He's too trusting. A neighbouring lord or baron comes to him in his room. He's alone and as the man kneels to kiss his ring he stabs Paul. He looks shocked as he dies. We go up into the light together."

Mary sighed deeply at this point and her whole body softened. There was no more to relive so she came out of trance, and with a mute voice began to process the experience. On one level she was shocked, but she now knew why her feelings towards Craig had been so extreme. No wonder she had felt that he couldn't be trusted.

At the start of Mary's second session she told me that Paul and she had decided to move in together as their relationship was feeling so 'right'. The only fly in the ointment was Craig. He had helped Paul to move in to their new house and she had been massively triggered, feeling churned up and angry all the time that Craig was around. Once she was in trance I asked her subconscious if the first past life that we had worked on was completely cleared of the negative effects it had upon her, negative effects connected to causing the issue with Craig, and it indicated (using the IMR) a 'no'. However, it didn't want to work on that same past life but it took us into another one. Initially this one felt lighter and happier. However, her mood soon darkened:

"I'm standing on a grass tennis court. I'm a woman, aged about 19, wearing a Victorian-type long dress. There are men wearing straw boaters near a small river. Behind us is a big country house. I feel happy, lively and jovial. I want to carry on playing tennis but a man wants me to go into a boat with him. He cajoles me until I relent and get into the boat with him. I wanted the action of the tennis, this is too sedate. We walk down a jetty on to a punt and he's using a pole to steer it. He's a friend; I quite like him and think that my feelings

could become romantic. He's aged about 30. I think it's Paul in this life. There are dark clouds in the sky so we go back to the shore, and sit and have a picnic on the grass. Suddenly he leans over and kisses me. I don't know what to do. The others have gone as it's raining and we're getting wet. We pack up the picnic stuff and go into a boathouse. I'm cold and wet and he suggests we undress. We take our clothing off and now we're naked. He's holding me – it's a nice feeling but I feel guilty. I feel torn as I think I'm in a relationship with another man. I see him in a red uniform, he's away at the moment and I'm supposed to be waiting for him to return. I know that he's Craig. I can't stop this but I know I should wait for Craig. We make love; it's exciting but afterwards I feel shame. He wants to see me again but I don't know, even though I'd love to."

Mary was restless as she relived all of this, a frown on her face as she felt the inner conflict inside her. I moved her on to the next significant event in that lifetime and she had sadness in her voice:

"I'm getting married to Craig but I don't want to. I'm making the commitment but I feel that I've betrayed myself. Paul is in the background all the time. I'm in bed with Craig but he's not gentle; it's not nice having sex with him. I'm closing down inside. I have three children to him but I feel dead inside. I have no love for Craig, only repressed feelings for Paul. I live like this for the rest of my life, and I'm old now, lying in bed waiting for death. What a waste of a life. I leave the body, and as I move into spirit I make the intention always to be the truth. My commitment to the truth is paramount."

This struck me as very significant as Mary is the most honest person I know, and her need to be ruthlessly honest with herself has always been something that I most admire about her. I wondered how much of that need to live in integrity had been formed as a result of that life. I was pondering this when she moved into another life, but we soon realised that her subconscious had spontaneously taken her back into the first past life we had opened up in the previous session. Her body became tense and her breathing quickened. Her jaw locked and she spoke in short, staccato sentences:

"I'm full of fear and dread. I'm remembering that in that past life Craig raped me – I feel it in my tummy and I feel so dirty I want to rip my womb out. I'm bathing in a tub. My maid is with me. We're laughing and joking. There's a knock at the door so I tell her to be quiet and not open the door as I don't want to be disturbed. The door opens – she hasn't locked it. He's standing there. I shout at him to get out. He comes closer. I see desire in his eyes. He lifts me up out of the water. We're both in shock. He pushes her out and locks the door. He carries me to my bed. I decide that it'll be more painful if I struggle so I just lie there. He removes his tights and pants. I can't do anything; I just wait for it to be over. I feel so much hatred for him. I shut myself down; it's as if I'm out of my body and I'm watching it happen. When he's finished there's a banging at the door. He lifts me back into the water and strokes the bed smooth. I'm still not present. He dresses and opens the door on my husband. He tells my husband a story about thinking that someone was in my room. My husband trusts him. I don't say anything as I'm still in shock and I don't want to upset my husband. Later that day my husband wants to make love with me but I've shut myself down. However, another time he does impregnate me and I have his child."

Mary's face was white and drawn throughout all of this, the tension in her body palpable. She was quiet for a few moments and then she began to cry, a painful sobbing that came from the depths of her being. Her body shook violently as she allowed the release of all of the emotional pain of both of the lives to take place. I sat quietly, comforting her with soft words, giving her permission to let go of the hurt that she'd had locked inside her for all of her life. Eventually, the release was complete and Mary sighed deeply and came out of hypnosis. We talked through her experience, and although she still felt uptight when she thought about Craig she also said that she felt lighter too.

We both felt that Mary needed a couple of weeks to process

the session, and when she came back she told me that the feelings toward Craig were still strong. This is quite usual, as sometimes it's only after we've worked through and 'cleared' several past lives that clients begin to notice an improvement in the problem that we're working on. Although she was a little apprehensive about what she'd uncover next, she also knew that we were making progress, and that it would only be a matter of time before her antipathy to Craig would be reduced. Mary went into a deep hypnotic state, and her subconscious took her into a new past life. She began to cry, and through her sobs she spoke:

"I'm on an operating table. There's a metal strap around my head. My womb's being cut open by a man and a baby removed. The baby's being taken away from me; it's tiny and there's lots of blood. At first I felt love and trust but now I feel the pain and grief of a betrayal. The man is a surgeon and I know that it's Craig. He's cut me open without any love for me and taken the baby away. He's leaving me to die. I'm remembering earlier in that life, when I was a young girl with pigtails, playing. I'm being watched by Craig and I get a sense that he's grooming me. I'm part of a good family, well-dressed and happy. He's about ten years older than me. He lives next door and then he goes away for a long time to study. He comes back to visit after I've grown up and he shows an interest in me. I become his wife but when I go to live with him he treats me badly, as if I'm just a housekeeper. I have to clean and scrub floors. He's not nice to me and he rapes me. I feel worthless and powerless. I feel angry. I'm on the operating table and I decide I don't want to live."

Mary's sadness began to soften, and she relaxed and breathed deeply as she moved through the death experience into Spirit. She remained quiet for a while and then she stiffened, her hands moving to her stomach. She had moved into another lifetime:

"I'm a man, a peasant working in the fields, scooping up hay with a pitchfork. A group of people come led by Paul. He's speaking the truth about the way we're exploited. They're good people, all farmers, and they're going to speak with the landowner to try to change things.

I join them. We're walking up a hillside and I see Craig on horseback. He's the landowner and he has his men with him. Paul tries to appease him but I don't think it's going well. Craig's stony-faced. He grabs a spear and stabs Paul in the chest. He falls to the ground, bleeding. We're all shocked. His men encircle us. I didn't come here to fight but to negotiate. Craig wants us to leave our fields and tend his crops to feed his soldiers. I try to move away but I'm singled out. He runs his horse at me and knocks me down. He's making an example of me to scare the others. His horse has its hoof on my stomach. I feel pressure there and pain. He's showing me no mercy. I'm not going to work for him, if I can't go back to my land I'd rather die. The horse's hoof is pressing down on my stomach. I'm determined not to give in. I despise him for the way he manipulates his power. I can feel my organs being crushed. I'm in the light now. It's over."

Mary let out a long sigh and relaxed in the chair. We finished the session and once more she felt that she had a lot of understanding about the situation with Craig. As she thought about him she no longer had a tight feeling in her stomach, which was her usual psychosomatic response whenever he came into her mind. She also looked a lot brighter too.

Mary returned one week later and told me that there had definitely been a major shift as a result of our last regressions. She was much less reactive whenever Paul mentioned Craig to her, and when Craig had visited their house she had only felt a small pang of tension in her stomach. She still found it difficult to be nice to him, but she felt that we had made major progress in the few weeks that we had been working together. After a short debrief, she lay back in the chair and I gently guided her into trance. Once she was sufficiently relaxed her subconscious took her back into another previous life:

"It's something like early-Victorian times and I'm a woman wearing a cream-coloured dress with a scooped neckline and my waist feels tight. I think I'm wearing a corset. I have a straw hat on and a bearded man wearing a top hat is bowing to me, holding my hand and

introducing himself. It's Craig. I don't like him. He's slimy and he has damp hands so I keep my gloves on. He wants to spend more time with me. I don't want to but I have to eat humble pie. Father made some bad decisions in a business venture and the business has collapsed. We've lost everything, including our house. I think Craig's manipulated things so he knew it would happen so he can have me. I have to go to him and his eyes light up as he talks about it. I feel very uncomfortable but I have no money and no home. I'm powerless. I resign myself to this as there's nothing else I can do." Her brows were knotted throughout all of this, her hands wringing nervously in her lap and her head was pushed back into the chair, as if trying to distance herself from Craig. A look of distaste grew on her face as she went on:

"He marries me. I feel I've sold my soul and have nothing but contempt for him. He parades me around as a trophy wife. Soon afterwards my father dies and I've been given a letter from him, apologising and explaining why the business deal went so wrong. I just feel numb. We live in a big house next to a lake, and one day Paul comes to work for Craig. He's a kind man and I like him a lot. Craig keeps going away, and Paul and I spend a lot of time talking in the garden. We enjoy our time together and I like his lightness. I fall in love with him. I'm touching his face and his hair but he says that he can't do anything because Craig's his boss and I'm married to him. I feel so sad. I start to withdraw; it feels as if a part of me is dying. I feel rejected by him and very hurt." A tear rolled down her cheek and her lip quivered as she went on: *"I find out that my husband has another woman. He's got a sexual disease too so he won't be touching me. His health isn't good. He spends a lot of time in London to be near the woman and a doctor. He's getting thinner and his face is drawn. He's dying. He tells me he's leaving the house in my name when he goes, but when he dies I don't have enough money to keep it. I have to sell the furniture – the upper floor is now empty. I live in the kitchen. I've let go of all the staff except for one maid and a butler. It's cold a lot of the time. We eat food that we grow and use wood from the forest, but I don't have enough to eat and I start to weaken. I blame him for*

this mess. I have a pain in my stomach and I get sick and die. It's over, I feel at peace now."

Mary relaxed and began to breathe deeply and calmly. Soon, however, she was moved into another life, initially remembering herself as a street urchin locked up in a prison. Her hands began rubbing her stomach, and every now and again she let out a moan:

"I've been here a long, long time. I've grown into a young man over the years. I'm all alone in a stone cell, dirty and with a long beard. High up in the wall are open windows with no glass in them. I stole a chicken because I was starving. It was Craig's so he locked me up to punish me. I have no energy and a pain in my stomach. I'm malnourished. I think that Paul is the jailer and we've developed a sort of relationship over the years. He's always fed me to stop me from starving to death. I would have died earlier otherwise. He had compassion but in effect he's only prolonged my suffering. I die eventually though as I'm so undernourished, and go up into the light. It's a relief."

Once more at the end of the session Mary was surprised at the depth of the connections between Craig and herself, but also at the way in which Paul was a significant player too in the past lives. As she talked about Craig she had no negative somatic reaction in her body which was unusual for her (before we started working on this she would feel an immediate churning in her stomach as soon as she thought about him).

At our final session Mary expressed amazement at how she had been since our previous one, as Craig and his son were both staying with Paul at her house for a few days and she had felt no aversion or animosity towards Craig. She told me that when Paul had asked her how she would feel if Craig stayed with them until his new home was ready to move into (and he had half expected her to react negatively when he asked her) she had shocked herself when she heard the words "no problems" coming out of her lips! She almost looked round to see who had said that before she realised it was her! She could not believe that all of her loathing, anger and repugnance of Craig could have been so reduced that it no longer existed. Although I was pleased that we had had such a good result, I just wanted to check with Mary's subconscious that there was nothing else to work on. If there wasn't then we would have just had an easy, relaxation-based session of hypnosis, so when she went into trance I asked her Ideo-Motor Response if there were any other past lives that we needed to explore, and it indicated that there was still one past life that required examination. Within a few seconds her eyelids began to flicker (a sign that she was visualising the images from the past life) and she spoke firmly but softly:

"I can see cobblestones and yellowy buildings and archways. I'm outside, wearing a yellow and red dress and holding a young boy by the hand. I'm quite well-to-do. The clothing is good quality. I'm about 23 years old. I have a tight bodice and a heavy, puffy dress with a frill around it and red shoes. We're rushing through the streets. I feel pressurised; it's important to get somewhere on time. I can see straw on the ground in a marketplace and there are unpleasant smells in the street, of life and of faeces. People are throwing waste water on to the street from the houses, using white bowls. The boy lets go of my hand and runs off. There are people everywhere and I can't see him. Now I'm torn – I have to find him but I have to be somewhere on time. Suddenly I see him. He saw a dog and he went to see it. He wants us to take the dog with us as he's wanted a dog at home. I agree he can have it so now I'm rushing with a dog and a boy, but our progress is slower now as they keep stopping. We're not going to be there on time. We arrive at some steps and knock on a big, black wooden door with studs on it. We go inside to an inner courtyard. There are people there, including women in varying states of undress. One woman has a breast exposed. This is a brothel. I go through another door and a man's sitting at a table with bags of gold. He says that I'm late and brushes my explanation aside. I feel tension in my stomach. I don't like him but he has power and wealth so I have to respect him. He's fat, wearing a black hat with a white feather in it. He has a white ruff around his neck,

a waistcoat and breeches and trousers that come down to the knees and buckles on his shoes. He has a big ledger on the table in front of him. I sense that I've been promoted from being one of the girls in the brothel. I'm now a lady's maid. He's counting money and he puts coins into a leather pouch and gives it to me. He says that if I'm late again he won't pay me and I'll be back in the brothel. I want to spit at him but I can't. It's been five years since I worked here; having the boy got me out of here. The boy is connected to a lady. Her husband came to the brothel and I fell pregnant to him." Mary paused before she went on: *"I go back into the market and buy a pheasant, a chicken and a brown-furred animal. I take them back to the big house where I live (it's like a castle) on the outskirts of the town and give them to the cook in the kitchen. I go to the stables and ask a man there to find somewhere to keep the dog so my son can visit him and play with him. I go up to the lady's room and dress her hair. She asks me how I'm feeling and I just say, 'Fine,' but inside I feel dead. There's no love or joy in my life, just responsibilities."*

Mary looked sad and was quiet for a few moments, as if taking stock of the life she was living. I asked her to become more aware of any connection to Craig in that life. Her voice hardened and her body stiffened as she remembered:

"In the first place I had to go to the brothel because I had no money. Craig is the fat, horrible owner of the brothel who paid me the money. He's teaching me how to behave with a man because I don't know anything. He's teaching me disgusting things. I feel it should be a woman teaching me. He takes great pleasure in demonstrating and making me do things on him. He's leering at me and making comments and movements. He disgusts me. He smells. I feel cold inside, but I know I have to earn money. I shut myself down. He's breaking me in. I have to open the buttons on his pants." She was writhing in the chair as she experienced this, her head moving from side to side as if trying to get away from something. Suddenly she screamed out, with venom and outrage in her voice: *"HE'S DISGUSTING. I don't want to be here but I have to stay, I'm powerless."* Tears rolled

down her cheeks as she continued: *"I shut my heart down to survive."* Slowly Mary recovered her composure and she moved on a little in time:

"The next morning a very wealthy, powerful man comes to the brothel. They tell me he's the king. I'm not interested so I stand back. Oh God, Craig is pointing to me and saying how about me? Oh God, no, no. I don't want it. He takes me into a room and I just play dead. I don't do any of the things I'm supposed to do. He has a nice body but I don't feel anything. Every week after that he comes back. Oh no, I have to endure this every week. The others are jealous of me because he only wants me. My stomach starts to swell. I'm no longer attractive to him and he asks Craig if I've had contact with any other men but I haven't. I'm only kept for him. They take me out of service and I get bigger and bigger. The king pays him money to keep me." Mary's body started to stretch out and her breathing came harshly through gritted teeth. She was twisting around as she lay in the chair. *"I'm having the baby. They give me some herbs. There's blood and water and a smell. I have a boy and they want to take him from me and give him to the queen as she's unable to have children but I say no. No way."* Her voice was strong and her jaw clenched. *"I'm not compromising on this. He's my baby and I'm keeping him. A few days later they take me to the castle and I'm told I have no rights. The boy will be given to her and will be told I'm his nanny. That's the compromise they're prepared to make. I know I have no choice; they could have just taken the baby away. This way I'm in a nice place and I have a nice room but I have to close my feelings down. I feel like a prisoner; I can't go because if I did I'd never see my son again. The king doesn't visit me for sex anymore either. He continues to go to the whore house but is more careful. The queen is happy to have a baby. I feel sorry for her as she's as powerless as me, just in a different way. She has to put up with him sleeping around."*

Mary relaxed and was quiet for a time. She sighed and spoke quietly:

"I've been very sick and I'm outside of myself, looking down at

my body now. I'm about 35 years old. What a waste of a life. I feel I compromised myself and I had to go into the brothel as I had no money. Then I had to go to the castle to be a lady's maid. I can hear spirit voices saying that I could have said no to the brothel and I could have worked on the land but I didn't feel I had a choice. I feel annoyed with them for saying this. They say I had other choices and they won't let me die. They say that it's not my time yet and I have to go back. I have to go back down and do it again." Suddenly she shouted and started to choke: *"I DON'T WANT TO GO BACK. I'm angry but it's as if I'm turned around and I go back into the body. It's cold. They've put something under my nose. They've brought a medicine woman in, and she's thrilled and amazed that I'm alive. Oh God, I have to endure this again. Well, I'm not standing for it. When I'm better I go to see the king and make some demands. He agrees with them, so I get a cottage in the grounds to live in, with furniture from my old room, food from the kitchens and water brought to the cottage. My son can still visit but I don't want any more visits from the king and queen. They think it's a miracle that I'm back from the dead so I get what I want. My life now changes for the better. I have a life of my own in the cottage. I paint – the light here is lovely."* Mary became emotional now, her voice coming between the sobs: *"I like the man who works in the stables; he's kind and gentle and he loves me, despite everything that's happened to me. He wants me to marry him and I'm trying to open my heart. It's very hard though because it's been shut down for so long. I want to open it but I can't; it feels like it's locked. I don't know how to show love. I can't open my heart to him so he finds someone else and marries them."*

She was unable to speak for a time as the emotion was so great. I allowed her the time to release the sadness and after a while the tears stopped flowing and she relaxed. She had again moved on in time, and even for one of my sessions what she experienced was very unusual:

"I'm older now – about 48 – I'm ready to go again. I'm in my bed and I drift up out of my body. This time they let me stay. The spirit

voices are there again. They're my guides. They say I had a choice about opening my heart and they talk about the importance of having the seed of trust. They're very thin blue forms. They put my spirit body on a bed and open my chest and take out my heart. It's as if they plug it in somehow to an energy source which has energy pulsing into it. They say it was faulty and they have to change its blueprint. They're going back, like on a timeline, looking for where the fault occurred. It's something that happened right at the beginning of time. It's as if something got into it and changed its structure. They're taking out something that looks like a grain of sand. The heart then becomes purple and they put it back into me with some golden light. They say the heart was faulty so it wasn't my fault. It's complete."

And so it was. Mary came out of trance, as surprised as me at what she'd experienced at the end of the session. I couldn't really analyse it as it may have been a metaphor for her healing or it may have been what actually happened to her whilst she was in Spirit. Whatever it was it made her feel quite whole inside and she felt extraordinarily at peace. The work which we had done had released her repugnance of Craig and she was able to enjoy her relationship with Paul knowing that Craig would not cause any conflict to come between Paul and her. I spoke to her a couple of years after we'd done the sessions and she told me that the 'Craig issue' been totally resolved for her, and that whenever Paul mentioned him or went off to spend time with him she felt completely at ease. Soon after our conversation Mary sent me an email:

> *Just as a footnote, 'Craig' stayed at our house with his son about 2 weeks ago, I was completely calm. Paul was also fast asleep in the morning, so I cooked breakfast for Craig and his son, and they left early. I felt nothing.*
>
> *Also Paul is to be best man at Craig's wedding. We will both be going to the celebrations – and **I am looking forward to them**!*
>
> *I have to say, that when I think about the past life experiences, I*

sort of remember them, don't remember how intense they were, and it feels like it happened to someone else.

The one thing that struck me though was the theme of powerlessness, it seemed to have all been triggered by the feeling of powerlessness when Craig showed up at the house with no warning and I was home alone (which explains me freaking out when this happened based on the previous lives and experiences), but that in every life, the feeling of powerlessness was connected to Craig and the feeling of love connected to Paul.

Epilogue

I do hope that you've enjoyed reading about my clients' experiences in past life therapy. I feel honoured to have helped so many people overcome their issues over the years, and if in some way this book helps more people to take the idea of reincarnation more seriously I will be happy.

Better still, if anyone as a result of this book has past life therapy and heals their issues, I will be overjoyed. Therapy is a way of helping human beings become more balanced. As individual people become more balanced the fact that we are all connected energetically means that the world becomes more balanced. This rebalancing of human beings is an important part of our spiritual growth in this Universe, and is an essential way to help humankind to survive the challenges that we face as spiritual species on this topsy-turvy, battered but benign planet. When we are more balanced as a result of therapy or spiritual growth we can learn to love each other. **Remember: therapy sets you free!**

6TH
BOOKS

ALL THINGS PARANORMAL

Investigations, explanations and deliberations on the paranormal, supernatural, explainable or unexplainable. 6th Books seeks to give answers while nourishing the soul: whether making use of the scientific model or anecdotal and fun, but always beautifully written.

Titles cover everything within parapsychology: how to, lifestyles, alternative medicine, beliefs, myths and theories.

If you have enjoyed this book, why not tell other readers by posting a review on your preferred book site?

Recent bestsellers from 6th Books are:

The Afterlife Unveiled

What the Dead Are Telling us About Their World!

Stafford Betty

What happens after we die? Spirits speaking through mediums know, and they want us to know. This book unveils their world...

Paperback: 978-1-84694-496-3 ebook: 978-1-84694-926-5

Spirit Release

Sue Allen

A guide to psychic attack, curses, witchcraft, spirit attachment, possession, soul retrieval, haunting, deliverance, exorcism and more, as taught at the College of Psychic Studies.

Paperback: 978-1-84694-033-0 ebook: 978-1-84694-651-6

I'm Still With You

True Stories of Healing Grief Through Spirit Communication

Carole J. Obley

A series of after-death spirit communications which uplift, comfort and heal, and show how love helps us grieve.

Paperback: 978-1-84694-107-8 ebook: 978-1-84694-639-4

Less Incomplete

A Guide to Experiencing the Human Condition Beyond the Physical Body

Sandie Gustus

Based on 40 years of scientific research, this book is a dynamic guide to understanding life beyond the physical body.

Paperback: 978-1-84694-351-5 ebook: 978-1-84694-892-3

Advanced Psychic Development
Becky Walsh
Learn how to practise as a professional, contemporary spiritual medium.
Paperback: 978-1-84694-062-0 ebook: 978-1-78099-941-8

Astral Projection Made Easy
and overcoming the fear of death
Stephanie June Sorrell
From the popular Made Easy series, *Astral Projection Made Easy* helps to eliminate the fear of death, through discussion of life beyond the physical body.
Paperback: 978-1-84694-611-0 ebook: 978-1-78099-225-9

The Miracle Workers Handbook
Seven Levels of Power and Manifestation of the Virgin Mary
Sherrie Dillard
Learn how to invoke the Virgin Mary's presence, communicate with her, receive her grace and miracles and become a miracle worker.
Paperback: 978-1-84694-920-3 ebook: 978-1-84694-921-0

Divine Guidance
The Answers You Need to Make Miracles
Stephanie J. King
Ask any question and the answer will be presented, like a direct line to higher realms… *Divine Guidance* helps you to regain control over your own journey through life.
Paperback: 978-1-78099-794-0 ebook: 978-1-78099-793-3

The End of Death

How Near-Death Experiences Prove the Afterlife

Admir Serrano

A compelling examination of the phenomena of Near-Death Experiences.

Paperback: 978-1-78279-233-8 ebook: 978-1-78279-232-1

The Psychic & Spiritual Awareness Manual

A Guide to DIY Enlightenment

Kevin West

Discover practical ways of empowering yourself by unlocking your psychic awareness, through the Spiritualist and New Age approach.

Paperback: 978-1-78279-397-7 ebook: 978-1-78279-396-0

An Angels' Guide to Working with the Power of Light

Laura Newbury

Discovering her ability to communicate with angels, Laura Newbury records her inspirational messages of guidance and answers to universal questions.

Paperback: 978-1-84694-908-1 ebook: 978-1-84694-909-8

The Audible Life Stream

Ancient Secret of Dying While Living

Alistair Conwell

The secret to unlocking your purpose in life is to solve the mystery of death, while still living.

Paperback: 978-1-84694-329-4 ebook: 978-1-78535-297-3

Beyond Photography

Encounters with Orbs, Angels and Mysterious Light Forms!

John Pickering, Katie Hall

Orbs have been appearing all over the world in recent years. This is the personal account of one couple's experience of this new phenomenon.

Paperback: 978-1-90504-790-1

Blissfully Dead

Life Lessons from the Other Side

Melita Harvey

The spirit of Janelle, a former actress, takes the reader on a fascinating and insightful journey from the mind to the heart.

Paperback: 978-1-78535-078-8 ebook: 978-1-78535-079-5

Does It Rain in Other Dimensions?

A True Story of Alien Encounters

Mike Oram

We have neighbors in the universe. This book describes one man's experience of communicating with other-dimensional and extra-terrestrial beings over a 50-year period.

Paperback: 978-1-84694-054-5

Electronic Voices: Contact with Another Dimension?

Anabela Mourato Cardoso

Career diplomat and experimenter Dr Anabela Cardoso covers the latest research into Instrumental Transcommunication and Electronic Voice Phenomena.

Paperback: 978-1-84694-363-8

The Hidden Secrets of a Modern Seer

Cher Chevalier

An account of near death experiences, psychic battles between good and evil, multidimensional experiences and Demons and Angelic Helpers.

Paperback: 978-1-84694-307-2 ebook: 978-1-78099-058-3

Readers of ebooks can buy or view any of these bestsellers by clicking on the live link in the title. Most titles are published in paperback and as an ebook. Paperbacks are available in traditional bookshops. Both print and ebook formats are available online.

Find more titles and sign up to our readers' newsletter at http://www.johnhuntpublishing.com/mind-body-spirit.

Follow us on Facebook at https://www.facebook.com/OBooks and Twitter at https://twitter.com/obooks.